PINK TOURISM
Holidays of Gay Men and Lesbians

To Andy and Claire with love

PINK TOURISM
Holidays of Gay Men and Lesbians

Howard L. Hughes

www.cabi.org

CABI is a trading name of CAB International

CABI Head Office	CABI North American Office
Nosworthy Way	875 Massachusetts Avenue
Wallingford	7th Floor
Oxfordshire OX10 8DE	Cambridge, MA 02139
UK	USA
Tel: +44 (0)1491 832111	Tel: +1 617 395 4056
Fax: +44 (0)1491 833508	Fax: +1 617 354 6875
E-mail: cabi@cabi.org	E-mail: cabi-nao@cabi.org
Website: www.cabi.org	

A catalogue record for this book is available from the British Library, London, UK.

Library of Congress Cataloging-in-Publication Data

Hughes, Howard L.
   Pink tourism: holidays of gay men and lesbians/Howard L. Hughes.
      p. cm.
   Includes bibliographical references and index.
   ISBN 1-84593-076-2 (alk. paper)
   1. Gay consumers.   2. Lesbian consumers.   3. Tourism–Marketing.
4. Gays–Attitudes.   5. Lesbians–Attitudes.   6. Sexual orientation.
I. Title: Holidays of gay men and lesbians.   II. Title.

   HF5415.32.H84 2006
   910.68'8--dc22

                                                                         2005035845

   ISBN-10: 1-84593-076-2
   ISBN-13: 978-1-84593-076-9

Typeset by AMA DataSet Ltd, UK
Printed and bound in the UK by Biddles Ltd, King's Lynn

Contents

Acknowledgements

This book, in many ways, marks another stage of a long, personal journey. Those who know me well will be aware of the nature of that journey. I gladly acknowledge the help, support and understanding shown by those who were with me on that journey; they will know who they are.

In addition, certain people have been particularly helpful with respect to the genesis and completion of this book: Philippa Hunter-Jones, a close friend as well as colleague, gave encouragement at the start when I did not really believe that such a book could be written, let alone by me. Much of the credit for the fact that it has been written at all must go to her. Philippa continued to 'have faith' throughout. Her warmth and sincerity are a delight to experience.

Danielle Allen, another friend and colleague, also inspired but, in addition, helped with some irritating but none the less essential tasks that ensured that the book was eventually completed. Her efficiency and enthusiasm are boundless, as indeed, are her geniality and compassion.

Rebecca Stubbs was Development Editor at CABI at just the 'right' time. Her enormous enthusiasm for the idea was encouraging and she progressed it through to contract with commendable swiftness.

Andrew Stokes, Managing Director of Marketing Manchester, has always encouraged my projects. His knowledge and expertise in this field are unsurpassable and he has always found the time in his busy schedule to listen to my ideas. He and his organization have, at all times, been generous with their assistance.

Nigel Morgan and Annette Pritchard of the University of Wales Institute, Cardiff, have been an inspiration. Their work in this and related areas has been ground-breaking. These delightful people continue to push forward the frontiers of tourism studies in a most remarkable manner.

Kevin has been part of the tourism experience for some time now but has, of course, had a much more significant role in my life than as a travelling companion. He has endured, with a good grace, trips which were not always of his own choosing. Kevin's endurance of a shared life is, to me, astonishing but joyfully appreciated none the less.

My appreciation, too, to several cohorts of undergraduate students at Manchester Metropolitan University who have tolerated (and, in a pleasing number of cases, shared) my enthusiasm for a study of gay and lesbian tourism. Not one has demurred at examining issues with which some may have felt uncomfortable. Credit to them all for being open-minded and for approaching issues in a mature way.

Ian Johnson, Principal Consultant of Out Now Consulting has been more than generous with his offers of assistance. He provided the results of a reader survey carried out in *Gay Times* and *Diva* in the period May to October 2005, for which I am very grateful. Unfortunately they were available too late to be incorporated into this book (www.OutNowConsulting. com).

Dominic O'Grady, Group Managing Editor of Gay Travel Guides, New South Wales, Australia, was also generous in his willingness to let me have access to the results of an international gay travel survey carried out on his behalf (www.gaytravelguides.info).

The library staff at Hollings campus of Manchester Metropolitan University are heroes of their profession. Led by Ian Harter, they have diligently, enthusiastically and cheerfully met every request for assistance.

The following graciously shared their views in short interviews (during 2004/05) about gay and lesbian tourism: Rob Harkavy, Respect Holidays; Malcolm Hardy, ManTrav Holidays; Andrew Roberts, AMRO Holidays; Michael Gibberd, Exclusively Gay Cruising; and Tony Bloomfield and Lorna Jasper, Village Travel (Manchester). My thanks to them for giving their time so readily and also for keeping my feet on the ground.

Grateful thanks is also given to those who gave permission to reproduce advertisements and other promotional material: Manfred J. Kaufmann, Manager Public Advertising, Vienna Tourist Board (Fig. 2.1); Andrew Roberts, General Manager, AMRO Holidays (Figs 3.1, 5.4 and 6.13); Andy Newman, Press Officer, Florida Keys and Key West Tourism Council (Figs 5.1, 7.3 and 7.4); Andrew Stokes, Managing Director, Marketing Manchester (Fig. 5.2); Ian Johnson, Principal Consultant of Out Now Consulting (Fig. 5.3); Michael Gibberd and Peter Russell, The Exclusively Gay Cruising Company (Fig. 6.1); Tony Bloomfield, Director and Lorna Jasper, General manager, Village Travel (Fig. 6.2); Neil Basnett, Away Gay Holidays (Figs 6.3 and 6.4); Rob Harkavy, Director, Respect Holidays (Fig. 6.5); Vicki, Proprietor, Bondi Hotel (Fig. 6.6); Heather and Helen, Proprietors,

Gabrielle's Hotel (Fig. 6.7); Stephen Joyce, General Manager, Trades Hotel and Rainbows Hotel (Fig. 6.8); Ronald Walgreen, Hotel New Amsterdam (Fig. 6.9); Lynn Mogell, Executive Director, Women Innkeepers of Provincetown (Fig. 6.10); Michael Williams, Executive Director, World's Foremost Gay and Lesbian Hotels (Fig. 6.11); Shaun, Brighton Wave Hotel, and members of the Gaydealsbrighton. co.uk (Fig. 6.12); Tobin, Proprietor, Village Lodge (Fig. 7.1); and Dale W. Dawursk, Desert Paradise Resort Hotel (Fig. 7.2).

Introduction

The aim of this book is to examine the holidays of gays and lesbians from, primarily, a marketing perspective. It also examines how marketing activity engages with and affects social issues relating to homosexuality.

The primary target audience for this book is postgraduate and second- and third-year undergraduate students on tourism, hospitality, leisure and recreation management courses. Some prior knowledge of marketing and of first-level tourism studies is assumed. None the less students on courses such as cultural studies, human geography and sociology should find it of interest and use. It may be that some of the content and approach is regarded as alien to their own discipline's perspective on homosexuality. They will find, hopefully, that it provides some constructive and thought-provoking illumination of issues of sexual orientation and contributes to further understanding of these issues.

Concepts and Terms

The statement of aim conceals several complications, not the least of which is what is meant by 'gays and lesbians'. This is an issue that will be explored in the next chapter, but, for the moment, 'gays and lesbians' can be regarded, in a commonly used sense, as referring to male and female homosexuals (though this term is also opaque), i.e. people who are sexually attracted to people of the same biological sex. The term 'holiday' is not so difficult to pin down, though 'tourism' is often used to mean holidays and can, on occasion, give rise to confusion. The technical use of

© Howard L. Hughes 2006. *Pink Tourism: Holidays of Gay Men and Lesbians* (Howard L. Hughes)

'tourism' is wider than holiday and includes (*inter alia*) business and conference trips and visits to friends and relatives, but it is also restrictive (at
least in the UK) in that it includes only trips that are of minimum 24-hour
duration or that involve an overnight stay (World Tourism Organization,
1981; English Tourism Council *et al.*, 2002); it therefore excludes daytrips.
In this book, the terms holiday and tourism will be used interchangeably
and tourism will usually refer to holidays, unless otherwise indicated.
The term 'gay and lesbian tourism' will also be used, though it was discarded by Cox (2001) in favour of 'gay holidaymaking', as the former term
was felt to imply a particular type of tourism involving holiday interaction with other gays or lesbians. This book deals with the widest holiday
experiences of gays and lesbians and not just with any one particular type
of holidaymaking that may be the focus of some gays and lesbians.

'Gay' and 'lesbian' are used here as they are more widely used than
'homosexual' in everyday usage, in the media and in academic studies.
'Gay' is sometimes used to cover both male and female homosexuals (as
in 'gays' or 'gay men and women') and in this book it will often be used in
this way as a 'shorthand' term. Usually, however, 'gay' will be applied to
men only, with women being referred to as lesbians. On occasion, the
catch-all term 'lesbian, gay, bisexual and transgender', or variations of it,
(usually abbreviated to lgbt or equivalents such as glbt, lgb or glb) will be
used in the book where it is used by others or where it seems appropriate
to encompass a wider population. The term 'straight' is in widespread
use to designate non-gays or heterosexuals and it too will, on occasion, be
used in this book.

The holiday experiences of those who are bisexual or transgendered
do not feature in this book. This is, in large part, because of the lack of
information about their holiday experiences; this omission does, though,
also conveniently mean that the need to consider the contentious nature
of bisexuality, in particular, and the distinguishing characteristics and
behaviour of bisexuals and transgender people is avoided. If bisexuality
is, for the sake of simplicity, regarded as being attracted (physically or
emotionally) to both the same and to the other sex, this may have been
experienced by most of the adult population at some time, either concur-
rently or separately. In surveys where people self-categorize their sexuality, the proportion that identify as bisexual is invariably low – typically
between 2% and 6% of the non-heterosexual population (Mintel, 2000a;
GL Census Partners, 2001, 2002; http://www.gaytravelguides.info, 2004;
Browne *et al.*, 2005). If a flexible notion of sexuality is accepted, then the
concept of bisexuality has very little meaning anyway (Horowitz and
Newcomb, 2001). Transgender is less to do with sexual orientation than
with gender identity.

The use of the word 'pink' in the title reflects the fact that there is a
widespread usage and recognition of the term 'pink pound' or 'pink dollar'
to refer to the purchasing power of gays and lesbians (though usually

particularly to that of men). Perhaps, more significantly, the colour has been adopted by homosexuals because of the inverted pink triangle that gay men were required to wear in the concentration camps of Nazi Germany. The triangle (upright) was reclaimed by gay activists in the 1970s and 1980s as a memorial to past persecution and as a symbol of community in continuing the struggle against contemporary oppression and, later, the campaign for action against AIDS. Lesbians were not required to wear a triangle that identified their sexuality but, if incarcerated as 'anti-social', wore black triangles. This colour, needless to say, has not been universally adopted as a sign of lesbianism. The use of 'blue' (boy) has been noted in reference to the purchasing power of lesbians as a counterpart to the association of pink (girl) with male homosexuals (Browne *et al.*, 2005). This usage is not common either. 'Pink', therefore, in the book title refers to both male and female homosexuals, though should not be taken to refer solely to economic matters. Other representations of homosexuality, such as the rainbow flag or the lambda symbol, are possibly more inclusive than 'pink' but were discarded for the title, as not being recognized as widely.

Limited Knowledge

Beyond such definitional and conceptual issues there is the practical matter that, to date, relatively little is known about holidays of gays and lesbians and related issues. Consideration of gays and lesbians in tourism studies in academic circles is relatively recent but is, none the less, a reflection of an increasing maturity of tourism research and education. Tourism studies are themselves 'new' but are maturing and, like tourism itself, increasingly acknowledge the fragmentation and diversity of tourist experiences. Issues such as gender and ethnicity are being examined within the tourism context and the dominance of an ethnocentric, patriarchal focus to tourism is being challenged (Kinnaird and Hall, 1994b; Stephenson, 2002). To some extent this is in response to a market imperative and a reflection of market recognition of change in tourism. Much of the limited information about gays, lesbians and their holidays has been the outcome of market research surveys by commercial organizations in order to assess the potential for targeting the gay and lesbian market. Academic studies of gay and lesbian tourism are, to date, limited. The earliest were published in the mid to late 1990s (such as Holcomb and Luongo, 1996; Hughes, 1997; Pritchard *et al.*, 1998), since which time there has been a relatively steady output including over 30 papers in academic tourism journals, an edited book (Clift *et al.*, 2002) and (in the UK) at least one PhD thesis (Cox, 2001). Whilst it is true that 'much of what has been written tends to define gay tourism through economic possibilities'

(Johnston, 2001, p. 187), the perspective is broadening. As this book nears completion, there is a prospect of at least two other books on gay and lesbian tourism being published in the near future; it's a little like waiting for a bus – none for ages and then several arrive at once! This growing interest in gay and lesbian tourism is welcome and, hopefully, these new publications and this one will complement one another and make a significant difference to this field of study.

In addition, material relating specifically to the holidays of lesbians is very limited in quantity and coverage. Much of the discussion in this book will relate therefore to gay men because of this and not because of some subconscious misogyny. The limited information about lesbians and their holiday experiences is a reflection of a more widespread lack of interest by market researchers in general and their perception of lesbians as being a market that is less worth pursuing than that of gay men (Sender, 2004). Tourism academic studies in general have also focused on the male (heterosexual) traveller.

Sexual activity *per se* has not been the focus of gay and lesbian tourism studies to date though it obviously features in some. They have considered the relationship between tourism and sexual orientation rather than sex tourism (purposefully travelling in pursuit of sexual encounter) or sex and tourism (sexual encounter whilst on holiday). There is, however, a small number of works touching on these aspects. The sex and travel experiences of gay men feature prominently in Luongo's (2004) edited book, though not from an academic perspective. The subtitle – *A Collection of Gay Travel Erotica* – gives a clear indication that this is a work that focuses on travellers' tales and narratives of sexual encounter whilst away from home. In the more academic sphere, Ryan and Hall (2001) focus on heterosexual issues in their book on sex tourism but do, none the less, devote a chapter to gay and lesbian tourism largely dealing with Sydney Mardi Gras and its political and social significance (and not, incidentally, with the sex aspect of gay and lesbian tourism). Clift and Carter's (2000) edited book on sex and tourism also has a heterosexual bias, though it does contain two chapters relating to sexual activity of gay men on holiday. Bauer and McKercher's (2003) edited book on sex and tourism ranges beyond this to 'romance and love', but it also is firmly heterosexually focused. The editors do acknowledge, however, that other topics could be explored 'such as the motivations and travel behaviour of gay men and women' (p. xvii). The core of this present book, however, is sexual orientation and holidays, not sex tourism or sex and tourism though both are, none the less, as likely to feature in holidays of gays and lesbians as they are for anyone else and they will be discussed where appropriate.

The apparent reluctance of tourism researchers to engage with gay and lesbian issues may simply be a reflection of the recent emergence of tourism studies generally, or may be a symptom of the fact that tourism research 'has tended to neglect the perspectives and experiences of marginalized groups' (Humberstone, 2004, p. 119). This, itself, is a reflection of power relations and the dominance of research agendas by a white, male, heteronormative perspective (Johnston, 2001). In addition, there may well have been a reluctance to research a field with which researchers might be personally associated, with a consequent risk of labelling and stigmatization. The recent (comparative) increase in gay and lesbian tourism research not only demonstrates a willingness to challenge dominant research agendas but perhaps more especially is a result of the challenge to dominant research paradigms. There has been a slow but steady acceptance of tourism research approaches other than those associated with positivism and its supposedly value-free, outside observer and interpreter overtones (Goodson and Phillimore, 2004). The willingness to embrace a view that 'reality' is a value-mediated outcome of a researcher–researched interaction is related to the new consideration of the greater diversity of tourist experiences.

Why is it Important?

Does it matter that gay and lesbian tourism is barely researched? It is likely that the holiday motivations and experiences of homosexuals are different from those of heterosexuals and, as a consequence, there will be an obvious imperative to determine those differences if academics and practitioners are not to continue dealing with tourists as an undifferentiated homogeneous mass. Differences are likely to arise as it is recognized that the meanings attached to tourism spaces and experiences are social–cultural constructions and that 'reality' lies in the lived experiences of people within their situations and contexts (Goodson and Phillimore, 2004; Humberstone, 2004). Social geographers (such as Bell, 1991; Bell and Valentine, 1995) have pointed out how the character of space is influenced by sexuality (and how that space may itself influence sexual identities); tourism has an obvious spatial dimension. It is already acknowledged that there has been an undue emphasis on the masculine aspect of tourism; tourism studies within the social sciences have produced 'hegemonic, disembodied and masculinist knowledge' (Johnston, 2001, p. 180). Women and men, however, experience tourism differently, and this has led to a relatively recent interest in the gendered construction of tourism and the need to explore the experiences of women in particular (Kinnaird and Hall, 1994b; Swain, 1995). Motivations, for instance, are 'constructed out of the social realities of the lives of those who participate' (Kinnaird and Hall, 1994b, p. 212) and those realities are the product of power and control. Tourism 'is built of human relations and thus impacts and is impacted by global and local gender relations' (Swain, 1995, p. 247); for 'gender', substitute 'sexual orientation'.

The determination of the differences is important because an 'analysis of gender is part of a wider concern with equity issues and social exclusion in contemporary societies' (Deem, 1999, p. 164). A study of sexual orientation and tourism, along with the study of gender differences, will not only illustrate the diversity of tourism experiences but also contribute to the wider debate about the more general inequalities arising from gender or sexual orientation. Tourism is 'an ideal vehicle' for this and will add to an understanding of the 'power dynamics' that have contributed to patriarchal and heteronormative societies (Swain, 2004, p. 103).

Sources

Although the academic interest in gay and lesbian tourism is relatively new there have, of course, long been publications written by gay men and lesbians about their travels or lives in foreign countries. Gertrude Stein (1874–1946), an American, lived with her woman partner in Paris for nearly 40 years. Their life together was featured in Stein's *The Autobiography of Alice B. Toklas*, published in 1933. Joe Orton (1933–1967) chronicled his gay sexual adventures in North Africa in his diaries, posthumously published in 1967, and life in inter-war Berlin was immortalized by Christopher Isherwood (1906–1986) in his *Berlin Stories*, published 1935–1939 and subsequently as the film *Cabaret*. T.E. Lawrence (Lawrence of Arabia, 1888–1935) was allegedly homosexual and published *Seven Pillars of Wisdom* in several versions in the 1920s and 1930s describing his military and espionage adventures in the Middle East. They have not necessarily dealt with specific gay or lesbian matters, nor been written with an overt admission of the author's sexual orientation.

Similarly, there have long been travel guides, such as *Spartacus*, written for lesbians and gays (in its 34th edition in 2005) and *Damron's Men's Travel Guide*, first published in 1964 and now in its 39th edition. The title of Van Gelder and Brandt's travel guide book (1991) poses a particularly relevant question: *Are You Two . . . Together?*, reflecting the hesitancy with which gay couples are often accepted on their travels. Sources such as these are used in this book, though it is recognized that they may well be partisan in their recommendations and comments and often are little more than listings. Listings are not necessarily representative of facilities or destinations.

Holidays have featured in gay and lesbian magazines (traditional and online) in the form of news items, as features about destinations and, of course, as advertisements. Holiday-related news items have appeared in the 'straight' press where particular issues have been considered worthy of a wider readership. There have also been gay and lesbian travel and destination features in a number of (broadsheet) newspapers, which are likely to attract an upscale gay and lesbian readership. Given the limited empirical work relating to gay and lesbian tourism these media sources are used, where appropriate, throughout this book but with due consideration for their reliability.

Some of the material in this book is derived from other non-academic sources, including web sites of tour operators and of destinations, and gay and lesbian information web sites. Material is also derived from newspapers and magazines, both 'mainstream' and gay and lesbian. These sources are acknowledged throughout, though reservations about the reliability of the sources are not always articulated. It is recognized that these sources may be less than objective and that they may have a particular agenda to pursue; they may be promotional of a place or of a cause. The basis for many observations and statements in these sources is unclear and is rarely equivalent to what would be expected in an academic journal. They should be treated therefore with appropriate caution. They are used, however, as they are often the only source of information about particular events or issues. They also serve to illustrate the current perspectives of the gay or general media on issues or events which will, in turn, colour readers' views. In the UK, there are currently several magazines targeted at the gay and lesbian market; most are 'lifestyle' magazines and include a mixture of fashion, entertainment and news items. Of these, *Gay Times* has the largest 'news' content and has been a significant source of material for this book. It has a circulation of about 60,000 (readership of 180,000) and has existed under its present title since 1984. Since 1994, it has had a sister publication, *Diva* (circulation of about 35,000), which is aimed at the lesbian market.

Approach

The purpose of this book is to examine and analyse holidays of gays and lesbians and related issues from a particular (marketing) perspective, though it is not a marketing handbook. Much of the little academic work that exists is speculative and polemic, reflecting the lack of research, either qualitative or quantitative, that has been undertaken to date. This book is an attempt to summarize what is known about gay and lesbian tourism (with all of the shortcomings relating to that knowledge) rather than to dwell too much on the hypothetical or theoretical. It will draw attention to both the limitations and strengths of existing work.

The origin of this book lies in research based in a university department of tourism management, and the book has a management and a particular marketing genesis and emphasis. As an evolving part of research studies in this department (and in other universities) it has become apparent that the diversity of tourism experiences is not only under-researched but also worthy of further investigation (as contended above). The reality of tourism continues to change and tourism studies need to keep abreast

of that reality whilst, at the same time, contributing to a greater understanding of the diversity and, in practical terms, to the future development of tourism activity.

The book will have an undoubted bias towards the observation of
gay and lesbian tourism from a UK perspective, but it will also draw on
material from other countries. UK experiences may not be universal, but
some issues will be common to many countries and the UK experience
will serve to illustrate those issues. Material from other countries (in so
far as it exists) will also be used to illustrate both commonalities and
differences.

This book attempts to summarize the 'state-of-the-art' with respect to
work on gay and lesbian tourism and to begin to bridge a gap in tourism
studies. In particular, it examines 'the market' and how it might be
targeted by suppliers. There is an examination of gays and lesbians as
tourism consumers and, specifically, how sexual orientation and societal
marginalization might influence consumer behaviour. Market segmentation has usually been undertaken by reference to socio-economic and
demographic, geographical, psychographic and behavioural factors but
'gay and lesbian factors', although possibly categorizable under the previous factors, may have an overriding influence. They have rarely been
examined separately as possible influences on holidaymaking.

Gay and lesbian tourism is occasionally referred to as a form of 'niche
tourism'. The terms 'niche markets' or 'niche tourism' more particularly refer
to 'types' of tourism such as interest in heritage, sport or arts (Robinson and
Novelli, 2005). In the latter part of the 20th century and early part of the
21st there has undoubtedly been a development and increased prominence of such new niche markets (special interest markets) as distinct
from an earlier importance of mass tourism. Gays and lesbians may enter
these niche or special interest markets like anyone else. It remains to be
seen whether or not sexual orientation influences choice of 'conventional'
holiday product or activity but also whether or not there is a special interest
gay and lesbian market in the sense of specific product or activity. This
book is a focus on tourism markets from a demand perspective rather than
from an activity or product (or niche market or niche tourism) perspective.

This book will reveal (as far as is known) the interrelationship
between sexual orientation and holidays, any distinctive 'needs' and
specific and differing meanings attached to the holiday, any distinctive
holiday patterns and any barriers to participation. If sexual orientation
does have an influence on consumer behaviour, then gays and lesbians
as potential or actual holidaymakers may require targeting, positioning
and product provision that differ from those adopted for the rest of the
population. The book will therefore assist in effective marketing to the
neglected gay and lesbian 'markets', but will also contribute to the further
development of tourism studies by demonstrating the diversity of tourist
experiences.

Such a particular management-oriented marketing approach is firmly within the 'tradition' of academic tourism studies: industry and applied managerial and economic perspectives. Tribe (1997) has observed that academic tourism studies comprise two fields: those of tourism business studies and those of 'the rest' associated with sociology, geography, etc. Studies have, however, crystallized around the former, which holds out the prospect of a coherent structure and framework. The contribution of 'the rest' is increasingly evident, however, in many aspects of tourism studies and can offer valuable insights into the phenomenon of tourism. Selby (2004), for instance, focused on the contribution that social sciences – especially sociology and human geography – can make to the study of urban tourism. His starting point was a growing existing literature on the topic that has focused on 'applied and pragmatic approaches . . . and (which is) atheoretical and descriptive' (Selby, 2004, pp. 1–2). This, he believed, has its place, but overlooks the contribution that social sciences may make to a more rigorous approach to the analysis of urban tourism. That, in turn, will lead to greater understanding, and ultimately to enhanced tourism practice. Smith (2003) identified a related situation with respect to cultural tourism. She adopted a similar approach to Selby's and discussed the contributions that fields such as cultural studies, sociology and urban planning can make to key issues that have largely been previously discussed in less theoretical terms. Theory and concepts are not explored for their own sake, but rather for their contribution to understanding of more practical matters.

The application of the social sciences is not, however, the purpose of this book. This is not to deny the contribution that social sciences can make, and some researchers have already adopted such perspectives for the study of gay and lesbian tourism. The further development and refining of these will undoubtedly lead to clearer foci for further research into determining the 'facts' and to greater insight into this area of activity. This book, however, has developed from awareness of a 'gap' in the management and marketing field.

This is not, though, solely a positivist, 'hard facts' book. Whilst focusing on management-oriented marketing, the book goes beyond this to examine issues such as the wider implications for gays and lesbians of such marketing and considers how marketing activity inter-relates and engages with social issues beyond those relating to the holiday experience itself. Tribe (2002) argues that tourism education – and thus tourism studies – should aim to produce a philosophic practitioner, a person who can 'tune into the bigger picture' (p. 349). Tourism education should be an amalgam of vocationalism, liberalism, action and reflection, so that the end product is a person who assumes 'responsibility for promoting the well-being of tourism's society and world and not just the profitability of individual firms' (Tribe, 2002, p. 351). It is this viewpoint that underpins this book. A further aim therefore is to consider the impact that marketing holidays to gays and lesbians might have on their lives in the wider sphere and what it means for homosexuality. These are matters that owe more to the view that 'reality' lies in the experiences of people and that the social world can be understood only from the point of view of those within it (Humberstone, 2004). The book, although focused on tourism, will, in addition, identify the contribution of tourism to a further understanding of the diversity of society and of issues of sexual orientation and homosexuality.

A Particular Disciplinary Approach?

Tourism studies are 'new' compared with disciplines such as geography or physics, and there has been some debate about whether tourism may be considered to be a separate discipline. It is more widely accepted that it is a field of study that draws on existing disciplines (Jafari and Brent Ritchie, 1981; Leiper, 1981; Tribe, 1997). Tourism studies, with their consideration of tourism consumers, travel and holiday destinations and experiences, have applied relevant concepts, theories and models drawn from disciplines such as geography, economics, psychology, sociology and anthropology. Selby (2004) contends there is no single unifying discipline on which to draw, and this book is no exception in this respect. Marketing too has been the subject of debate as to its status as a discipline; notwithstanding that, it too is clearly derivative of several existing disciplines in the same way as tourism is. There is a certain inevitability therefore about the multidisciplinary nature of this tourism book.

The book also draws on ideas and issues from other multidisciplinary fields of study such as lesbian and gay studies and gender studies. These fields, as are tourism studies, are also 'new', having also emerged from disciplines (especially sociology) such as those contributing to tourism and have no common theoretical core or single methodology (Plummer, 1992; Weeks, 2000; Pilcher and Whelehan, 2004). There is much within 'mainstream' lesbian and gay studies that deals with related matters, though not directly with the interrelationship between tourism and sexual orientation. There are some noticeable exceptions, such as nine papers in the special issue of *GLQ* in 2002 (vol. 8, issue 1–2). The relationship of space and sexuality as studied by geographers has been particularly helpful, though not, for the most part, focused on tourism *per se* (e.g. Bell, 1991; Bell and Valentine, 1995; Ingram *et al.*, 1997; Binnie and Valentine, 1999; Valentine, 2000; Puar *et al.*, 2003). There is by now, with the growth of lesbian and gay studies, a large amount of published material that approaches homosexuality from psychological, sociological and political perspectives and relates to gay and lesbian lifestyles. There is, also, an increasing body of work that discusses marketing to gays and lesbians (e.g. Wardlow, 1996; Kates, 1998; Lukenbill, 1999) and the economic aspects of homosexuality (e.g. Gluckman and Reed, 1997a; Badgett, 2001). Useful historical and contemporary accounts and analysis of gay and lesbian life in particular places (home and abroad) include Drucker (2000a) on the 'third world', Jackson and Sullivan (1999a) on Thailand and Higgs (1999a) on large cities throughout the world. Similarly, there are a number of helpful and insightful accounts and analyses of places with gay and lesbian significance such as Newton (1993) on Cherry Grove (Fire Island), Cunningham (2004) on Provincetown and Boyd (1997, 2003) on San Francisco.

The book will therefore utilize 'facts' about lesbian and gay tourism, drawn from a variety of sources including market research studies, within an analysis based on the academic study of marketing which also utilizes, where appropriate, ideas and issues from other disciplines and fields such as lesbian and gay studies.

Structure of the Book

Chapter 2 discusses the nature of homosexuality and some of the features of gay and lesbian life that are believed to have most significance for tourism. It may be that many readers of the book are very familiar (either personally or through academic study) with this, in which case the chapter can be passed over. Experience suggests, however, that many students are not particularly well informed, or have a baggage of half-truths and stereotypes. Studying and analysing the holidays of gays and lesbians in such a situation can result in bizarre outcomes. The material in Chapter 2 is not comprehensive and it is not the thorough discussion that many would wish it to be. Inevitably, too, it is a simplification – and hopefully not too much of a misrepresentation – of a complex matter.

The following four Chapters (3–6) deal specifically with gay and lesbian tourism, before a return to more general issues in Chapters 7 and 8. In Chapter 3, existing work on the demand side is considered. This includes the size of the market and the holiday profiles of gays and lesbians, especially the frequency of holiday-taking and accommodation used. There is a substantial input relating to what is argued to be the particular significance of holidays for gays and lesbians. The chapter concludes with a consideration of sex in tourism, an issue that is often thought to be central in this type of tourism.

Chapters 4 and 5 move the focus to where gays and lesbian tourists go on holiday. It is argued that risk plays an especially important part in the destination choice process for homosexuals and an overview of those risks is given. Some of the more evident risks encountered are discussed, especially the reactions of local residents.

In Chapter 5, it is indicated that where gays and lesbians go on holiday is difficult to determine directly. There are a large number of indirect sources for this information, however, and these are reviewed.

The remaining part of the chapter includes a description of some of what are widely believed to be the more popular destinations.

The supply side is examined in Chapter 6. The approaches of tour operators and of accommodation providers, in particular, are discussed and their particular reactions (if any) to the demand for holidays from gays and lesbians. The chapter also includes an analysis of sights and events, such as the Gay Games and Pride festivals, that are likely to stimulate travel by gays and lesbians.

The following two chapters (7 and 8) return to a more general consideration by placing material discussed in Chapters 3–6 within a wider context. These chapters contain more analysis and commentary than do the others. Issues are dealt with here rather than in the preceding chapters, as the issues arise from matters discussed in more than one chapter. In addition, it is the combined influence of some of these matters that bears upon the issues. A full discussion of issues is dependent, too, upon a prior consideration of marketing, as some of the more significant issues arise from this activity. Much of Chapters 3–6 is based on the assumption that there is, in some form, a gay and lesbian market to be targeted and this, and related matters, are discussed in Chapter 7. This chapter deals with marketing, in part, from a general perspective, though the aim is to illuminate and analyse some of the issues that have arisen in earlier chapters. It also illustrates approaches to marketing of holidays to gays and lesbians.

The material in Chapter 8 continues, and develops further, discussion of issues of significance which may seem to be of little, if any, immediate or obvious relevance to marketers. The consideration of tourism in Chapters 3–6 does, though, have implications not only for marketers and tourism studies academics, but it also serves to reveal further dimensions of homosexuality and the relationship of gays and lesbians to heteronormative society. A study of tourism by gays and lesbians has consequences that go beyond tourism. In particular, it is suggested that not only does tourism have a particular meaning for homosexual life, it is also an important arena where dissonance between homosexuals and heterosexuals is confronted and addressed. There are implications (both favourable and less so) of tourism that reach beyond the immediate concerns of those directly involved.

In the final chapter (9), the existing work on gay and lesbian tourism is briefly summarized, issues arising from it are revisited and implications drawn out.

Self and a Deeper Purpose

As a final observation, it is pertinent to acknowledge the significance that many researchers attribute to lesbian and gay studies, a significance that lies in the potential to counter the current social situation of homosexuals. This book is not a research monograph and it largely reports on and discusses the work of others. As such, there is a reasonable expectation that it would be characterized by a relatively neutral, 'outsider's' approach. None the less, no author can remain 'un-situated'. 'In terms of why we research what we do, one cannot . . . ignore the personal' (Hall, 2004, p. 148). The decision to write this book, the choice of issues and of the studies and sources to be included and the interpretation and use made of those in the book are inevitably personal and, however unconsciously, reflect an agenda. Some readers may detect a particular empathy or bias in places or throughout; as far as is humanly possible the book has been written with the objectivity and distance that are expected of an academic researcher. Inevitably, 'self' has informed the work; the book is written from the perspective of a male homosexual of 'mature' years who came late to allowing others to know of his sexual orientation.

There is no attempt, however, to disguise the fact that this book is written with the conscious hope that it might make a modest contribution to 'a distinctive form of politics . . . which simultaneously affirms the validity of homosexual life choices and confronts the various forces of power which deny lesbian and gay life chances' (Weeks, 2000, p. 6). No excuse is offered for this. 'We think that gay and lesbian studies should deal with research questions that might contribute to countering discrimination against homosexuality and to fostering its expression and to promoting sexual diversity' (Schuyf and Sandfort, 2000, p. 219).

A note on UK and US terminology

There is a confusing difference in the US and UK usage of the term 'resort'. In the US it refers to a complex of tourist villas or similar accommodation or an all-inclusive hotel (similar to the old UK 'holiday camp'). A US resort hotel has a focus on providing recreational facilities such as swimming pools, golf courses and similar sporting amenities in addition to the 'usual' hotel services (Lundberg, 1994). A particular type of resort hotel, the casino hotel, has an emphasis on entertainment. There are 'resort hotels' in the UK which tend to be positioned as a country club with up-market clientele (Roper, 1996). In the UK 'resort' usually refers to a coastal town that is a tourist destination (though it may also refer to a mountain or rural town). Both the US and UK usages of the term serve convenient purposes and it would not be helpful to abandon one use in favour of a 'new', but unfamiliar, term. In this book, therefore, the term will be used in both senses, with appropriate clarification at relevant points. Hopefully this will avoid confusion and ensure understanding, whilst maintaining the familiarity of well-used and long-accepted terms.

There may be some (but lesser) confusion about the term 'accommodation' which, in the UK, covers both a single place and several places to stay. The plural version 'accommodations' (unfamiliar in the UK) is frequently used in the USA.

There should be no difficulty arising from the usage of 'holiday' and 'vacation'. These terms will be used interchangeably and, usually, as and when used by others.

Homosexuality – its Nature and Characteristics

2

Introduction

This chapter is meant as background to the following chapters that deal specifically with tourism. It is necessary to discuss terms such as gay, lesbian, homosexual and queer in order to clarify the focus of the book. In addition, this chapter will discuss issues associated with gays, lesbians, etc. that are of continuing significance for the lives of such people and which have a particular relevance when tourism is considered. The chapter is written for those with little prior knowledge of the issues and is not meant to be comprehensive either in breadth or depth. Inevitably, it simplifies what are often complex arguments and concepts. The chapter is lengthy but is not an inclusive overview of gay and lesbian issues. It focuses only on those issues that are believed to be of significance when considering tourism.

Two Views on the Nature of Homosexuality

Homosexuality may be defined in a fairly simplistic way as individuals having sexual desire for, or sexual activity with, persons of the same biological sex. Such individuals may not, however, necessarily think of themselves or identify as homosexual. There is a strong body of opinion amongst sociologists that homosexuality as an identity is something that has emerged only recently (Schuyf, 2000). This view – a 'social constructionist' view – is in contrast to the 'essentialist' view that there has always been homosexuality at all times and in all places. Many 'apologists' have referred to same-sex relationships and sexual practices in societies throughout recorded history, often focusing upon Ancient Greece, in particular (Bravmann, 1994). These have frequently referred to emotional ties and affection, however, and not solely to sexual acts.

This essentialist–social constructionist debate is not one that attempts to explain the cause of same-sex attraction, though there was a connection with some recent studies which suggested a biological causation of same-sex desire. The LeVay study (1991) claimed that there was a difference between gay men and heterosexuals in the size of the part of the brain (hypothalamus) that is linked to sexual behaviour. Hamer *et al.*'s study (1993), showed a greater presence of particular genetic markers in some gay men. None of these studies is conclusive, but they have strengthened the case for those who support a 'biological determinism' or essentialist view of homosexuality. It suggests that sexuality is not a matter of choice but is, in some way, pre-determined. This has an appeal in as much as the individual's homosexuality is innate and is something over which he/she has no control; as a consequence, it strengthens the case against condemnation and for remedying inequalities (Halwani, 1998). Views on the causes of homosexuality have tended to polarize into a 'nature versus nurture' debate. Suggested 'causes' have included parenting styles, birth order, parental age, sex abuse in childhood, relationship with parents (dominant mothers and weak fathers) and unsatisfactory relationships with the opposite sex (Sandfort, 2000; Robinson, 2002). The question of the causes of homosexuality is, however, a separate issue from the essentialism–constructivism debate, though there is a tendency for essentialists to consider differences as innate and biological.

The social constructionist view (drawing upon symbolic interactionism) has been developed since the late 1960s by a number of individuals, including Foucault in France and McIntosh and Weeks in the UK. They relate the emergence of the concept of 'the homosexual' to the desire of 19th century psychologists and 'sexologists' to identify, categorize and ultimately to condemn some 'categories' as disordered. Homosexual acts have always existed but the identity of the homosexual is regarded as a 19th century invention (Weeks, 1992). The initial use of the word 'homosexual' is credited to the Austro-Hungarian, Kertbeny (1824–1882) in 1868–1869. The terms lesbianism and sapphism came into use between the 1870s and 1890s. They derived from Sappho, who was born on the Greek island of Lesvos, in about 630BC, and established a community of women there after the death of her husband.

Only since the 19th century have individuals been identified as, or have identified themselves as, homosexual. Any variation of desire or behaviour from the supposed norm, such as homosexuality, was labelled 'aberrant', 'deviant' or mentally ill. It was important to have criteria for identifying such an individual and this encouraged interest in 'scientific' bases for classification. Homosexuality, in effect, became a mental illness, with the consequent belief that homosexuals could be subjected to treatment in an attempt to 'cure' the disorder. The German psychiatrist Krafft-Ebing (1840–1902) was foremost in attempting to categorize sexual 'disorders', and his initial view that homosexuality was caused by moral degeneracy or mental illness was widely accepted. The American Psychiatric Association did not de-classify it as a mental disorder until 1973, and the World Health Organization not until 1992 (Mind, 2002). 'Cures' for homosexuality have included electroconvulsive therapy, aversion therapy, surgery (including lobotomy), chemical castration and hormone treatment.

It is argued that a person will only identify him/herself as homosexual if that concept exists in a society (Horowitz and Newcomb, 2001). The concept, however, has not always existed and it does not exist everywhere even now. A person may or may not be born with a same-sex emotional and physical preference, but identification as a homosexual is something a person chooses to do, or has forced upon him or herself. Essentialism is associated with an individual recognizing and accepting a given sexuality. Social constructivism entails a more fluid concept, where identity is the outcome of an interaction between the individual and the social environment, the outcome of which will depend on the specific social and historic context. Homosexuality becomes less a sexual category or sexual preference and more an identity.

Identity

'Identity' is itself not a particularly clear concept. It has many different meanings, but basically it is to do with who or what a person thinks he or she is – a 'sense of self' – self-identity. Identity is 'a socially constructed myth about shared characteristics, culture and history which comes to have real meaning for those who espouse it' (Altman, 2001, p. 86). This is constructed by reference to the outside world: an individual distinguishes the factors which make him or her 'the same' as others and which differentiate him or her from others. Identity gives a feeling of 'belonging' to a particular community and of 'not belonging' to others. Even if individuals resist categorization, others will impose it on them. There are many reference points, including ethnicity, sex, class, religion and age for identity formation, of which sexual orientation is but one. The idea that it might be an issue in identity or even a key element of identity is a relatively recent one – from the late 1960s, as a central one around which people constructed their lives – and largely in the Western world (Altman, 1997). Same-sex desire can now be a central and defining component of identity for some (Robinson, 2002). None the less, sexuality is but one aspect of a person's identity and, as a consequence, there will be no one 'gay identity': homosexuals do not share a common core of experiences, interests and way of life (Richardson and Seidman, 2002).

The identity of 'homosexual' has been supplanted since the mid-20th century by that of being 'gay'. There is no commonly accepted definition of the word or agreement about its origin as applied to homosexuals. (It has been used as a coded sexual reference since the 19th century, at least, and as a coded reference to homosexuals since at least the 1920s. The view that it is an acronym for 'good as you' has little foundation.) It is sometimes used to cover both male and female homosexuals (as in 'gay men and women'), though it is more frequently applied to men only, with women being referred to as lesbians. 'Gay' and 'lesbian' are now more widely used than 'homosexual' in everyday usage, in the media and in academic studies. When the term 'gay' is used alone it is not always clear what the intended meaning is, though it would often appear to be used in its inclusive male and female sense. The term gay appears to have gained widespread usage because of its more positive resonance compared with previously commonly used, pejorative terms for men such as faggot, poof, pansy and nancy-boy, or dyke for women. Gay is also commonly used to refer to men who not only have a same-sex sexual preference, but are also 'open' about it and have a lifestyle built primarily around that sexuality.

The fluidity of social constructivism has a counterpart in 'queer theory'. Although the word 'queer' has long been applied to gays and lesbians, often in a derogatory sense, queer theory is not confined to gay and lesbian identities. It is based on the idea that identities are not fixed but are a 'performance' – actions produce sexual identity. Identity is performative, it is what a person chooses to do rather being 'a given' (Butler, 1990); it is produced through behaviour that projects a particular identity. Queer theory acknowledges that a person's (sexual) identity is not fixed and no individual can be categorized. There is a wide range of choices which are open to people. Rather than a simplistic, heterosexual–homosexual binary divide which envisages heterosexuality as the norm and homosexuality as marginal, sexuality is envisaged as a continuum. Sexuality is fluid and there is a multiplicity of sexualities which may apply to any one person at any particular time and circumstance. Inevitably, individuals are 'forced' by convention, when seeking an identity, to fit themselves into one of the generally recognized categories when, in reality, sexuality is a much more fluid, diverse and imprecise concept (Horowitz and Newcomb, 2001). Many will find comfort and stability in an identity, a concept which is inclusive through identifying commonality between people. It can, though, be coercive and exclusionary for those who cannot readily identify with a specified identity (Plummer, 1992; Connell, 1995; Esterberg, 1997). The term 'queer' has, incidentally, been reclaimed by some gays and lesbians as a term of pride. The term features as a strapline in advertisements promoting Vienna to the gay and lesbian tourist market – see Fig. 2.1.

A number of studies have confirmed the imprecise and personal nature of identity. In one, women identified as lesbian despite having relationships with men or having had no sexual experience with other

Fig. 2.1. Press advertisement produced by the Vienna Tourist Board, Austria.

women; others identified as heterosexual, despite having had sexual experiences with women (Golden, 1994): sexual encounters had been removed from the heart of sexual identity. Women who identified as lesbians in another study did so on differing bases, such as sexual relations or emotional relations, or friendships and social relationships (Esterberg, 1997). For some, the self-identification derived from feminism and the desire to disrupt gender expectations, to challenge patriarchal society and to demonstrate the ability to choose their relationships. Some feminist lesbianism was associated with anti-capitalism and a stand against the subordination of women to men (Esterberg, 1997).

Community

An individual identity also involves a feeling of belonging to a particular 'community' of people with similar characteristics and behaviour. The term community is increasingly used to refer to 'imagined communities' (Anderson, 1991), a concept that referred specifically to nation states which are themselves constructs based on a supposed internal homogeneity that distinguishes the citizens from others. A gay or lesbian community can be an imagined construct in the same way: any one individual may not even meet or know fellow members of that community, but all share a common perception of what it is to be gay or lesbian and therefore share a feeling of belonging (Esterberg, 1997). Lesbians in Brooklyn perceived themselves to be members of a community even though they may never have known most of their fellow members (Rothenburg, 1995).

Despite many diverse lifestyles, there may be a sense of common cause and identity among large numbers of gays. Some have gone so far as to envisage the existence of a 'quasi-ethnic community', especially with respect to the USA (Higgs, 1999b; Wright, 1999). Cox (2001), too, suggests that the shared meanings of homosexuals may constitute a sense of 'gay ethnicity'. Negative aspects may, however, play as large a part as positive in forging of community; alienation from society may encourage a common identity as 'victims' (Seidman *et al.*, 1999). Field (1995) sees the nucleus of a gay community as being a sense of shared oppression. Unlike ethnic minority communities, gays and lesbians do not have a homeland – a country in which ancestors lived – to which they can look for a sense of who they are. They may, though, perceive certain places as gay and lesbian 'homelands' – a dream or fantasy – thus stimulating migration (or tourism) to particular centres associated with gay and lesbian life which hold out the prospect of constructing an identity (Cant, 1997; Stephenson, 2002).

Undoubtedly communities – in the sense of concentrations of gays and lesbians living in particular geographical areas – do exist (see later, this chapter). Quite often, however, communities (especially lesbian) are 'overlapping friendship networks, and sometimes exclusive ones at that, with multiple centres and fuzzy boundaries' (Esterberg, 1997, p. 175). The community of gays and lesbians may take the more intimate nature of a circle of friends. A sense of belonging may apply more to friends than to a wider heterosexual society or biological family, especially if the family experience has been one of rejection (Nardi, 1992; Cox, 2001). They often have a sexual dimension as a starting point, but subsequently offer lasting, long-term opportunities for social support.

Identity and others

Defining oneself as gay or lesbian is often regarded, perhaps simplistically, as a stage process moving from a personal awareness of 'difference', through accepting that sexual identity, integrating into concept of self, through to disclosure to others (Horowitz and Newcomb, 2001). Part of this process may involve associating with other gays – 'validating others' – against whom a person can judge and test his or her identity and be accepted. An identity is constructed not only by relating positively to the characteristics of some, but also through acknowledgement of difference. From a social constructionist perspective, the individual is more actively involved in this process of establishing an identity than simply discovering, by stages, a pre-existing sexuality.

Awareness of sexual orientation commonly occurs in teen years (Warner *et al.*, 2004) and the process of adjustment is often made difficult as family or peer support has frequently been unlikely, at least initially. There is also a lack of ready reference points about what homosexuality or gay lifestyles might entail. Most people are raised in a heterosexual family unit and, beyond that, in a heteronormative world – where heterosexuality is the norm. It is not easy to gain an insight into the 'alternatives', other than through representations in the media, which are often stereotypical. As a consequence, there may be confusion about how to live as a gay person. Further confusion may arise as the heterosexual model of long-term relationships is not obviously apparent in the gay world, and casual encounters are an important part of the experience (Connell, 1995). In societies where heterosexuality is legitimized and homosexuality is regarded in negative ways, identifying as gay or lesbian becomes a particularly difficult issue to address which can give rise to problems associated with stress and self-esteem (see later, this chapter).

Even when a person self-accepts as homosexual there may be considerable reluctance to allow others to be aware of it. 'Coming out' is a common term used to refer to the process of revealing sexual orientation to others, though it is also used to refer to defining oneself as gay or lesbian (Valentine and Skelton, 2003). Being 'in the closet' is a term widely used when sexual orientation is not revealed. Fear of rejection and disapproval may induce individuals to continue to conceal. Coming out may be a selective process with identification as homosexual to some people and not to others. Marriage to a person of the opposite sex and maintaining a lifestyle that is ostensibly heterosexual may be a common form of being 'not out'. Concealment of sexuality (being 'in the closet') is common; nearly two-thirds of young people in Northern Ireland did not feel able to tell their parents when they first came out, but confided first in friends (YouthNet, 2003). None the less, several surveys of older gays and lesbians suggest that families were supportive. In a survey of adults in Wales, people were much more likely (about 80%) to have come out to parents, siblings and children than to anyone else (Robinson and Williams, 2003). In a similar study in Scotland, between a quarter and a third of people concealed their sexuality from employers and work colleagues (Beyond Barriers, 2002). The US GL Census 2004–2005 showed that gays and lesbians were more likely to be out to friends than to immediate family or to work colleagues.

Leisure, Gay Space and Identity

Leisure has a significant role to play in the development of identity, as it offers opportunities for freely performed behaviour which can have positive influences on self-perception (Haggard and Williams 1992; Wearing and Wearing, 1992). A number of studies have shown how young gay and lesbian people, in particular, have used leisure to negotiate their understanding of themselves; leisure offers choice about who to socialize with (Kivel, 1994; Kivel and Kleiber, 2000). Some, however, have reported difficulties and how the choice of leisure activities had been constrained through fear of exposure or of homophobia (Johnson, 1999). Both positive and negative experiences applied to adult gays and lesbians too (Jacobson and Samdahl, 1998; Markwell, 1998). The leisure sphere of bars and clubs may be particularly important for gay and lesbian identity formation, at least for those old enough to frequent them. Gays are socialized into new sub-culture through bars and clubs – these fulfil a function of creating a sense of community (Haslop *et al.*, 1998).

Gay space is generally characterized as a concentration of bars and clubs, but also saunas, cafes, shops, residences and public space (streets, parks, squares, etc.) for social interaction (Hindle, 1994). It is also popularly referred to as the 'gay scene'. Gay space, whatever form it takes, is of great significance for gays and lesbians. In a heteronormative world, gay space provides the opportunity to relate to other homosexuals and to validate one's own identity. It also enables gays and lesbians to 'be themselves', so that behaviour can change between gay and straight places. It brings a sense of belonging to a community and confers a sense of empowerment. It is also where gays and lesbians can hopefully be safe from physical and verbal abuse: 'queer spaces create a strong sense of empowerment that allows men to look past the dangers of being gay in a city and to feel safe and at home' (Myslik, 1996, p. 169).

Gay space has historically, for men at least, been associated with public 'cruising areas' of parks, beaches and public toilets (Humphreys, 1970; Higgs, 1999b). These were particularly important meeting places for participation in casual sex before the development of the commercial gay scene and the legalization of homosexual sexual activity. Despite such changes, many gay men continue this challenge to heteronormative values of the use of public space; it not only facilitates physical gratification but also contributes to a sense of community (Markwell, 1998; Howe, 2001). In parts of the world where such developments have not occurred, cruising areas retain a special importance.

Place and space are considered to play an important role in the construction of identity (Forest, 1995). Most public space is masculine- and heterosexual-dominated, something that is so deeply ingrained that it is not seen by most (Myslik, 1996). Public space is kept free of passion or expressions of 'abnormal' sexuality. Most issues to do with sexuality are associated with private sphere – the home – and homosexuality is tolerated only if it remains in private (Duncan, 1996; Brickell, 2000). Public space is a place of tension and conflict; it potentially becomes a site for opposition where non-heterosexuals can claim space for themselves (Valentine, 1996; Pritchard *et al.*, 2002; Rushbrook, 2002). Heterosexual residents of Le Marais district in Paris have expressed their opposition to the development of gay space there (Sibalis, 1999, 2004). There is a desire to create spaces in which non-heterosexuals can give expression to their sexuality; these spaces are usually leisure spaces (including tourism) (Visser, 2002).

Young people in a study in Birmingham (UK) regarded the local gay scene as a space in which they could be 'authentic'; it was considered liberating, tolerant and open (Holt and Griffin, 2003). They did recognize, however, that inclusion was related to clothing, class, age and ethnicity and, as a result, many gays and lesbians who did not 'conform' could feel excluded. Young people may turn to the gay scene rather than to family in order to establish their own identity. Gay space (or gay scene) can play a crucial role in this, though it may also be 'risky' space in that often represents a particular gay or lesbian identity to which some may have difficulty relating (Valentine and Skelton, 2003).

Though gay space can lessen isolation, can contribute to identity and a sense of community and can confer strength and protection, it does also project a particular image of gays and lesbians. Newton (1993), for instance, held that Cherry Grove contributed to an image of gays as young, white, male, promiscuous, artistically inclined and middle class. Sibalis (1999) has argued that gay space can create a separatist homosexual identity and discourage integration; the cost is isolation from the rest of society.

(See Chapters 7 and 8 for discussion of the view that gay identity is bound up with consumerism.)

The emergence of Le Marais as gay and lesbian space in the 1990s is considered to have contributed to a sense of gay identity in France (Sibalis, 1999). This, like much of gay space in the UK, is predominantly commercial rather than community-based or residential. In the USA, in particular, some gay spaces cover large geographical areas, to encompass residential areas and towns that are not confined to the leisure-related gay scene (Sibalis, 2004). Cherry Grove on Fire Island (off the south coast of Long Island, New York) was, from the 1920s, one of the first communities where it was possible to be openly gay, though initially confined to a limited, relatively wealthy, segment of society. The Grove is a summer vacation destination but a gay and lesbian residential (though often seasonal) population was soon established. It, along with neighbouring Pines, became dominated by gay and lesbian tourists and residents by the 1960s.

It is estimated that gays and lesbians comprised 30–40% of the population of West Hollywood (California) when it became incorporated as a separate municipality in 1984 (Forest, 1995). This 'independence' lent legitimization to gay identity and, indeed, the gay press had been at pains to project an image of the city that drew on 'desirable' qualities of a gay person (qualities such as creativity, progressiveness, responsibility and orientation towards entertainment and consumption). Perhaps one of the best-known gay and lesbian neighbourhoods is the Castro district of San Francisco. This residential area has, since the 1970s, become an area where the homosexual population outnumbers that of others. An infrastructure of

Fig. 2.2.   Castro Street, San Francisco, California, USA.

gay- and lesbian-related and owned businesses and leisure venues give the
neighbourhood a distinctive character. Rainbow flags along the main street,
Castro Street, are clear signifiers of the area's character – see Fig. 2.2.

It is argued that 'urbanisation is a precondition to emergence of a significant gay subculture' (Sibalis, 1999, p. 11). The opportunity to adopt a
gay or lesbian identity may be restricted in rural areas for many reasons,
including the limited prospects of encountering other gays and lesbians
and a less liberal attitude towards non-heterosexuality (Kramer, 1995).
Large towns and cities have the advantage of a large population where a
diversity of experiences exists and is tolerated and the possibility of
adopting anonymity in relationships, especially when developing one's
own sexuality. They offer a wider selection of partners and the potential
to break free from restrictions. Casual sex, as well as community, is typically more likely in cities (Knopp, 1995; Bouthillette, 1997; Aldrich, 2004).
Cities have been such key sites in developing the modern concept of the
gay identity that this identity has become associated with becoming a
'sophisticated' urban dweller (Binnie, 2000).

Lesbians and gay space

Much gay space tends to be male-dominated – at least in outward signs
such as bars and clubs, which for lesbians are uncommon. This may be
explained by women perceiving public space as being unsafe, and therefore

there is a greater tendency to develop private social networks and family for leisure and for nurturing identity (Peake, 1993; Jacobson and Samdahl, 1998; Elwood, 2000). Women – heterosexual and homosexual – may have a fear of possible male violence in public space, especially city centres, and therefore that space is used carefully (Scraton and Watson, 1998). Lesbians, in a UK survey (Mintel, 2000b), were noticeably less frequent users of bars and clubs than were gay men. In addition, lesbian identity is less focused on sexual activity or consumption in the way that gay men's is (Bouthillette, 1997). The same Mintel survey showed that lesbians were less likely to be single than men (29% compared with 40%), more likely to be in a relationship and therefore less likely to go out and socialize. It may be, too, that women have lower discretionary incomes than men or are not as interested in domination through territorial presence as are men (Valentine, 1995). Even where some commercial provision exists, lesbians may feel less inclined to frequent that scene once a partner has been found (Pritchard *et al.*, 2002). The lack of commercial representation of lesbianism may also be partly explained by feminism's anti-capitalist and anti-consumerist elements (Forsyth, 2001). Lesbian communities appear to be more loosely organized groups of women than actual spatial communities (Schuyf, 1992).

Lesbians do, though, also concentrate residentially (e.g. Park Slope, Brooklyn, the heaviest concentration of lesbians in the USA outside San Francisco, where lesbians have been active in gentrification), but lesbian leisure and residential areas are of a comparatively low profile (Rothenburg, 1995; Valentine, 1995; Forsyth, 2001). Even in those areas 'support groups run by lesbians for lesbians are important sites around which communities are imagined' (Valentine, 1995, p. 102). The invisibility of lesbian space can mean less contestation of space than may be evident for more male-oriented gay space.

A Universal Phenomenon?

There is little doubt that same-sex attraction and sexual activity occur in every society throughout the world, though the social constructionist perspective would suggest that 'a homosexual identity can only exist in those societies in which the homosexual categorization is acknowledged' (Horowitz and Newcomb, 2001, p. 15) and, as a result, the concept of homosexuality – as it is known in North America and Western Europe – may have little meaning elsewhere. In many societies in the non-Western world, same-sex sexual activity may occur without any identification by self or by society as 'gay'. It may be acceptable in some societies for individuals to marry but maintain same-sex sexual relationships during that marriage: the whole concept of sexuality may be more fluid. In Thailand, for instance, an identification as either gay or straight is unusual, and more subtleties in sexuality are recognized (Jackson and Sullivan, 1999b). According to Drucker (2000b) sexual identities transfer more slowly and change more across nations than do products, and domestic factors have an over-riding influence. Altman (1997) acknowledges that whilst most homosexual encounters in Asia, for instance, are by people who would not define themselves as gay or lesbian, the continent is, none the less, witnessing a growing commercial gay scene and more men, in particular, are accepting an identity based on sexuality.

Cultural and economic factors may inhibit the development of a gay identity. In Latin America, marriage and family-building remain priorities and a person's same-sex activities will remain unremarked as long they remain discreet (Murray, 1992). The idealization of family life and marriage, alongside a recognition of same-sex activity as something that most people can experience, is common to many cultures and the concept of a homosexual or gay identity is unfamiliar in such cultures. Although homosexuality is known in all societies, the concept of a 'gay identity' is a Western import (Altman, 2001). (See, also, Joseph and Dhall, 2000 for India; Chou 2000, for China; Cantu, 2002 for Mexico; Arguelles and Rich, 1984 and Lumsden, 1996 for Cuba; and Tuller, 1996, Healey, 1999 and Baer, 2002 for Russia.)

Some cultures have been more tolerant of same-sex activity than others, but its open expression is especially stigmatized in patriarchal societies characterized by 'machismo' values, where both women and homosexuals were consigned to positions of inferiority. A reluctance to adapt the concept of a gay identity in France, however, has little to do with patriarchy or homophobia and more to do with anti-Americanism, and also the French tradition that rejects minority rights in favour of universal rights. The American model of 'gay' is regarded as 'the physical embodiment of forces that allegedly threaten to undermine the very foundation of the French Republic' (Sibalis, 2004, p. 1753).

It is claimed that the toleration of same-sex activities has always existed in most societies: 'the notion of exclusive heterosexuality in pre-colonial sub-Saharan Africa is not borne out by the evidence . . . It is clear that in many communities same-sex relations were closely interwoven in the social fabric' (Mburu, 2000, p. 182). Further it is often claimed that it is only with colonialism (especially British) and the spread of Judaeo-Christian religion during the 19th century, in particular, that stigmatism appeared (Altman, 2001; Naphy, 2004). Anti-homosexual laws, along with harsh punishments, were introduced into societies where same-sex activity had been previously tolerated; the censure of homosexuality is regarded as a Western import (Gevisser, 2000).

Many formerly colonized nation states have turned the argument around by claming that homosexuality did not exist within their societies in pre-colonial times and that it is homosexuality that is a Western import and a corrupting influence (Potgeiter, 1997). It is a convenient approach to rally people against Western society and to distract from real issues. Some of the best known of these arguments include the views of President Mugabe of Zimbabwe, who is quoted as saying that homosexuality 'is unnatural and there is no question ever of allowing these people to behave worse than dogs and pigs ... We have our own culture and we must rededicate ourselves to our traditional values' (quoted in Gevisser, 2000). Accusations of homosexuality were levelled against a former deputy prime minister in Malaysia and the ex-president of Zimbabwe in the late 1990s, at what were clearly politically motivated trials (Altman, 2001; Gronchfelder, 2003). The visibility of gays and lesbians in the USA and Western Europe is considered by some in Russia to be symbolic of those societies' failings (Baer, 2002).

Gays and Lesbians as a 'Market'

For some time, gays and lesbians have been identified as a group of people worthy of singling out and targeting as consumers, and as a separate market segment. Whether or not sexual orientation is a valid basis for market segmentation is an issue that will be discussed later. (See Chapter 7 for further discussion of market surveys.) 'The gay marketing moment', as this new interest is termed (Gluckman and Reed, 1997b), has arisen because of a belief that it is 'a dream market' (*Wall Street Journal,* 18 July 1991, cited in Badgett, 1997a). There has been a consensus that gay males in particular (and lesbians less so) are high-earners, have large discretionary incomes, more discretionary leisure time and have attitudes and interests that mean a predilection to be high-spenders. A supposed lack of children is believed to explain, in part, different spending patterns and outlooks (Stormbreak, 2000). UK market research reports, for instance, have suggested that 'gay people ... tend to spend their personal disposable income differently and appear to maintain a more youthful spend for longer' (Mintel, 2000a, p. 1) and are 'individualistic and style-conscious' (MAPS, 1998, p. 22). In attempting to persuade that the gay and lesbian market was worth pursuing, one survey suggested that 77% 'indulge themselves' and 68% upgrade to latest models and more gays and lesbians 'like to keep up with latest styles and trends' (24% compared with 17% of heterosexuals) (Witeck-Combs Communication and Harris Interactive, 2005).

Numbers

Estimates of market size will be influenced by views on numbers of gays and lesbian and their earnings. There are obvious difficulties in determining the size of the homosexual population. National population censuses do not identify sexual orientation (though it may be possible currently to identify same-sex couples), and estimates therefore depend on sample surveys. In any survey there is a strong possibility of non-disclosure, individuals may not even identify as homosexual regardless of the nature or frequency of sexual feelings or activity and there is, of course, no agreed definition of homosexuality. Respondents to surveys may be asked about their same-sex sexual activity or attraction – whether they have ever had any, or still do so, or have only ever had such experiences, and so on. Some confusion arises because various researchers choose to adopt different criteria within these as an indicator of homosexuality. Further, respondents may be asked to self-identify by sexuality category. There will, though, be no necessary connection between same-sex sexual activity or attraction and self-identification as homosexual or gay, especially given the social constructionist perspective discussed earlier. Self-identification approaches usually result in low estimates and will have less significance in societies where the concept is not acknowledged than in countries of North America and Western Europe (Fejes and Lennon, 2000). As it becomes easier to be openly gay, or the concept comes to have relevance to people, estimates of numbers may increase.

There is a widely quoted estimate of the homosexual population at 10% which is associated with the Kinsey report of sexual behaviour of US males, published in 1948. This 10% referred to those who had 'more or less' exclusive homosexual relationships for 3 years, but was only one of several figures from Kinsey. Only 4% claimed exclusively homosexual relationships but 37% had reported at least one homosexual experience. It is now generally accepted that Kinsey's work lacks credence, as it was based on biased, non-random samples of volunteers and not on a representative cross-section (Pruitt, 2002). In a national survey (over 11,000 people) of the general population in Britain, just under 1% of men and only 0.2% of women said that they had been attracted only to the same sex (Erens *et al.*, 2003). A further 5.3% of men and 9.7% of women did, however, acknowledge having been attracted at least once to the same sex. When sexual experience was considered, just over 8% of men and nearly 10% of women admitted to ever having had a sexual experience with a same-sex partner; these figures fell to 6.3% and 5.7% in respect of same-sex 'genital contact'. Another UK survey asked respondents to self-identify, with the result that 3% identified as homosexual and 3% as bisexual (Yates, 2002). Representative surveys in the USA report between 1% and 3% of the population had 'self-identified and had same-sex sex in previous year'; the proportions were higher over a longer time span or if measuring sexual desire (Pruitt, 2002). One review of estimates of the extent of homosexuality in North America showed they ranged from 0.2 to 37% of national populations (Banks, 2003). The UK government, in its proposals for same-sex civil partnerships, estimated that 5% of the population (over 16) in Great Britain was gay, lesbian or bisexual (Department of Trade and Industry, 2003).

Whilst recognizing the difficulties of estimating the size of the homosexual population, any estimates that do emerge have significance for businesses that believe homosexuals constitute a market segment. They also have meaning for gays and lesbians themselves, who may be encouraged by an awareness of the existence of similar people. It can also influence the political process – the greater the number, the greater the political influence the minority may have, whereas if numbers are low, those unsympathetic to homosexuality can dismiss gays and lesbians as an insignificant minority. The wide variety of figures quoted in different sources often reflects the interests of particular parties: anti-gay groups give low estimates whereas pro-gay groups give estimates up to 10%, often without any qualification (Pruitt, 2002).

Witeck-Combs Communication and Harris Interactive (2003b) estimated the US lgbt market size as 15 million adults (7% of adult population), with a 'buying power' of US$485 billion, which was larger than that of Asian-Americans (US$344b) but less than that of African-Americans (US$688b) or Hispanics (US$653b). Stormbreak (2000) estimated the UK gay and lesbian market at about 3.2 million (7% of the adult population).

Incomes and spending

Many surveys, especially in the USA, have consistently shown that gays and lesbians have above-average incomes. A survey in the early 1990s (by 'Overlooked Opinions') showed that gay and lesbian households in the USA earned 41 and 26%, respectively, above the national average (http:// www.commercialcloset.org). In a more recent study of 60,000 North American households in 2003, the average annual household income for gays was US$61,300, compared with US$56,900 for heterosexuals; 19% had postgraduate degrees compared with 12–14% of heterosexuals (Kolko, 2003). They were also more likely to agree with statements such as 'like to show off my taste and style', 'am influenced by what's hot and what's not' and 'constantly looking for new ways to entertain myself' (Kolko, 2003). A survey of exhibition attendees in London showed that most worked in managerial or professional occupations or were office workers. Earnings averaged £30,000 compared with a national average of £18,000, and gay men earned more than lesbians (Stormbreak, 2000).

At face value, it could be expected that a same-sex, two-person household would have a higher income than a heterosexual, two-person household. Women tend to have lower earnings than men and therefore any male + female household might be expected to have lower earnings than a male + male household, especially if the female is currently unemployed for 'domestic' reasons. By the same reasoning, a female + female household would be expected to have lower earnings than both a two-male house-hold and a male + female household where all are working. This reasoning, however, does not necessarily relate to single people and it may well be the case that homosexuals, for whatever reason, have higher earnings than their heterosexual counterparts (see below). Lesbians, for instance, might experience fewer interruptions in their careers and be able to progress further and more quickly, or might feel impelled to seek higher income occupations because marriage is not an option (Dunne, 1997).

Determining the size or any of the characteristics of this market is obviously problematic, given the difficulties of definition and disclosure mentioned earlier. Some surveys are more rigorous than others, but it remains that describing this market is virtually impossible. The issues that have arisen in interpreting these surveys are by now well known, so much so that any conclusions should be drawn from them only with a great deal of caution (see Chapter 7).

Badgett (2001) has identified a number of, what she termed, 'myths' relating to the economic position of gays and lesbians. In particular, she has demonstrated – through a series of rigorous studies in the USA – that gays and lesbians are not typically affluent and well educated, that many do have family responsibilities and they are not typically consumption-oriented. She highlighted the weak underpinning of the early US studies that led to the generation and perpetuation of the positive profiles. She questioned why it might be expected that gays and lesbians choose to achieve higher educational qualifications and to enter mainly service, professional and managerial occupations. Badgett could find no obvious justification for this, especially as many will have made choices before identifying as gay, and other factors are much more influential (Badgett, 1997a; Badgett and King, 1997). Her own – and similar, more representative – studies showed that gay men earn less than heterosexuals with the same backgrounds such as education (with discrimination and fear of exposure being critical factors) – gay male earnings were 4–27% less than hetero men; lesbians' earnings were about average for females. It is possible that two-man households will have higher earnings than straight households (though even that is not shown unequivocally in studies), especially given the tendency for average female earnings to be lower than male. Two-woman households are likely to have earnings and disposable income below either, especially if there are children in the household. A study using the UK Labour Force Survey was able to compare the earnings of same-sex couples (assumed to be homosexual) with those of opposite-sex heterosexual couples. It was established that 'gay men [couples] suffer from a pay disadvantage compared to non-gay married and co-habitees but lesbians have a clear earnings advantage' (Arabsheibani *et al.*, 2004, p. 352).

Regardless of incomes, it could be that gays and lesbians have tastes, product preferences and spending patterns that differ from their straight equivalents. It is argued by some that even if incomes are not much different from those of heterosexuals, households may be smaller (perhaps a single person), with fewer dependants, and therefore discretionary income is higher and distinct consumer attitudes and buying preferences result (Witeck-Combs Communication and Harris Interactive, 2003b). Lukenbill (1999) argued strongly that 'the power of the mind-set of the gay or lesbian consumer and how he or she differs from the heterosexual consumer cannot be underestimated' (p. 90). This he attributed to the particular coping systems gays and lesbians have had to adopt which, in turn, have a significant effect on purchasing behaviour and decisions.

In fact, it may be becoming increasingly difficult to distinguish the lifestyles of gays and lesbians from those of heterosexuals. Simpson (2004), for instance, identified the 'metrosexual': gays and straights with discretionary income who have a concern for their appearance and who 'pursue pleasure'. Badgett (2001) was particularly critical of what she termed the 'gay marketing moment' and was wary of subscribing to the widely accepted view that gay and lesbian households have purchasing preferences and patterns that differ from those of equivalent straight households. No studies unequivocally show this to be the case, or at least they only show a partial picture because of the inherent bias of the samples. The picture of high-spend, hedonistic, fashion-conscious, trendsetting individuals will be representative of some parts of the whole gay and lesbian population, but there are obvious problems when they are presented as, or understood to be, 'typical' (Gluckman and Reed, 1997b). In some instances it has been concluded that product purchases and purchase criteria of gays were not particularly distinctive and were similar to those of equivalent heterosexuals, especially young singles.

Partners and children

One of the few features of gay and lesbian life that can be determined from some national censuses is the number of same-sex partnerships, at least in the sense of same-sex households. The USA 2000 census indicated there were 594,000 same-sex couples, of whom 301,000 were male and 293,000 female (Rubenstein *et al.*, 2003). Of these, 35% had a college degree, compared with 28% of married couples, though average (median) earnings were about the same. Forty-five per cent lived in urban areas and 41% in suburbs compared with heterosexual couples, at 35 and 46%, respectively. An earlier study had shown that about 25% of US same-sex couples were living in ten large cities, including New York, Los Angeles, Chicago, Washington, DC and San Francisco (Black *et al.*, 2000). Apart from the obvious issues of disclosure, there is a further caveat to make regarding this and other national censuses that collect these data, which is that the sexual orientation of the couples is not known (not all will be homosexual) and not all partners live together. The UK Census 2001 identified 78,552 people in same-sex couples (England and Wales only). Other surveys have also endeavoured to identify same-sex relationships: in the 2000 Stormbreak survey (UK) 83% of females and 51% of males were in a 'strictly or mainly monogamous' relationship, though there was no indication of whether men regarded themselves as being a 'household'. In a Pride festival survey in Brighton (UK), nearly 60% of gay men and just over 70% of lesbians were in same-sex relationships. Over half of the men lived with their partner but typically for less than 4 years (nearly all respondents were aged 16–45) (Browne *et al.*, 2005). It is not too clear from such surveys whether 'partnerships' refer to sexual partners or to relationships that are more aptly conceived of as 'a household', which usually (though not necessarily) entails living at the same address. It is none the less apparent that lesbians are more likely than gay men to have 'a partner' and to have longer-lasting relationships and, if having more than one sexual partner during a year, to have fewer than gay men.

A UK study based on the national Labour Force Survey identified 795 cohabiting same-sex couples out of 360,000 respondents. Same-sex couples were particularly likely to live in cities: 35% of male couples lived in London compared with 9% of heterosexual couples (Arabsheibani *et al.*, 2004). They also typically had higher educational qualifications (36% had degree or above compared with 15% of non-gays) and more were in professional, managerial and intermediate occupations (44% of males and 37% of females compared with 35 and 21% of non-gays, respectively).

It is significant that several studies identify gays and lesbians as having children or having with children living within them. In the USA 2000 census one-third of female same-sex households and over 20% of male same-sex households included children. Over 60% of respondents to an lgbt survey in Wales were in a same-sex relationship and over a third had children in the household (Robinson and Williams, 2003). The 1996 New Zealand census showed that 28.5% of female couples and 11.6% of male couples had children in the household (Hyman, 2001). The Brighton Pride festival survey (UK) indicated that 2% of gay men and 14% of lesbians had dependent children (Browne *et al.*, 2005). Other US surveys suggest that a significant proportion of gay and lesbian households have children living within them, though there was usually a much higher proportion of lesbian than of gay households indicating this (GL Census Partners, 2001, 2002, 2004–2005). It would be rash to assume that the earnings or spending patterns of these households conformed to the marketers' dream consumer. Noticeably, between 11.6 and 17.2% of gay men in the USA and between 21.6 and 28.7% of lesbians confirmed that they had been previously married (Black *et al.*, 2000).

Disapproval and Discrimination

Human Rights Watch (2002) concluded that 'in virtually every country in the world people suffered from *de jure* and *de facto* discrimination based on their actual or perceived sexual orientation' (p. 1). Five of the 13 countries (Bulgaria, Cyprus, Estonia, Hungary and Lithuania) which were seeking accession to the European Union in 2004 had, at that time, discriminatory provisions in their criminal laws.

Gays and lesbians experience a certain degree of disadvantage in most societies (Amnesty International UK, 1997; Amnesty International, 2001). This can take many forms, including attitudes of grudging acceptance, disapproval and intolerance, as well as more explicit forms such as discrimination in employment and service provision, physical or verbal abuse, and unequal legal rights – including criminalization of same-sex sexual activity. In the UK, for instance, all male homosexual physical relationships were criminalized by the 1885 Criminal Law Amendment Act and remained so in England and Wales until 1967, when private homosexual acts between consenting male adults (21 and over) were de-criminalized. The law was not changed in Scotland until 1980, and until 1982 in Northern Ireland. These laws had applied only to males. Offences such as 'gross indecency' (any form of gay sex) and 'importuning for an immoral purpose' remained, however, and were used, in particular, in prosecutions relating to group sex and 'cruising' or sex in public places. These were specifically homosexual offences with no equivalent law affecting heterosexuals. The offences were removed in 2004 and the age of consent was lowered to 18 in 1994 and to 16 in 2001 (17 in Northern Ireland), to become the same as that for heterosexuals.

The UN Declaration of Human Rights, 1948 did not acknowledge the issue of sexual orientation as such, though, in 2003, a draft resolution on human rights and sexual orientation was introduced at the UN Commission on Human Rights. It was proposed by Brazil and seconded by South Africa, but opposed by Pakistan, Egypt, Libya, Saudi Arabia, Malaysia and the Vatican, and this opposition was sufficient for the resolution to be lost (Baird, 2004). Currently, homosexuality is illegal in about 80 countries (including India and Singapore) and is punishable by death in nine (including Iran, Afghanistan, Saudi Arabia and Pakistan) (Baird, 2004). Most disapproval and censure is directed at male homosexuals rather than at lesbians; the UK legislation, for instance, was directed solely at males.

Even where homosexuality is not specifically proscribed by law, other non-specific laws relating, for instance, to immoral behaviour or corruption of minors may be invoked (Mogrovejo, 2000). Strong cultural prejudices may also remain in 'traditional' societies such as in a number of Latin American countries, where disapproval may manifest itself as harassment and various forms of discrimination. Homosexuality continues to be problematic in many countries, and gay and lesbian visibility is limited.

These disadvantages faced by gays and lesbians may be the outcome of homophobia, 'the irrational fear of, or aversion to, homosexuals or homosexuality', and of heterosexism, 'the belief that heterosexuality is normative and non-heterosexuality is deviant' (Banks, 2003, p. 13). Most societies are inherently heterosexist. Enemies are labelled as homosexuals; homosexuals are blamed for disasters, misfortunes and general problems in society – AIDS, decline of family and family values, decline in morality, natural disasters, etc.! A US religious fundamentalist group were alleged to have blamed Hurricane Katrina, which devastated New Orleans in 2005, on the upcoming gay celebration, Southern Decadence (Swift, 2005b). Rulsan Sharipov, a campaigner for human rights in Uzbekistan, was arrested for homosexuality (which is illegal) and sex with minors, and was sentenced in 2003 to 5½ years in prison (Smith, 2004a). He later escaped and was granted political asylum in the USA. Politicians in several Southern African countries have made homosexuals scapegoats for the spread of the HIV/AIDS epidemic (Long, 2003).

Masculinity and homosexuality

As seen previously, much of the antagonism towards homosexuality arose during the 19th century, and it seems initially to have been associated with effeminacy. Ulrichs (1825–1895) considered that homosexuality arose from an innate biological condition, but characterized it as being a female soul in a male body – the 'third sex' (which he labelled 'Uranian'). As such it could be conceived of as a threat to masculinity. Connell (1995) identified a gender hierarchy, at the top of which is 'hegemonic masculinity', some of the characteristics of which are physical toughness and strength, non-femininity and denial of vulnerability and emotion. Hegemonic masculinity is a standard by which others are judged and through which unequal power relationships are maintained. 'Subordinated masculinity', which includes homosexuality, covers a range of behaviour that does not match up to this ideal – men who lack masculinity (Pilcher and Whelehan, 2004). Homosexuals may be particularly threatening for heterosexuals given the fluidity of sexuality and the varied experiences of people over time – anyone can experience same-sex attraction and it may be this 'repressed' or 'latent homosexuality' that causes homophobia to be so virulent at times. In addition, homosexuality is perceived to be a 'threat' because gays and lesbians (unlike women, disabled or ethnic minorities) cannot be easily identified: 'border anxiety is present when the other is least visible' (Johnston, 2001, p. 193). A person may be able to conceal his or her homosexuality and this may make it more threatening as a consequence; it is the 'hidden threat'. It could be everywhere and everyone, including oneself, and that makes it more difficult to react to and deal with.

A dominant effeminate identity remained well into the 20th century, but in the 1950s and 1960s male homosexuals adopted styles of clothing, body language, gestures and ways of speaking that were less feminine (Gough, 1989). Male homosexual relationships were also identified less as short-term liaisons between masculine (dominant) males and effeminate (subservient) males and more as longer-term, egalitarian and romantic relationships between masculine males (Humphries, 1985; Higgs, 1999b; Drucker, 2000b).

Although anti-homosexual legislation has generally focused on male sexual acts, and male gay lifestyles have been more flamboyant and conspicuous, lesbians continue to experience social disapproval. Women are socially subordinate in most societies and many societies and religions have sought to limit women's role by defining it in terms of reproduction. As a consequence lesbians face the double 'burden' of being female and (usually) non-reproducers (Altman, 2001). Mizielinska (2001) argued that lesbians feel particularly excluded in Poland. This is a particularly patriarchal society and the whole concept of the nation state and its post-communist constitution is based on masculine values (under the influence of the Catholic Church).

Reactions and attitudes

In a survey in England 'gay or lesbian people' were identified by 17% of respondents as being a group towards whom they 'felt less positive'; this was similar to 'ethnic minorities' at 18% (Stonewall, 2001). 'Travellers and gypsies' and 'refugees and asylum seekers', however, headed the list with responses of 35 and 34%, respectively. More positive feelings were held by women, younger people and by those with higher educational qualifications. People who knew someone who was gay or lesbian also had significantly more positive feelings. The study identified 'joined-up prejudice': people expressing less positive feelings towards any one group were likely also to have similar feelings about other groups. For example, those who were prejudiced against ethnic minorities were twice as likely as others to be prejudiced against gays and lesbians also (prejudice was defined as feeling less positive towards a group of people: Valentine and McDonald, 2004). A survey of residents in the city of Glasgow (Scotland) revealed that 31% would be concerned if lesbian, gay or bisexual people moved next door to them (Beyond Barriers, 2003).

There is an evident difference between men and women not just in attitudes towards homosexuality in general but also to male and female homosexuality in particular. In a British survey, sex between two men was considered to be 'mostly or always wrong' by nearly half of men whereas only 38% felt this way about sex between two women (Erens *et al.*, 2003). Women felt equally about both – only 27% considered same-sex sex to be 'mostly or always wrong', and this was so for both sex between two men and sex between two women. In this study it was also evident that younger and more educated people were more tolerant. The acceptance of gay men by heterosexual women and having a gay male friend has been attributed not only to their low 'threat' and, stereotypically, to their sense of fun but, more cynically, to being 'part of making claims to a contemporary and cosmopolitan identity' (Casey, 2004, p. 454).

Respondents with religious affiliations (especially non-Christian) were generally less tolerant in the British survey mentioned above (Erens *et al.*, 2003). Religious organizations frequently exhibit unsympathetic attitudes. The Roman Catholic Church, for instance, as recently as 2003, described homosexual acts as 'intrinsically disordered' and any state recognition of same-sex relationships as the 'legalisation of evil' and 'approval of deviant behaviour' (Offices of the Congregation of the Doctrine of the Faith, 2003, paras 4, 5 and 11). A further edict the following year attacked the effects of feminism because, amongst other things, it made 'homosexuality and heterosexuality virtually equivalent' (Offices of the Congregation of the Doctrine of the Faith, 2004, para. 2). The ordination of Gene Robinson – an openly gay man – as bishop of New Hampshire by the US Episcopal Church in 2003, and same-sex blessings in Canada, gave rise to considerable tension within the Anglican Church. Resistance to the moves by, in particular, evangelical Anglicans and leaders of the church in Africa, led to the prospect of schism within the Church (Bates, 2005a). 'In the context of human history and culture, it is the [Judaeo]-Christian response to homosexuality that has been abnormal and unnatural' (Naphy, 2004, p. 269). A mass demonstration in Madrid against legislation to allow marriage for same-sex couples in Spain was organized by Catholic bishops led by the Archbishop of Madrid (Tremlett, 2005). There is a strong view that the relative lack of progress in terms of pro-homosexual legislation in the USA is associated with the influence of 'Christian conservatives' (Goldenberg, 2003; Rodgerson, 2004a). It was significant that the Governor of Texas signed a resolution to ban same-sex marriages in the state (and also to introduce stricter abortion limits) in a ceremony that was held at an evangelical school in Fort Worth in 2005 (Wilson, 2005). The limited development of a homosexual culture in Belfast (Northern Ireland) has been attributed, in part, to the strong link between church and state (Kitchin, 2002).

Attitudes would, however, appear to have become more positive over time. In Britain, for instance, the proportion of the population that considered homosexuality to be 'always' or 'mostly' wrong had fallen from 70 to 47% between 1985 and 2002, and a third felt it was 'not wrong at all' (Evans, 2002). There was, once more, a marked relationship with age and education. In Australia a 1995 survey found that 56% of adults believed sexual activity between two men was 'absolutely wrong', though this figure had fallen over the previous 10 years (Sullivan and Jackson, 1999).

In the USA, there would appear to have been a significant shift amongst the general population towards supporting equal rights for gays and lesbians (in housing, employment and family issues, etc.). Attitudes towards homosexual behaviour have shown less change: during the 1970s and 1980s, according to one survey, the proportion of the US population that disapproved of same-sex relationships fluctuated between 67 and 75%, but during the 1990s there was a noticeable fall to 58% (Yang, 1999). A Gallup Poll in June 2003 revealed that 59% of Americans believed that gay sex between consenting adults should be legal, compared with only 33% in the 1980s (Goldenberg, 2003).

It is significant that studies in the USA (and subsequently in the UK) have suggested that a gay population is a key indicator of a city's 'creative potential' (Florida, 2002). The homosexual population of a city was considered to be a good measure of diversity which, along with influences such as ethnic make-up and the 'creative class', demonstrated an open, welcoming and innovative environment leading to enhanced economic growth. By these criteria, San Francisco headed the 'creativity index' in the USA, and Manchester in the UK. The 'gay index' element of this creativity index was, however, based solely on the national census figures of same-sex partnerships (see earlier).

Even supposedly positive views about gays and lesbians can be stereotypical and as damaging as negative views. 'For example, gays and lesbians are described as "happy" or "fun" and heterosexual women talk about valuing gay men for their supposed feminine qualities' (Valentine and McDonald, 2004, p. 10).

Gays and lesbians have experienced discrimination in the workplace also. This may occur as failure to be employed or promoted because of sexual orientation or as harassment whilst employed (Badgett, 1997b; Mims and Kleiner, 1998; Robinson and Williams, 2003; Arabsheibani *et al.*, 2004). Until 2003, UK employers had been able to discriminate in employment matters on grounds of sexual orientation, though under pressure from the European Union this has now been remedied. Discrimination in the provision of goods and service on grounds of sexual orientation (though not ethnicity) does, however, remain legal.

Abuse and stress

Negative attitudes towards homosexuality may manifest themselves in physical and verbal abuse (it has been argued that coping with this can be regarded as a positive developmental experience; Myslik, 1996). Over a third of gay men in a British survey had experienced violence and over 70% had been verbally abused because of their sexuality in the previous 5 years (Mason and Palmer, 1996). In another survey (England and Wales), about one-third of gay men and lesbians had experienced recent attacks or damage to property and between one-third and half of these were attributed to sexuality (Warner *et al.*, 2004). Higher proportions had experienced insults and 51% of men and 30% of women had been bullied at school. More than half of gays and lesbians in New South Wales (Australia) had experienced some form of homophobic abuse, harassment or violence in the previous 12 months (New South Wales Attorney General's Department, 2003). Although hate crimes (based on personal characteristics of the victim) were decreasing in number in Florida (USA), those where sexual orientation was a factor increased from six in 1996 to 55 in 2003, and had risen from 2.8 to 20% of the total over that period (Office of the Attorney General, State of Florida, 2004). In the UK there had been, until 2005, no allowance for the homophobic factor in law, in the same way that there had been for 'racially aggravated offences' (assaults or harassment) since 1998. Courts can now, however, impose higher penalties for offences motivated by sexual orientation.

Physical abuse is experienced by a (high) minority of gays and lesbians, but the fear of it can have a significant effect on the behaviour of many more. Verbal abuse is far more common, but issues that are of most concern to gays and lesbians are often less personal ones. Over 60% had felt that certain public statements made about 'morality of homosexuals' and articles in the media or portrayals of homosexuals on television had amounted to 'serious' discrimination (Robinson and Williams, 2003).

Even on the supposedly liberal atmosphere of university campuses, gay and lesbian students in the USA experienced problems (Rankin, 2003). Over a third reported harassment and 20% feared for their safety. As a consequence, many (51%) concealed their true sexual identity. This is a common coping strategy in the face of homophobia. Mason and Palmer (1996) reported that gays and lesbians frequently not only avoided public displays of affection and attempted to avoid 'looking gay', but also avoided telling others about their sexual orientation. 'Visibility is implicated in homophobic violence and hate crime' (Corteen, 2002, p. 260) and, as a consequence, gays and lesbians adjust outward signs of their sexuality. Unlike many other personal characteristics associated with appearance, sexual orientation can be concealed, but this very act of concealment can itself be stressful.

Gays and lesbians (and bisexuals) may face particular pressures of physical and verbal abuse and a general marginalization in heteronormative societies which may contribute to mental and emotional distress (Mind, 2002). Those who seek to deny their sexual orientation may experience high levels of stress and tension, low self-esteem and even self-hatred and 'internalized homophobia' (Sandfort, 2000; Mind, 2002; Banks, 2003). They, and those who do identify as gay or lesbian, often face the need to engage in concealment and to engage in avoidance strategies, all of which not only reinforce feelings of injustice, but also contribute further to stress and low self-esteem. This may manifest itself in a greater incidence amongst gays and lesbians of illicit drug use, alcohol abuse, depression and suicide (Banks, 2003). There is some evidence to suggest that this is the case, but it is not clear-cut; Sandfort (2000) suggested there was little evidence supporting the alcohol and drugs scenarios, but rather more for an anxiety disorder and suicide scenario. Research amongst young lgbt people in Northern Ireland revealed that 44% were bullied at school and 29% had attempted suicide (YouthNet, 2003).

A US study of (15–22-year-old) men who have sex with men identified a greater usage of illicit drugs than other studies had determined amongst the general youth population. Two-thirds reported using an illicit drug in the previous 6 months and over one-quarter reported frequent use (Thiede *et al.*, 2003). Consumption of alcohol was about the same as that of the general population, though another study suggested that the incidence of alcoholism amongst gays and lesbians was twice that of the general population (Mind, 2002). The fact that the opportunity to socialize with other gays arises primarily in gay space of bars and clubs will have facilitated access to and usage of alcohol and drugs. Drug and alcohol use may, in turn, increase the likelihood of high-risk sexual activity. One study of Latino gay men in the USA suggested a relationship between high risk of HIV infection and high personal experience of homophobia (but also of racism and poverty) (Diaz and Ayala, 2001).

A study of the mental health of gay, lesbian and bisexual men and women in England and Wales reported 'high rates of planned and actual deliberate self-harm and high levels of psychiatric morbidity . . . among gay men (42%), lesbians (43%) and bisexual men and women (49%) compared with previous community studies of [predominantly] heterosexual people' (Warner *et al.*, 2004, p. 483). One-quarter of gay men and 31% of lesbians admitted to having attempted suicide. There was an apparent relationship between these high rates and factors such as physical and verbal abuse and bullying which were, in turn, associated with sexual orientation.

Acceptance

Apart from the shifts in attitude that are evident in some polls, progress continues to be made in legislative spheres and elsewhere. An indicator of progress in the USA is the US Supreme Court declaration in 2003 that anti-sodomy laws in 13 US states (including Texas) were unconstitutional. This may well, however, have accounted for a drop in support for homosexual relations being legal from 60% of Americans in May 2003 to 48% later in the year (Grossman, 2003). None the less, Human Rights Campaign (a gay and lesbian rights group) reported that the majority of the largest US companies exhibited some aspects of non-discrimination, though most lacked commitment to full equality in their employment policies (Adetunji, 2002). By 2003, over 40% of Fortune 500 companies (the largest

US companies by revenue) offered same-sex couples employment benefits that were equal to those of heterosexual couples. United Airlines had been one of the first airlines to offer equal benefits (health and pension rights) to partners of same-sex couples as to heterosexual couples, albeit under pressure from a 1996 San Francisco ordinance requiring all businesses to comply (Campbell, 1999). It is not uncommon for some US organizations to recommend boycotts of companies that show favour in some way to homosexuals. The American Family Association, for instance, proposed a boycott of Ford in 2004 because of the company's donations to gay rights organizations and its advertising in gay-oriented publications.

The UK gay and lesbian rights' organization, Stonewall, has identified a number of companies and organizations that are particularly gay- and lesbian-friendly, as demonstrated by factors such as sexual orientation policies, equal benefits for same-sex couples, diversity training, etc. (Stonewall, 2005). They include city banks, government departments, airlines (such as American Airlines at number 14 and British Airways at 88) and retailers (such as Marks and Spencer at 45). The Co-operative Bank (UK), which has taken a particularly strong ethical view about its business, considered that the homophobic views expressed by the organization Christian Voice were such that it could no longer accept them as customers (Anon., 2005a).

There is no universal agreement that same-sex marriages are a desirable goal for gays and lesbians, but their existence may be interpreted as an indicator of acceptance. In 2005, same-sex marriages were permissible in The Netherlands, Belgium, Spain, Canada and in the US state of Massachusetts, with a number of countries and states allowing various forms of partnership agreements. Denmark, Norway, Sweden and France (since 2000) have provision for civil unions for same-sex couples, and the UK introduced civil partnerships, which are very similar to marriage, in 2005. The issue of same-sex marriage licences in February 2004 by San Francisco mayor Gavin Newsom was, however, halted by the Californian Supreme Court (Quittner, 2004). US polls show that over one-third felt there should be no legal recognition of same-sex relationships, a further third supported civil unions but only 25% accepted that same-sex couples should be allowed to marry (Witeck-Combs Communications Inc., 2004).

There have been, therefore, many advances in many countries in the legal framework affecting homosexuals and in public attitudes towards them, so that, for some, being gay and lesbian has 'become a positive experience bringing no more problems than any other way of living and loving and often some advantage' (Plummer, 1992, p. 22). Gay and lesbian magazines are on open sale in UK national newspaper chains. A UK national newspaper ran an article in 2003 of interviews with 'Britain's 20 most outstanding homosexuals', stating that 'gay and lesbian culture has never been as visible and confident as it is now' (Lutyens, 2003, p. 29). Interviewees included male and female national politicians, comedians, a designer, a civil servant, an artist, a novelist and businesspeople. Sympathetic portrayals of homosexuals on television have been credited, at least in part, for the greater acceptance of gays and lesbians as has been, less explicitly, business recognition of gays' and lesbians' purchasing power. There are undoubtedly more individuals in the public eye who are open about their homosexuality. Several of these are actors or singers such as, in the UK, (the late) Nigel Hawthorne, Ian McKellen, Sandi Toksvig, Neil Tennant (Pet Shop Boys), Stephen Gately (Boyzone) and Will Young. Others who have not concealed their sexuality include Chris Smith, one-time Cabinet Minister in the Labour government, Brian Paddick, Deputy Assistant Commissioner of the Metropolitan Police (London) and many businesspeople. There are (or have been) gay characters in the most popular British television soaps (including *EastEnders*, *Coronation Street* and *Emmerdale*). The television series *Queer as Folk*, which graphically chronicled the lives of gays and lesbians in Manchester (England), was transmitted on the national UK television network, Channel 4, in 1999. It was later shown in the USA and initiated a long-running US five-series equivalent, set in Pittsburgh. The high visibility of some television characters and television personalities has not always been welcomed, however. Criticisms have been wide-ranging and have focused on perpetuating certain stereotypes through emphasizing issues such as effeminacy or promiscuity. The personal makeover television programme, *Queer Eye for the Straight Guy*, has presenters who epitomize the creativity, sensitivity and effeminacy of stereotypical gay men.

Political movements

Undoubtedly political campaigning has had an impact on the situation. Popular mythology places the start of the gay rights movement at the Stonewall 'riots' in New York in 1969. Police had attempted to shut down the Stonewall bar in Greenwich Village, and this resulted in violent confrontations over 5 nights. This stand against police harassment is, in turn, is alleged to have inspired a highly visible mass phase of organization for gay rights. The 'riot' has been commemorated by a parade in New York every year since 1970 and, in 2000, the Stonewall bar was declared a national historic landmark.

There were obviously movements seeking gay rights prior to this. It is claimed, for instance, that the period of the late 1950s and early 1960s saw significant advances made in San Francisco through bar owners' legal actions against police and municipal policies (Boyd, 2003). The Mattachine Society (founded in Los Angeles in 1950 by Harry Hay) was one of the earliest gay movements in the USA, but its activities were necessarily discreet and largely involved pressure for legal change. The founders, however, were Marxists and came under the scrutiny of the Un-American Activities

Committee in 1954 during the period of Senator McCarthy's communist 'witch-hunt' in the USA (Spencer, 1995). The Mattachines sought the assimilation of gays into society, a policy now, ironically, adopted by 'right-wing' conservative gay observers. Up to the mid-1960s it was the leading gay organization in USA, but after Stonewall it failed to adapt to radical militantism and faded away (www.sbu.ac.uk).

In the UK, the Homosexual Law Reform Society (HLRS) had been established in 1958 (mostly by people who were not homosexual) with the purpose of persuading Members of Parliament (MPs) of the case for law reform, as recommended by the Wolfenden report of the previous year (Spencer, 1995). It was an 'elitist' rather than a grass-roots organization. After the (partial) legalization of male same-sex acts in 1967, the HLRS lost impetus and the North-Western Homosexual Law Committee (formed in Manchester in 1964) became the Committee (later Campaign) for Homosexual Equality (CHE) in 1969. This was a more radical, grass-roots organization, democratically controlled and gay-driven (Horsfall, 2004). Despite some militant activity it was still committed to reform rather than to revolution. The same approach characterizes Stonewall, the UK pressure group founded in 1989 as a response to Section 28 of the Local Government Act, 1988; the purpose of this Act was to stifle discussion of homosexuality in schools and, in effect, to suggest the unacceptability of homosexuality as a family relationship. Stonewall's strategy remains relatively low-key, in the belief that favourable outcomes are more likely than through direct action that might alienate public opinion. Its approaches include the lobbying of MPs and the raising of public awareness through education, 'discreet' campaigning and enlisting the assistance of 'personalities' in conveying its message.

Left-wing ideologies have characterized groups more committed to direct action, alternative 'community' and lifestyle and to the celebration and continuation of 'difference' (Goldstein, 2002). The Gay Liberation Front (GLF) arose in New York (in 1969) immediately after the Stonewall riot and was a 'fighting organization born in the streets and spent most of its time fighting in the streets' (Halifax, 1988, p. 28). A considerable emphasis was placed on 'coming out' as a first step in liberation. GLF was established in Britain in 1970 but its influence, as in the USA, was short-lived. Its activities ranged beyond a concern for 'pure' gay issues and 'GLF horrified the established gay reform groups of the time such as CHE . . . CHE viewed GLF's street campaigns and denunciations of the system as the sort of activity that gave gays and lesbians a bad name' (Halifax, 1988, p. 31). In the USA it allied itself with organizations such as the Black Panthers and, in the UK, it was involved with support for industrial disputes and trade union strikes. GLF activists were out and proud. 'Instead of gay people having to justify their existence, GLF demanded that gay-haters justify their bigotry' (Tatchell, 2004c, p. 82). Visibility is regarded as being particularly important; coming out is a political action that demonstrates existence and pride whereas by 'acting straight', gay men contribute to the *status quo* (Kirby and Hay, 1997). Outrage!, established in the UK in 1990, claims to be community-based and is dedicated, in contrast to an organization such as Stonewall, to 'radical, non-violent direct action and civil disobedience' (http://www.outrage.nabumedia.com).

Advances may well, however, have been accompanied by a retreat from the ideals and vision of liberation pioneers. The gay movement began on the political left along with civil rights and women's movements, but there has been a relatively recent emergence of gay conservatism such as that associated with Andrew Sullivan (1995). He and similar writers have been termed 'gay cons' (Robinson, 2005), 'homocons' (Goldstein, 2002) and 'hetero-homos' (Tatchell, 2004c) and the whole phenomenon termed the 'new homonormativity' (Duggan, 2002). Their arguments are that homo-sexuals need to become more respectable by restraining sexual behaviour (promiscuity) and being less effeminate (men) or mannish (women). These assimilationists favour homosexuals becoming more like and liv-ing a life like heterosexuals; there is essentially no difference between gays and straights (other than sexual preference) and 'equalizing' legis-lation is a sufficient goal. The aim is policies that work within the existing political framework, though critics argue this upholds the dominant hetero-normative assumptions and principles. 'Most queers no longer question the values, laws and institutions of mainstream society. They happily settle for equal rights with heterosexuals' (Tatchell, 2004c, p. 82).

Liberationists promote a rather more radical approach, which is the cultural and structural transformation of society rather than working within existing structures (Rimmerman, 2002). The assimilationist approach is seen as leaving 'repressive' structures unchanged, which inhibits the move towards a goal of freeing gay identity from consumerism, ending discrimination and hate crime and acknowledging a variety of sexual identities and behaviours instead of endorsing a neo-heterosexual existence (Goldstein, 2002).

Conclusions

What it means to be homosexual is not as clear-cut as some might imagine. The conventional distinction between heterosexual and homosexual is something that is relatively recent and conceals what is a complex diver-sity of feelings, attitudes and activities. Despite this there are individuals who choose to identify, or are identified, as homosexual, gay or lesbian; to some extent a gay or lesbian identity is a matter of choice. Given the domi-nance of heterosexual norms, identifying as homosexual and living as a homosexual often require reference points that are available only in gay space. This space (also known as the gay scene) is primarily a leisure space and has an important role in facilitating the acceptance of a gay identity.

There remains considerable disapproval of and discrimination against gays and lesbians, and gay space has an equally important role to play in enabling gays and lesbians to escape from that disapproval. Disapproval and discrimination stimulate a desire to 'escape' to other places even though they may only be in the same town. The marginalization of gays and lesbians in many societies can create particular difficulties in terms of adjustment and self-acceptance and may generate excessive stress and low levels of self-esteem furthering the desire to escape.

There would seem, therefore, to be a 'travel' imperative in the lives of many homosexuals – a need to find space where acceptance and safety are paramount. Some communities and societies are more accepting than others though, in general terms, acceptance and toleration of homosexuality has increased and discrimination lessened in countries such as the USA and the UK. Same-sex attraction and activity are universal, and homosexual activity may well be tolerated in many societies. Openly gay lifestyles are most obvious, however, in North America and Western Europe, and the concept of a 'gay identity' is very much restricted to these parts of the world.

Notwithstanding some of the wider societal issues that relate to homosexuality, there has been a popular perception of gays (and to a lesser extent, lesbians) as having relatively high levels of discretionary income and living lives that are 'unburdened' by children. These features, combined with a belief that gays and lesbians adopt a different, more carefree, hedonistic and style-conscious approach to life generally, have contributed to the view that spending patterns are different from those of the rest of society. The basis for these assertions lies in market research surveys which may well be flawed (see Chapter 7). In addition, more rigorous studies in the USA, in particular, suggest that these popular assertions are ill-founded. There are also a number of gays and, more so, lesbians that have children in their households.

It does appear that gays and lesbians are more likely to be urban dwellers than are the rest of the population. Some evidence suggests a residential concentration in large towns and cities compared with the more suburban and rural distribution of others. Given the importance of gay space this is not too surprising.

Considering the nature of homosexuality it is not surprising that relatively little is known of the 'market characteristics' of gays and lesbians, or that there are perceptions that are poorly based. This includes views on the size of the homosexual population; apart from the fact that the concept is difficult to define, many will not choose to acknowledge it to others. None the less, many of the assertions about homosexuals probably apply more to men than to women. Lesbians, for instance, seem to be less inclined to frequent the gay scene, and are more likely to seek long-term relationships than are men.

The significance for tourism of these features of homosexuality will be examined in the following chapters.

Gay and Lesbian Tourists – Profiles and Reasons

3

Introduction

This chapter focuses on certain demand aspects of gay and lesbian tourism. It examines market size and growth, the holiday patterns (or profile) of gays and lesbians, along with an identification of patterns that are specific to males and to females. In addition, the reasons for holiday-taking will be examined and any that are particularly important for gays and lesbians will be identified. The chapter will conclude with a consideration of the sex dimension of gay and lesbian tourism and its implications.

In the previous chapter, the nature and characteristics of homosexuality were examined in order to provide a context for the remaining chapters relating specifically to tourism. There is obviously a great deal of (almost inevitable) uncertainty about the market as it relates to homosexuality, and information about 'the market' relating to gay and lesbian tourism is also limited. As with information about homosexuality generally, it is almost impossible satisfactorily to draw a line around the chosen study area. There is no agreement about being able to categorize people according to their sexual orientation, so that identifying the size of the potential market is itself fraught with difficulty. In addition, there are significant issues relating to determining the actual pattern of tourism by gays and lesbians not the least of which are the problems in obtaining data that are representative of the gay and lesbian population (however defined). There are, in fact, few studies of the market and most available information is derived from market research surveys by commercial organizations rather than from academic studies, and these are frequently focused on the USA. These market research surveys are invariably limited in their

© Howard L. Hughes 2006. *Pink Tourism: Holidays of Gay Men and Lesbians* (Howard L. Hughes)

coverage of gays and lesbians and deal with particular respondents who share common characteristics, but who may well have little in common with others in other surveys and are (probably) unrepresentative of the general homosexual population (see Chapter 7 for further discussion of market surveys). Whilst many of these surveys acknowledge their short-comings, the information within them is frequently quoted and used with little or no qualification. In addition to this, there are frequent assertions made about the market which are actually based on little research as such, but which are anecdotal or based on personal experience or on some general feeling that they are true.

The material that does exist is very positive in that there is agreement, for instance, that the market is growing, that gays and lesbians are fre-quent travellers and are high-spend and that the market is resilient in the face of factors that have an adverse effect on other tourism. It needs to be noted that when commentators and survey results refer to the 'gay' or 'gay and lesbian' market, it is not always clear who is being included – homosexual men or women separately or together – and, as a consequence, statements and data need to be interpreted cautiously. Such evidence as exists usually relates predominantly or solely to men, and it may be inferred from many comments that they refer to gay men only.

Market Size and Growth

Observations on the market typically refer to it as 'one of the fastest growing niche markets in the international travel industry' (Ivy, 2001, p. 338) and as 'increasing at, or above, the rate of mainstream travel' (Wood, 1999, p. A110), though how this has been determined is not made clear. Not only is it a market that is believed to be growing but it is also considered to be a profitable one (Holcomb and Luongo, 1996; Clift and Forrest, 1999a; Wood, 1999). This view is shared by tourist boards such as the Australian Tourist Commission and Tourism Queensland: 'the gay and lesbian market has been acknowledged throughout the tourism industry as a profitable niche segment' (Tourism Queensland, 2002, p. 1). 'When a city like Pittsburgh develops a special gay travel market strategy, you know something's up . . . The reason for this interest in gay and lesbian travel marketing is simple: money' (Johnson, 2005a). It is considered also to be a sizeable market: the value of the US market has been estimated at US$54 billion, which represents 'an estimated 10% of the US travel industry' (Community Marketing Inc., 2003) (it is not obvious how this percentage is derived). Data from Australia would suggest lower magnitudes: expenditure by gay tourists was estimated to be less than 2% of total domestic tourist spend (Roy Morgan Research, 2003). Overseas visitors to Australia who identified as gay or lesbian for the International Visitor Survey comprised only 0.6% during 2002, the year of the Gay Games VI (http://www.atc.australia. com, 2004); this obviously may be an understatement of the actual proportion.

The gay travel sector is also considered to be particularly resistant to recession and other influences such as terrorism and epidemics that might ordinarily have adverse effects on the tourism market (Holcomb and Luongo, 1996; Community Marketing Inc., 2003; Trucco, 2004). It is claimed, for instance, that 79% of US gays and lesbians did not alter their travel plans after 9/11 and, rather cynically perhaps, it may have been situations such as this which caused many in the tourism industry to direct their attention to this market (Van Drake, 2003). A similar view is expressed by Quest (1998): 'The importance of this market is likely to increase especially if economies continue to slow down and traditional families find annual foreign vacations too expensive. Then the selling to those with money will truly begin' (p. 2). Also, gays and lesbians are believed to offer the advantage of flexibility, that families may not have, to travel off-peak.

Holiday Profiles

The basis for such optimism lies in the perceived tourism patterns of gays and lesbians. There is a common perception that gay men are frequent and intensive holidaymakers. It was stated, for instance, in a report by the US National Tour Association (NTA) that 'this market likes to travel and has the money and time to devote to that end' (National Tour Association, 2002, p. 1). The British Tourist Authority (BTA, now VisitBritain) concluded, in a study of the gay market in the USA, Australia and Germany, that 'not only did gay travellers have a higher than average disposable income but crucially they showed high indices of overseas travel, coupled with a tendency to spend longer abroad' (Wood, 1999, p. A107).

Community Marketing Inc. have conducted annual gay and lesbian travel surveys in the USA since 1994/95; their data underpin many of the comments and observations of others (including the NTA). Their 2001–2003 surveys showed that 97% of US gays and lesbians had taken a vacation in the previous 12 months compared with a national average of 64% (Community Marketing Inc., 2003). Similarly, a UK survey showed that 72% of gays took a holiday compared with 61% for the population as a whole, and 24% took three or more holidays compared with 11% for the whole population (Mintel, 2000a). An international online survey of gay travellers (38% living in Canada, 31% in the USA and 20% in Australia) showed nearly three-quarters took two to six vacations a year and over one-third took four to six (http://www.gaytravelguides.info, 2004).

One study in the USA did, however, show that a lower proportion of gays, lesbians and bisexuals (glbs) than of heterosexuals had taken a pleasure trip in the previous 2 years (22 and 17%, respectively, had taken no such trip) (Witeck-Combs Communications and Harris Interactive, 2003a).

Also, glbs had taken fewer pleasure trips than heterosexuals. A similar survey in Australia concluded that the number of leisure trips (lasting at least one night) taken by gays was no different from that taken by other (heterosexual) survey respondents (Roy Morgan Research, 2003).

Surveys suggest that foreign holidays are more likely for gays and lesbians. US gays were much more likely to take an international holiday than were the rest of the US population: 72% compared with 9% (Community Marketing Inc., 2001); 84% had a valid passport compared with the US national average of 29% (Community Marketing Inc., 2003). Another UK survey reported that, over a year, gays took one domestic holiday, two overseas holidays and three short breaks, though it made no comparison with the rest of the population (Stormbreak, 2000). Nearly 60% of Canadian gay travellers had taken seven or more vacation trips in Canada over the previous 5 years and 41% had taken seven or more abroad (http://www.gaytravelguides.info, 2004). Australian gay travellers were also more likely than the rest of the population to have travelled overseas or interstate: 12% of gays had travelled overseas compared with 8% of all (Roy Morgan Research, 2003). It was also concluded in this survey that gays had a greater preference for short breaks (usually holidays in cities) than did the rest of the population (Roy Morgan Research, 2003).

Gays are also believed to have a different travel pattern for business trips. In the USA, they had taken an average of seven trips in the previous 2 years compared with two trips by other travellers (Witeck-Combs Communications and Harris Interactive, 2003a). It was suggested that this could be explained by the limited family commitments of gays which caused them to be asked to take such trips or which enabled them to do so more readily.

There are no comprehensive data indicating which countries generate the largest number of gay and lesbian tourists, though it is widely believed that the USA and Germany are two of the main sources of domestic and international tourism. In 2002 (the year of the Gay Games VI in Sydney) the largest single generating countries of gay and lesbian tourists to Australia were the USA (22%), New Zealand (13.8%) and the UK (11.2%) (http://www.atc.australia.com, 2004). This is an isolated study and the inward tourism reflects the particular event as well as the particular geographical position of the country and its anglophile ties.

Accommodation

There are mixed views on the accommodation used by gay and lesbian tourists. The MAPS (1998) survey reported that apartments were popular with British gays and lesbians: 46% of respondents had stayed in apartments abroad and 20% in apartments in the UK. This was believed to be a reflection of demand for privacy and freedom. Most (66%), however, according to an international online survey of gay travellers, stayed in hotels and motels, followed by 'with friends and relatives' (13.5%) and B&Bs (12.9%) (http://www.gaytravelguides.info, 2004). Forty per cent had stayed in gay- or lesbian-operated or -owned accommodation and over 60% believed that being gay- or lesbian-operated or -owned was 'very' or 'somewhat' important. Whether or not accommodation was gay- or lesbian-exclusive was of importance to between only 30 and 40% of Australian gays and lesbians (Tourism Queensland, 2002). Those who did show a preference for it (mostly singles) did so because they felt more comfortable and relaxed and enjoyed the feeling of support and tolerance; it was also an opportunity to meet others. Key factors in choice of accommodation were price, location (close to beach, shops, nightclubs, etc.), 'friendliness' of the proprietor and other guests and personal referral. Many wished to avoid family-style properties where they might feel uncomfortable, though some lesbians holidaying in family groups may seek out accommodation that is child-friendly. Significantly, 'fair treatment of people like me' was a more important factor in accommodation choice for gays and lesbians (30%) than it was for heterosexuals (24%) (Witeck-Combs Communications and Harris Interactive, 2003a) (see also Chapter 7 for further discussion of 'gay-friendliness').

Friends may be expected to feature highly in the accommodation used by gays and lesbians (Valentine, 1995). Friends are often seen by gays and lesbians as proxy family and relationships are maintained for lengthy periods of time. This, along with bonds forged through the international 'imagined community', means there is an 'international family of friends who provide travellers with places to stay, eat and socialize' (Nardi, 1992, p. 112). Van Gelder and Brandt (1991) felt strongly that this feeling of community would ensure that 'you may be a foreigner but you won't be a stranger' (p. xvi). Friends rather than family are obvious travelling companions if only because, for most, family in the 'legal', heterosexual sense does not exist. The young male segment of the market is probably 'heavy with singles' (National Tour Association, 2002, p. 2), at least in the sense of being uncommitted to a sexual or life partner, though they are probably travelling with friends. Travel with others – whether friends or partners – is especially likely, it is believed, in the case of lesbians (Tourism Queensland, 2002). One-quarter of gay and lesbian international travellers to Canada visited alone and half travelled with one other companion (http://www.gaytravelguides.info, 2004).

Influencing Factors

The apparent tourism profile of gays and lesbians has led a number of observers to view tourism as an inextricable part of the gay lifestyle: 'travel and tourism have come to represent a significant dimension of contemporary western gay culture' (Visser, 2002, p. 85): 'we'll give up coffee before we'll give up travel' (Roth and Luongo, 2002, p. 131). What is it that drives gays and lesbians to exhibit such travel patterns?

The common views of gay and lesbian incomes and attitudes which were discussed earlier recur to explain the holiday profile: 'gay male couples have higher average incomes than their heterosexual counterparts . . . They have both more discretionary time and money for travel' (Holcomb and Luongo, 1996, p. 711). Community Marketing reports on the upscale characteristics of the gay traveller: the 2001–2003 surveys indicated that 76% had household incomes above the national average of US$40,000; 82% were college or university graduates (national average is 29%); and 67% belonged to frequent-flyer programmes (national average of about 25%) (Community Marketing Inc., 2003). Gay and lesbian visitors to a beach in Florida were highly educated, had high household income and were young and urban (and white) (Philipp, 1999). In a review of gay tourism globally, Russell (2001) echoed the general perceptions that 'gay people have relatively higher disposable incomes and that they tend to be early innovators of new products and services. The gay community is often considered a trendsetter' (p. 38). The MAPS (1998) report considered that gays and lesbians had become 'innovators and flexible thinkers', largely because of their rejection by the rest of society (p. 16).

A small-scale magazine survey in New Zealand (response of 161 from 4000) showed that, despite the limited incomes of respondents to that particular survey, there was a willingness to spend on vacations. This was explained by gays and lesbians having 'a predilection for consumer goods, travel and the visual arts . . . [and are] . . . a segment with enviable levels of intellect and discrimination for the suppliers of tourism services and products' (Wiltshier and Cardow, 2001, p. 122). A high level of education may in itself make people more aware of the world and stimulate travel (Roth and Luongo, 2002). It is possible that being an 'outsider' and experiencing 'difference' at home makes gays and lesbians more willing to accept and embrace 'difference' associated with travel to other places and cultures (Bledsoe, 1998a).

An inevitable link: homosexuality and travel

It may be, however, that this apparently high demand for travel arises from a fundamental feature relating to homosexuality. This is what Aldrich (1993) describes as the 'traditional homosexual dilemma . . . the yearnings of a man whose desires make him socially deviant and who must flee to some other place to act upon them' (p. 4). It has previously been noted that homosexuals may need to search out gay space in order to be able to relate to the concept of a homosexual identity and to escape the heteronormative constraints on behaviour. 'Movement offers sexual dissidents a means of escape and of self-realization' (Binnie, 1997, p. 240) and 'we travel great distances in order to live in the ways that enhance further contact with one another' (Ingram, 1997, p. 27). As it is possible to be gay or lesbian only in some places and not others, this may entail seeking out the nearest gay space, which may well be a single local bar or social organization. At another level, it may mean spending leisure time in an environment such as a 'gay village' of more numerous venues or even migrating to a town or city with such extensive gay space (Cant, 1997). Gay men living in a US town considered that their lives as gay men were tied to leisure and leisure travel (Herrera and Scott, 2005). They commonly travelled to large cities for the gay scene and felt able to express their sexuality in such a safe environment where they could develop skills that enabled them to cope with life at home and develop 'pride' in being homosexual. They also, through travel, established networks of friends which helped them cope. Nestle (1997) lived in the Lower East Side of New York and, for her, the 'deepest joy' was a bus and subway trip at weekends through Brooklyn to Riis Park (south Long Island): 'this tired beach . . . was my first free place where I could . . . kiss in blazing sunlight the salt-tinged lips of the woman I loved' (p. 66).

Even for those who have not been particularly restricted at home, travel can be an exposure to different perspectives on sexuality. In his journey to Russia Tuller (1996) 'experienced, in startling and unexpected ways, a different kind of sexual freedom than I had found in the golden gay enclaves of New York and San Francisco' (p. 42) and was 'exhilarated . . . to discover that my sexuality was more nuanced and complex than I had assumed' (p. 290).

The adoption of a gay identity may itself be conceptualized as 'a journey from another place to where one now is' (Connell, 1995, p. 157). Brown (1998) makes a similar analogy: 'we have one country, one set of behaviour, one tradition in which we are raised and, to which, for a time we belong . . . but we as lesbians have another country to explore, the one in which we "live really"' (p. viii). At a functional level, however, and because gay space is limited and is more likely to be found in larger urban areas, the achievement or fulfilment of gay identity actually often involves travel (however short the distance) and is thus, in practice, a form of tourism (Hughes, 1997). It may also be the case that tourism (travel and overnight stay), rather than short-term and episodic travel, is an important way in which this may be achieved (Visser, 2002). 'The holiday can provide a further opportunity to be gay and provide the only, or extra, opportunity to validate identity by living and playing over a continuous period of time, in gay space or at least a place that is gay-friendly' (Hughes, 2002b, p. 299).

AMRO, a UK tour operator targeting the gay and lesbian market, uses the strapline 'travel with us and be yourself' (see Fig. 3.1), which highlights this fundamental link between homosexuality and being away from home.

Fig. 3.1. Press advertisement produced by AMRO Holidays (UK) showing range of holidays offered.

Mythical places

Rojek (1998) has pointed out how, in the mid- and late 19th century, tourism to places such as Tangiers, Casablanca, Cairo and the Italian Riviera became associated with emancipated lifestyles and popular with tourists who were anxious to escape convention, whether ethnic or sexual. Homosexual men have long gone abroad from Britain in order to escape the rigours of the law and/or social disapproval. Oscar Wilde, the 19th century playwright, holidayed with Lord Alfred Douglas in Algiers in 1895, where a major attraction was the availability of young men for sexual purposes. After Wilde's release from prison in 1897, he and Douglas went to Naples, another place (along with Capri) that was popular with homosexuals. Wilde lived the last few years of his life mainly in Paris, a city that Wilde had said, in earlier years, 'pleases me greatly. While in London one hides everything, in Paris one reveals everything' (quoted in McKenna, 2004, p. 223).

In his study, Cox (2001) concluded that there were opportunities to participate in gay culture that were not available at home, and that being away from home provided the ideal opportunity to 'experiment' and to come out or consolidate a sexual identity. He felt that his research showed that the significance for gay men lay more in identity than in sexual activity. 'Holidaymaking provides gay men with significant opportunities to experience a range of sexual cultures that may bring important changes in their individual and collective sources of gay identity' (Cox, 2001, p. 3). Gays and lesbians may well only 'find themselves' when somewhere other than their home environment. Newton (1993), in her study of Cherry Grove (Fire Island, New York), pointed out how 'resorts like Provincetown (Massachusetts), Key West (Florida) and the Grove were (and, to a large extent, still are) the only public places gays could socialize and assemble without constant fear of hostile straight society' (Newton, 1993, p. 2). Although Newton (1993) considered that within the 'seaside ghetto' of Cherry Grove some fundamental aspects of modern gay identity evolved, it was limited and there was a reluctance to engage with the political activity of the 1970s. In Philipp's (1999) survey of gay and lesbian visitors to a beach in Florida, 54% were more 'out' than they usually were at home and most would display gay and lesbian symbols whilst in the area (though most were restricting themselves to the gay beach and immediate vicinity).

Some places have become endowed with a particular ethos as gay or lesbian Meccas – as idyllic communities where it is perceived that gays and lesbians can live, work and play openly – and, as a consequence, they have become especially attractive as places for gay and lesbians to visit. Some, such as San Francisco, can take on the role of 'homeland' similar to that of ethnic minorities (Howe, 2001). The reputation of San Francisco as a gay Mecca may owe much to the publicity associated with the high-profile public struggles over civil rights from the late 1950s onwards (Kitchin, 2002; Boyd, 2003). The novel *Tales of the City* (published 1978), and several successive novels in the same series by Armisted Maupin, which graphically described the gay life of San Francisco, must have also contributed to its iconization as a 'gay capital'. The adaptation as a television series shown in many countries – including the USA and the UK in the mid-1990s – will have added to this. The analogy of the homeland is not complete, though, given that it is not related to ancestral 'roots'. Such homeland travel is usually perceived to be non-touristic and is associated with becoming, if only temporarily, a local, though this may not occur in practice and the reality may not live up to the dream (Stephenson, 2002). Lesvos, as the birthplace of Sappho, has also become an 'imagined' lesbian Mecca – a place of symbolic meaning and of pilgrimage (Kantsa, 2002). Sappho, apart from establishing a community of women here, was also allegedly an accomplished poet and music composer. Very little is actually known about her life and little of her poetry exists and, to a large extent, the significance lies in a 'fantasy' constructed by two French women in the early 20th century. Some of the early visitors in the 1970s saw the Greek island as a place with a tradition of same-sex practices and where it was possible to have a separatist community where women might live independently in an atmosphere of love and freedom. Unfortunately this coincided with a more general expansion of tourism on the island which meant the fantasy could not be readily fulfilled (see Chapter 4).

The 'other'

The attraction of travel to gays and lesbians has also arisen out of other fantasies – the construction of 'the other' – places where it was imagined that same-sex activity was common or not proscribed and even openly accepted, and where locals were especially 'innocent' about sexual activity and would willingly enter into relationships with foreigners.

There has been a representation of Mediterranean countries in literature, film and music as places where homosexual love was more acceptable than it was in northern European countries (Aldrich, 1993). In part, this was accounted for by romanticized views of classical Greece, but also by a perception of societies that were more liberal and less restrained in their emotional and sexual lives, as well as the reality of a more lenient approach by the law. Photographs of Sicilian and Sardinian naked or semi-naked youths, often in classical Greco-Roman poses, taken at the end of the 19th century by von Gloeden received wide circulation in 'respectable' circles and furthered the myth of the 'sensuous Latin'. Southern Italy was also idealized in the pre-World War I books of Norman Douglas: 'each Italian boy, youth and young man glitters and glows and glowers in Douglas's supple prose, attracting new travellers . . . decades after he and those lads are long gone' (Picano, 1998, p. viii). There is a persistent image of same-sex relationships in Ancient Greece which continues to influence present-day tourists and tourism promotion (Bravmann, 1994).

Myths of sensuality (usually associated with 'primitiveness' and a lack of 'civilization') existed about other places too in the 19th and early 20th centuries and, in particular, about Africa and the Middle and Far East as convenient rationalization for colonization (Aldrich, 1996; Altman, 1997). By defining other societies and cultures in these ways, the 'West' was helping define its own self-image as more civilized and superior; the construction of identity involves establishing opposites, the 'others' (Said, 1978). Sir Richard Burton (1821–1890), a Victorian explorer and writer, believed 'pederasty' – homosexual practices – was common in what he termed the 'Sotadic Zone', which included Spain, Italy and Greece and countries on the northern shore of the Mediterranean as well as, amongst others, parts of the Middle and Far East. His translation of *Arabian Nights* (1885) included a 'Terminal Essay', discussing this at great length. More recently, the published diaries (1967) of the British playwright, Joe Orton (1933–1967), described in graphic detail his sexual encounters with local youths in Morocco.

Myths may bear little resemblance to the reality but they have none the less led many to migrate or to holiday: 'homosexuals beat a path to Tangiers to follow in the footsteps of Bowles and Burroughs, Kerouac and Orton' (Aldrich, 1996, p. 190). The myths persist and there remain 'romanticised views about homoeroticism in many non-western cultures' (Altman, 2001, p. 92) even though homosexuality is far from being universally accepted or tolerated in 'paradises' such as Morocco, Philippines and Thailand. Eastern Europe (including Russia) was also conceptualized in the 18th century as an 'oriental other' sphere (Bunzl, 2000) and, more recently, as an economically and culturally backward place (Baer, 2002).

A number of Western writers have pictured sexual identity as being more fluid in Russia (Tuller, 1996). Prague, the capital of the Czech Republic, is perceived as a place of sexual licence, innocence and availability with men relegated to 'boys' for use and purchase by tourists (Bunzl, 2000). Cantu (2002) believes that US gay tourists hold a similar 'exotic other' view of Mexico as a homosexual paradise where sexuality exists in its 'raw' form. Gay guidebooks represent Mexican men as sensual and sexual. This representation of local gays as a fetishized object in an 'exotic paradise' may be perceived to be a form of neo-colonialism, a colonial construction of adventure with the prospect of taboo sex (Puar, 2002b).

Gayness and Other Reasons

What is it, therefore, that gays and lesbians look for on holiday? Are the reasons for holidaying any different from those of the rest of the population? Most studies suggest that gays and lesbians go on holiday for the same reasons and choose to experience the same type of holidays as the rest of the population. The categorization of gay and lesbian holidays by Tourism Queensland (2002) into 'partying holidays' and 'relaxation or getaway holidays', though an obvious simplification, could be equally applicable to a heterosexual market. The Mintel report (2000a) also showed that the range of holidays experienced by British gays and lesbians was similar to that of the whole population and gave detail of the type of holiday. Beach and city breaks (at 25 and 23%, respectively) were the most popular types of holiday for gays and lesbians, followed a long way behind by lakes and mountains (7%), adventure and sport (5%), gay themed (4%) and gay special event (1%). The proportion taking city breaks (23%) was greater than that for the population as a whole (9%). This may be due to the fact that cities have some form of gay space that is an attraction in its own right or because of the intrinsic attractions of cities, including arts and culture in which gays are purported to have a particular interest generated by comparatively high levels of education (Roth and Luongo, 2002). There is a belief that many gays – especially in the US market – have sophisticated tastes and a strong interest in arts and culture when on holiday (Wood, 1999). A study (of gays and lesbians) by Pritchard *et al.* (2000) confirmed that the reasons for going on holiday were similar to those expressed by non-gays. There was, however, an emphasis on the desire to 'escape', the need for 'safety' and a need for gay space where there would be no requirement to suppress sexuality. The BTA's research confirmed that US gay travellers wished to experience Britain's tourist assets much as any other traveller did but they also placed a premium on gay-friendliness (Wood, 1999; see also Community Marketing Inc., 2003).

Descriptions of destinations in the gay press cover the 'usual' attractions, such as museums and art galleries in cities and beaches or scenery elsewhere, and would appear to confirm that gays and lesbians go on holiday to do and experience the same things as everyone else. These articles do, though, generally also contain detail of gay space. In the Mintel (2000a) study, the existence of gay venues at the holiday destination was an important choice factor for about half of UK respondents, though this was less important for females (important for 63% of males and 47% of females) and applied equally to beach and city destinations. Only a very small proportion (about 4%) required a 'gay-themed' or gay-centric holiday.

In the holiday decision process, dimensions of 'gayness' appear to have some significance. This was confirmed by Clift and Forrest (1999a) in their study that sought to determine influences that underlay the holiday decision. In 'planning a holiday', gay men rated rest and relaxation, comfort and good food as the most important factors and these were no different from what the responses of heterosexuals might be expected to be. A relatively low proportion of gay men identified opportunities to have sex on holiday as important in planning a holiday, though it was important to be able to socialize with other gay men in gay space: 36.6% rated this and 39.1% rated 'gay culture and venues' as 'very important' compared, for instance, with 70.2% rating 'opportunities for rest and relaxation' and 29.3% rating 'opportunities to have sex'. Factors such as gay venues, good nightlife and socializing with other gay men were, though, more important to those who visited 'gay' destinations than to those who did not (Clift et al., 2002).

The reasons for going on holiday and the type of holiday chosen appear to be common to both homosexuals and heterosexuals, but there is also a particular need to be, at least in part, with other gay persons and have access to gay space or to gay-friendly places or, at least, to avoid homophobia. The Mintel (2000a) report concluded that there was a definite determination amongst gay men and lesbians not to visit countries perceived to be homophobic: over two-thirds of men would not go to such a place. Whilst on holiday gay men will expect to be able to escape from the features of life at home that cause difficulties and force them to adopt avoidance and denial strategies. The choice of destination is therefore likely to be influenced by perceptions of the gay-friendliness of a place. The push factors that are specific to gay men create a desire to ensure that destinations visited are 'safe' and 'comfortable'. Gayness – or gay dimensions of a holiday and destination – can take several forms. These will include tolerance, acceptance and gay-friendliness on the one hand and, on the other, actual gay space in the form of gay and lesbian venues. This space would itself be an indicator of tolerance and gay-friendliness.

Dimensions of gayness on holidays

Gay dimensions or gayness will perform a dual function for gay and lesbian tourists: a dual function of 'paradise' and of safe haven. For gays and lesbians who have 'problems' at home (such as not being open about sexuality), it is an 'escape' to a different environment and provides an opportunity to be oneself. It is of importance for the establishment and confirmation of gay identity. For those who do not have such problems, it is a necessary requirement that the holiday should provide an environment which is at least as satisfactory as that at home. Its existence in other places, if not in the physical and spatial sense, then at least in the sense of tolerance and acceptance is a significant draw in its own right for those who experience intolerance and disapproval at home. It also has a significance for those with more favourable home circumstances, as they would not wish to visit destinations on holiday that are less agreeable.

For some tourists, a toleration and acceptance of gays and lesbians may be sufficient but, for others, it may be necessary for there to be physical gay space in the form of bars, clubs, restaurants, accommodation, etc. This in turn, may be used or not used and simply read as a sign of acceptance. Further, the gay space may be used for the 'usual' tourist demands or may be a focus for casual sex. Gay space will probably be more important for 'partying holidays' than for 'relaxation or getaway holidays' where scenery, cultural facilities and shopping are significant (Tourism Queensland, 2002). Gay space is not, in such cases, the main attribute looked for but is a pre-requisite for other factors such as sun, culture or heritage. Gay space will be more determinant, however, for others. It may be a key issue when sexual activity features as a significant factor in the reason for a holiday (though gay space and sexual activity do not necessarily go together). Gay tourist guidebooks often identify (if not focus on) places for cruising – casual sex (Howe, 2001). Whilst 'gay tourists travel to Cape Town mainly for its natural, cultural and historical attractions' (Visser, 2003, p. 186), gay visitors to Amsterdam, for instance, may be particularly interested in the sexual opportunities offered in such a tolerant city (Duyves, 1995; Hughes, 1998). Whatever the nature of 'gayness' sought, the fact that gay space and gay-friendliness are not universal means that 'some places that are popular for the travelling public in general . . . may not be considered as desirable by some gay travellers' (Ivy, 2001, p. 352).

Undoubtedly, some homosexuals will seek to avoid the gay scene totally when on holiday, especially if that scene has been a factor of everyday leisure life or if they were seeking some form of adventure holiday. Despite having written in gay magazines about the more hedonistic type of holiday, one gay man claimed that 'my dream is to escape from the homo metropolis and head for wilderness' (Tatchell, 2004a, p. 117). This he found on a hiking holiday on Madeira, a Portuguese-speaking island with no gay bars or hotels venues, though with a gay beach.

There are then several 'types' of holiday undertaken by gays and lesbians. These, apart from the gay space element and a few other exceptions, are likely to be similar to those of the rest of the population: beach holidays in a warm climate, city breaks, cruises, and so on. How these relate to 'segments' of the gay and lesbian market is unclear. It is possible that beach and partying holidays will be appealing to younger gays (and less so to lesbians?), and more cultural holidays will be popular with older gays. It would, however, be too simplistic to segment the market by age and sex alone and there are other factors (such as class and ethnicity) whose influence is as yet undetermined.

Cox (2001) concluded that 'there is no such thing as a typical gay holiday' (p. 249) and, from the above discussion, it is possible to identify several forms of gay or lesbian holidays. A distinction frequently made is between holidays that are no different from those of the rest of the population and holidays that have a distinctive gay or lesbian element (Clift *et al.*, 2002a; Puar, 2002b). Even in the first case, however, it may be that 'expressions of a gay identity have to be managed' (Cox, 2001, p. 249). The second category of holiday may run on a continuum, depending on the extent of the gay or lesbian element. The continuum will include holidays that are, in varying degrees, 'gay-related' and where tolerance, gay-friendliness or gay space are important but do not necessarily dominate other requirements. Other holidays will be 'gay-centric', where gay space and experience is the key factor in decisions. This latter is similar to what Cox (2001) termed a 'gay holiday'. He also identified holidays where gays, whilst not immersing themselves wholly in gay life, might seek to gain entry to 'authentic' gay life in the destination.

Lesbian Holidays (See also Chapters 5 and 6)

There is little published material available that would provide a basis for a detailed discussion of holidays undertaken by lesbians. It is evident that the market surveys that have been discussed rarely distinguish holiday experiences of gay men from those of lesbians, often because the number of women responding to these surveys is small. There is also a lack of academic studies dealing with lesbians and tourism (Puar, 2002c). There is, though, no more reason to believe that lesbians' holiday profiles are the same as those of gay men's than there is to believe males and females generally have the same motivations and behaviours.

The limited data are a reflection of a greater visibility of gay men within the homosexual leisure sphere, but are also indicative of the fact that regardless of sexual orientation, 'tourism research has traditionally failed to recognize women as a specific market segment' (Aitchison, 1999, p. 28). There has, though, been a relatively recent interest in the issue of gender in tourism and, within that, in the experiences of women. These studies have not been lesbian-specific and it would be unwarranted to assume the conclusions of these studies could be applied to lesbian tourism, but they may none the less have the potential to contribute to an understanding of it.

Women, leisure and travel

Kinnaird and Hall's (1994a) pioneering collection of essays on gender and tourism include one chapter (out of ten) that focuses on women as travellers compared with several relating to women in the labour force. That deals primarily with the common topic of women travellers of the past and their writings. There is a significant body of work that relates to the historical dimension of 'women travellers' – women who have, in the past, travelled and written about those travels in diaries, letters and books (Hall and Kinnaird, 1994). Robinson (1990) describes, individually, the writings of about 400 women travellers. Their writings reveal a 'consistent role of tourism as a source of independence for 19th and 20th century women' (Butler, 1995, p. 489). They saw travel as an opportunity to escape from domestic environments and the constraints, routines and expectations of women (Birkett, 2000; Gibson, 2001). They may well have been from privileged backgrounds and were often conventional in respect of their 'imperialistic' views of some of the societies they encountered, but their writings were often particularly significant. Most of the early writing about the Balkans, for instance, has been by women (Allcock and Young, 2000).

The emerging work on women and tourism suggests strongly that women and men experience tourism differently. 'Tourism revolves around social interaction and social articulations of motivations, desires, traditions and perceptions, all of which are gendered' (Kinnaird *et al.*, 1994, p. 24). In addition, historically, men have been travellers and the role of women in tourism has frequently been that of employees in the industry or as a 'submissive' part of local society to be experienced, especially in promoting 'exotic' destinations (Apostolopoulos and Sonmez, 2001; Gibson, 2001). 'In many societies, being feminine has been defined as sticking close to home. Masculinity, by contrast, has been the passport to travel' (Enloe, 1990, p. 21).

Women's leisure also differs from that of men. There is a relative lack of leisure opportunities for women and, because of a male domination of public leisure space, women's use of it is restricted geographically and temporally (Deem, 1996; Gibson, 2001). 'The fear of violence, sexual harassment and rape is a constant and all-pervasive restriction upon the actions of women . . . Monitoring and avoiding these risks take on a more unknown character whilst travelling . . . The characteristics of hegemonic masculinity can be seen as constituting a threat' (Black, 2000, p. 260). Independence is inhibited and women when travelling, especially solo, engage in risk-reduction activity over and above that of men by developing strategies to keep them safe (such as choice of transport or accommodation) and constructing mental maps of surroundings in terms of potential danger (Gibson, 2001).

Some other key issues to emerge from studies include the conclusions that women place more importance than do men on relationships and social obligations as an important part of the holiday experience, and that women with young children frequently continue to accept the domestic role of caring and taking responsibility for others whilst on holiday (Davidson, 1996). Single women without dependants or male partners were believed to have more relaxed, fulfilling and 'escapist' holidays than did other women (Deem, 1996). A study of the holiday experiences of university-educated women in the USA concluded that the most popular benefits derived from holidays were considered to be experiencing natural surroundings and seeking educational experiences (Pennington-Gray and Kerstetter, 2001). Increasing knowledge of other places and intellectual enrichment were not considered important.

Lesbian tourism

There is little detail from surveys about the detail of lesbian tourism as such. The development of the feminist lesbian movement (however defined) globally and of activist networks may, though, have stimulated some lesbian tourism (Puar, 2002c). The UK Mintel (2000a) survey is one of the few that has distinguished between gay men and lesbians with respect to holidays. Most respondents to the survey were male but 41% were classified as 'gay or bisexual female'. Females were slightly less likely than males to have taken a holiday in the last 12 months (71 compared with 74%) and less likely to have gone on beach holidays or city breaks (25 and 20% compared with 29 and 30%, respectively), though what other holidays they did go on was left unspecified. Lesbians (and female bisexuals) considered that it was less important than did men that there should be gay venues on holiday (55% compared with 64%). They were also slightly less likely to book with a gay-friendly company and were slightly more likely to want to stay in gay-friendly accommodation, to want more diverse gay holiday products and not to visit a homophobic country.

   In the USA, Community Marketing considered that it was possible for the first time to separately identify the responses of gay men and lesbians in their 8th survey (2002–2003), and concluded that there are 'two very distinct markets, male and female'. Of the 1500 respondents, 21% were lesbians and separate responses were given for some, though not all, of the questions. Lesbians were less likely to have a passport (57% compared with 88% of gay men) and spent less on their holidays (39% spent over US$2500 per person per vacation though 64% of men did this). Lesbians were more likely than gay men to look for a 'relaxing holiday' (68% compared with 56%) and less likely to choose somewhere they had been before (57% compared with 67%). Otherwise, their concerns were similar, though the survey suggested that lesbians might be slightly less concerned for 'safety', for the holiday being 'affordable' and about holidaying in order 'to learn about local culture'.

Evidence is limited and equivocal but there would seem, therefore, to be some differences in the holiday profile of lesbians and gay men. Lesbians will be subject to the dual influences of being both female and homosexual and their holiday profile can be expected to reflect and be explained by this. It has been noted earlier that lesbians are less likely than gay men to be participants in the gay scene and to frequent gay space. They are, too, more likely to be looking for or be in more stable relationships and be less concerned with casual relationships (sexual or otherwise). It is possible that frequency of holiday-taking is lower and holidays are taken more with partners than is the case for gay men. Given the difficulties faced by women travellers (homosexual and heterosexual), it might be expected that as a generalization, lesbians will be less interested in the gay space type of holiday and more focused on lower-key types of holidays that serve to nurture existing relationships. The presence of children in some lesbian households will have an obvious effect, but may also promote a demand for holidays where families with two female adults are not regarded as unusual.

Sex and Tourism

It has already been suggested that sex is not an obviously dominant reason for gay and lesbian tourism (Clift and Forrest, 1999a). Even for US circuit parties (see Chapter 6), sexual activity is apparently low on the list of reasons for attending (Mansergh *et al.*, 2001). In their work on the sex–tourism relationship, Ryan and Hall (2001) concluded that 'one of the great myths of gay lifestyles [is] . . . that it is full of single gays and lesbians who are seeking casual sex' (p. 103).

The sexual behaviour of gays and lesbians even when not on holiday is not a well-covered issue. In the UK, the Sigma surveys of gay men's sexual behaviour gives some indication and seems to suggest a fairly high incidence of sexual activity (though comparison with activity of unmarried non-gays would give greater significance to the data) (Reid *et al.*, 2004). The mean age of survey respondents in 2003 was 33; 84.4% of respondents had had sex only with men in the previous 12 months and 9.5% with both men and women. Only 18% had had sex with one man only and about one-quarter of respondents had had sex with 13 or more men in the previous year. Clift and Forrest's survey (1999b) of gay men revealed that about one-quarter of their respondents had had no new sexual partner (when not on holiday; time period not specified) but one-third had had one to three new sexual partners and 21% had had ten or more.

With respect to tourism it might be expected that the incidence of sexual activity (however defined) would be higher. It has already been suggested that gays and lesbians may go on holiday to seek opportunities that are unavailable at home. This may include sexual encounter as much as it might include socialization of a non-sexual nature with other gays. Sex and tourism are frequently related, though the exact nature of this relationship is complex. There is a considerable variety of experiences that might be envisaged. For some tourists, having sex whilst on holiday may be a reason for travel and for others an encounter that might be opportunistic (Oppermann, 1999). In some cases, usually prostitution, sexual encounters may involve monetary payment. There are other dimensions to the relationship including its duration, the nature of the activity and whether voluntary or exploitive (Ryan and Hall, 2001; McKercher and Bauer, 2003). Relationships may be between tourists and locals or between tourists themselves. In the case of heterosexual tourists the most common sexual interaction in leisure travel is probably between tourists themselves, either with existing partners (perhaps increased frequency) or with new partners (Carter and Clift, 2000).

Without further related research evidence it is impossible to generalize about the sexual motivation or behaviour of gays and lesbians on holiday. It is possible, though, that whatever the motivation, sexual encounters of gays and lesbians on holiday are mostly with other (gay and lesbian) tourists. This scenario is plausible given the number of like-minded gays and lesbians who may view holidays as opportunities for experiences denied or difficult to obtain at home.

Regardless of sexual activity, commercial organizations and destinations use erotic images and the allure of sexual activity to attract tourists, gay and straight. Gay and lesbian tour operators and destinations that target this market use images of good-looking individuals or same-sex couples in advertisements, in much the same way as do those targeting similar heterosexual customers – usually young singles. Beyond that imagery, however, there is usually little further implication of holiday sex; the equivalent of the manifestly hedonistic package holidays such as those associated with Club 18–30 (Thomas Cook) does not exist.

Heterosexuals, sex and holidays

Evidence about sexual behaviour of heterosexuals on holidays is a little more available than is that for homosexuals, but is still limited. The papers in Clift and Page (1996) were all mostly focused on heterosexual tourists, but shared a common view that there was a paucity of studies of sexual behaviour of tourists. There was some agreement, though, that holidays are opportunities for relaxing behavioural norms and that tourists do make new sexual contacts and may take greater risks in those contacts. Holidaymakers have reduced perceptions of the consequences of sexual activity and some – especially heterosexually orientated holiday companies – encourage sexual activity. Most papers agreed that casual sexual encounters appear to be part of the desired holiday experience. It is not always clear how the situation when on holiday, in terms of numbers of sexual partners and the level of unprotected sex, compares with that at home. There were considerable differences in the studies, however, in figures quoted relating to proportions of tourists who had sex whilst on holiday and with whom and how many partners. Some suggest that the number of travellers (usually focused on young travellers) who had sex with new partners whilst away is low but many studies none the less report a 'high' level of unsafe sex. Drug and alcohol use may be associated with unsafe sex: a general lowering of inhibitions and increased recklessness on holiday. Some holiday sex may also be related to 'romance' and not regarded as casual sex, and the need for safe sex is neglected.

A study of British heterosexual young people on 'dance holidays' in the Balearics showed that the proportion who had sex on holiday was lower than those who had sex at home (50% compared with 67%) and the average number of partners was fewer; usage of drugs and alcohol was much higher, however (Elliott *et al.*, 1998) (these were young people who were on dance holidays and may therefore have been less interested in sex on holiday than were other young holidaymakers). A similar study of British young (16–35) holidaymakers on Ibiza (though not with a focus on dance holidays) found that most had visited for 'the music' and only 15% were 'looking for sex', though this reason was given by 22% of men and only 4% of women. The majority of all respondents had travelled to the island without a partner (Bellis *et al.*, 2004). Just over half had sex at least once during their stay and 13.5% had sex with between two and five sexual partners, and the number of partners during a 10-day holiday was, on average, equal to that in the previous 6 months. In a survey of UK tourists on Tenerife (Canary Islands), average age 30, it was reported that 35% had had sexual intercourse with a new partner whilst on holiday (Batalla-Duran *et al.*, 2003).

Males were shown to be more likely than women (20.8 compared with 3.7%) to have sex with a new partner during a vacation break (the Spring Break) in a study of heterosexual US students in Florida (Josiam *et al.*, 1998). The number of new sex partners (per week) during the break was significantly higher than the number at other times (for men, 1.5 compared with 0.2). Sexual relationships and motivations are not confined to men, however. In a study of female (heterosexual) tourists (single or travelling alone) in Jamaica and the Dominican Republic, 31% had engaged in one or more sexual relationships with local men during the holiday and one-quarter of these reported two to five partners (Sanchez Taylor, 2001). The women who had sexual relationships with local men were more likely to have made several visits to the Caribbean in the past. In another female-focused study, heterosexual women tourists who had sexual intercourse with a new partner on their trip often associated this with a strong physical attraction, but it was also regarded as signifying commitment (Thomas, 2000). It was shown in a further study of the relationship between 'beach boys' and female tourists in the Dominican Republic that the women regarded it as more of a romantic relationship than did the male tourists in their encounters with female sex workers (Herold *et al.*, 2001). In the study of women tourists who had sex with Caribbean local men, most did not regard the men as prostitutes, despite having given cash, gifts or meals to them (Sanchez Taylor, 2001). Relationships were more usually described as a 'holiday romance' or 'real love'. Jeffreys (2003), however, considered that women remained the exploited partner in such relationships.

Gays, lesbians, sex and holidays

Some gay and lesbian destinations do have word-of-mouth reputations as places where casual sex is possible and this aspect undoubtedly has significant influence on destination choice for some, though there is no hard 'evidence' for this. Some of these reputations are rendered explicit – as in the case of Fire Island – in books, television programmes and popular pornographic films or novels. Fire Island has had a reputation for outdoor cruising and 'recreational sex' ever since the 1930s and entered popular mythology as a sexual heaven (Newton, 1993). Provincetown (Cape Cod, Massachusetts) has not had the same reputation but it too has outdoor cruising areas which are, for instance, mentioned in a recent travel book by Cunningham (2004).

Media articles about holiday products or destinations do, though, sometimes pick up on the sexual angle. In an article about Gran Canaria in a mainstream UK national newspaper, a journalist commented 'as far as I can see gay holidays are designed with two things in mind: to allow gay men to spend the daytime ogling other men in Speedos without having to switch on their gaydar and to spend the night trawling the bars trying to identify each other fully clothed . . . Sex is readily available' (Wells, 2002). Alternative Holidays' resort holiday in Sardinia in 2004 was described in a travel article in *Gay Times* as 'a sun, sand, sea and (hopefully) sexy holiday with 500 other gay men from all over the world . . . [where] the only other people on the island will be the 5000 US marines holed up in the nearby nuclear submarine base' (Tatchell, 2004b). The resort holiday (in Sicily) was described the previous year in a national newspaper as 'a week of freedom, giddiness and, yes, shagging' (McLean, 2003). Fire Island has been depicted as 'renowned for beach parties, drugs, wild sex and beautiful boardwalks' in the (UK) *Pink Paper* (Czyzselska, 2003). The ramparts of Ibiza Old Town were identified as a traditional cruising area in an article in the UK gay magazine, *Attitude* (June 2004).

Tourist guidebooks are rather more likely to mention sexual opportunities. *Spartacus*, for instance, identifies places, such as parks and beaches, for cruising – for casual sexual encounters. The extracts from the work of gay and lesbian writers in Bledsoe's (1998a, b) two edited collections frequently include reference to, though do not focus on, sexual encounters during travels. Luongo's more recent edited book (2004) is explicitly 'a collection of gay travel erotica'.

In the Brighton (UK) survey of gay men, half agreed that there were more opportunities for sex on holiday and nearly 40% were more sexually active on holiday than at home (Clift and Forrest, 2000). Of those who had been on holiday at least once in the previous year, half had been with a new sex partner on holiday and, of those, half had sex with three or more partners; 60% of those having sex with a new partner had penetrative sex. Not surprisingly, men holidaying in 'gay destinations' were more likely to have new partners and to have more partners. Sexual activity was also associated with being on holiday alone or with a friend, with 'gay life' as a motivation for holiday and also with a high number of sex partners at home. 'Gay men are considerably more likely than heterosexuals to have sex with new partners on holiday' (Clift and Forrest, 1999b, p. 290). A survey of gay men carried out at travel fairs in London (1997–1998) was similar in content to that of the Brighton survey (Clift *et al.*, 2002a). Findings were similar in that nearly half had a new sexual partner whilst away and 30% had four or more new sexual partners, though just less than half of those having sex with a new partner reported having penetrative sex. Of these, one-third had penetrative sex with three or more new partners. In a sample of US circuit partygoers, 67% had had some form of anal or oral sex during the circuit party weekend (Mansergh *et al.*, 2001).

Sex tourism

Sex tourism is often thought of as travel which occurs with the prime purpose of having sexual encounter whilst away, and this usually on a commercial basis. Invariably sex workers and tourists are unequal in terms of economic power, though this is not overtly acknowledged and the relationship is often rationalized as a 'natural' one, readily and freely entered into. Thailand has a long-established reputation for sex tourism, both heterosexual and homosexual (Sanders, 2002). Homosexuality is not illegal and there is a considerable degree of toleration of the commercial venues ('host bars', bars offering 'go-go' dancing and sex shows, saunas, massage parlours) and services provided for both heterosexual and homosexual clients. Sexuality is fluid in this culture and the polarization into hetero and homo is not prevalent. Participation in homosexual acts is not particularly proscribed, provided it is discreet. Many male sex workers do not associate their male sexual activity with homosexuality and continue to have a sex life with women. Most clients are domestic and it would appear that tourists are opportunistic users of an existing sex industry (McKercher and Bauer, 2003) though 'the male sex industry in Pattaya also depends heavily on overseas tourism' (McCamish, 1999, p. 169). As well as the gay scene in Bangkok, Chiang Mai's (Thailand's second largest city) gay nightlife – although smaller – is focused around male prostitution, with few non-prostitution gay venues (De Lind van Wijngaarden, 1999). This, too, is sustained by demand from tourists, especially from the rest of South-east Asia and Japan. Pattaya, a beach resort south-east of Bangkok, is well known for a ready availability of male commercial sex workers (McCamish, 1999). In some cases, long-term relationships between workers and foreign tourists have been established – either for a lengthy period over the duration of the trip or on a regular recurring annual basis. Relationships were often perceived by both tourist and local as involving affection, emotional attachment and commitment, rather than as being sex-based.

The Czech capital of Prague has been labelled 'the preferred site for Austrian gay male sex tourism' (Bunzl, 2000, p. 70). A study of this tourism showed that most such tourists were middle-aged, and without any previous familiarity with Central and Eastern European countries. Many of the Czech 'boys' did not perceive themselves to be gay and the Austrian and German clients were reluctant to see the 'boys' as prostitutes or to admit to the possibility that money was a significant factor in the relationship. They regarded the Czechs as exotic but innocent 'others', and as idealized locals who were untainted as yet by the capitalist and consumerist West, and who could show uninhibited affection and have unrestrained sex.

Sexually Transmitted Infections and Holidays

Any consideration of the sex–tourism relationship invariably gives rise to the issue of sexually transmitted infection (STI), including HIV and AIDS. One paper that reviewed relevant studies (relating to heterosexual travel) concluded that 'travel abroad seems to be responsible for a small but increasingly important proportion of acute STIs in the UK' (Rogstad, 2004, p. 215). It is considered that tourists are more likely to engage in unsafe sex whilst on holiday than when at home. This is attributed to many factors, including increased alcohol consumption and drug usage, as well as a greater number of sexual contacts and/or increased frequency of sexual activity. Sex tourists often think of contacts as friends rather than prostitutes, and therefore there is less need for safe sex. Women tourists who had sex with Caribbean men without using condoms were usually those who saw the relationship as 'real love' (Sanchez Taylor, 2001). A higher incidence of STIs in some destination countries may also add to the risks of infection on holiday (Carter and Clift, 2000).

The survey of British heterosexual dance holiday tourists confirmed that unsafe sex whilst on holiday was more likely than when at home. Condoms were used by only 27% (of those sexually active) on holiday but by 40% at home (Elliott *et al.*, 1998). The Florida study of students, however, reported that condom usage was higher during the holiday break than otherwise: just over half reported always using condoms compared with only one-quarter pre-break, though 21% claimed never to use condoms during the holiday break (Josiam *et al.*, 1998). Of young heterosexual tourists surveyed on Ibiza 44% had unprotected sex during the holiday (Bellis *et al.*, 2004). This was most likely amongst those who had a large number of sexual partners both on holiday and at home, thus raising significantly the possibility of transmission of STIs. The incidence of unsafe sex amongst those who had homosexual sex (15%) was slightly higher than that for heterosexuals. 'Epidemiological studies of UK residents who acquire STIs often identify sexual contact abroad as a risk factor for infection ... and the risk posed by international transmission has now been recognized in UK health policy' (Bellis *et al.*, 2004, p. 43). It should be noted, however, that some proportion of STIs acquired whilst not in the UK could be due to inward migration or to employment abroad as much as to holiday-taking. 'High frequency of diagnosed HIV infection in black African communities in GB is, in part, due to recent migration to the UK from sub-Saharan African countries with high prevalence' (Fenton *et al.*, 2005, p. 1252).

The Brighton survey and London travel fair surveys of gay men showed that 14–15% (of those who had sex with a new partner on holiday) had unprotected penetrative sex and this was more likely for those who had passive penetrative sex (Clift and Forrest, 2000; Clift *et al.*, 2002a). It was considered that gay men were less likely to take risks in sexual encounters than were heterosexual tourists: 'they are ... far less likely to engage in unprotected penetrative sex' (Clift and Forrest, 1999b, p. 290). Only 10% agreed that they were more likely to take sexual risks on holiday, whereas over one-third would take more precautions if having sex on holiday. Although not directly connected to tourism, it is reported that more than half of HIV-positive men had reported unprotected anal sex with at least one man (and 22% with five or more) in the previous year (Reid *et al.*, 2004). Whether or not these contacts were on holiday is unknown.

US circuit parties may well carry a high risk. Between 13 and 25% of US circuit partygoers report being HIV-positive (Ghaziani, 2005) and over one-quarter of circuit partygoers in a sample of men, from San Francisco, had unprotected penetrative sex during party weekends. This increased to nearly half for those who went to multiple sex parties (Mansergh *et al.*, 2001). It was concluded that 'the likelihood of transmission of HIV and other sexually transmitted diseases among party attendees and secondary partners becomes a real public health concern' (p. 957). This was unlikely to have been helped by the reported high use of recreational drugs (see Chapter 6).

STIs and other diseases have often been portrayed as something that can be attributed to 'outside'; early recorded epidemics of syphilis were linked in the 16th century with Columbus and the New World (Carter and Clift, 2000). Similarly, the origins of HIV and AIDS have been located in 'primitive' Africa (Black, 2000) and the Third World is perceived as the location of disease (Patton, 2000). In a variation on that theme, USSR authorities insisted that HIV was an 'imported' affliction (from decadent capitalist countries) and illustrated the dangers of consorting with foreigners (Tuller, 1996). Developing countries now see it as Westerners seeking sex who bring it in (Patton, 2000).

Not only have infections such as HIV been regarded – from a neo-colonial perspective – as the purity of the West being despoiled by the less developed world, but HIV has also been associated particularly with 'promiscuous and perverted' gay men. The route of the virus from equatorial Africa to Europe and the USA is unclear, though once out of Africa, gay tourists appear to have contributed to its spread (Shilts, 1988). A US airline steward, Gaetan Dugas (labelled 'Patient Zero'), was one of the first AIDS patients in the USA (diagnosed in 1980) and was a contact common to many early AIDS patients in the USA. He travelled widely and admitted to having had about 250 male sexual contacts in a year. The first case of AIDS reported in Australia was an American visitor and all 20 AIDS cases (men) in 1983 reported having had sex with American men in recent years. Many of the early European cases were among gay men who had visited New York and San Francisco. The earliest HIV patients in the USA, Western Europe and Australia were men who had had sex with other men and, not surprisingly, it was perceived to be a 'gay disease'. Its incidence worldwide currently is such as to give the lie to this assertion, as the number of infected adult heterosexuals and of children far exceeds that who have contracted the virus through male homosexual sex, but travel has undoubtedly contributed to its spread. In 2004, only 28% of the new HIV cases in the UK originated in the gay population and similar numbers of Britain's gay and Black African populations are now affected by the virus (Scott-Clark and Levy, 2005).

In the UK 69% of UK-born men with heterosexually acquired HIV (2000–2002) were infected through sex abroad (22% in Thailand), as were one-quarter of the infected women (Rogstad, 2004). The contribution of holiday travel movements to the spread of HIV is unknowable given the influence of urbanization and migration, the movement of migrant workers, refugees and troops, the impact of wars and of changes in sexual behaviour in societies (Patton, 2000; Altman, 2001). Some idea of perspective, however, may be gained from the Brighton gay men's survey: only 17% of those who had who reported an STI in the previous 5 years believed that it was contracted on holiday (Clift *et al.*, 2002a).

Perversely, a belief that HIV prevalence was low in Dublin was attracting gay men to the city and leading to an increase in levels of STIs such as syphilis and gonorrhoea amongst gay men who felt less need to take precautions (Young, 2000).

Conclusions

There is some evidence to show that the gay holiday market is strong in the sense of growth, durability and intensity. The evidence relates more to gay men than to lesbians and probably relates (in its strongest form) more to US males than to gay men elsewhere. Compared with the rest of the population, gay men are considered to have a greater likelihood of having taken a holiday and of having more holidays per year. There would also seem to be a particular interest in international travel and in city visits and short breaks. This optimistic scenario has been explained by high income levels, unrestricted leisure time and the pursuit of a high-status, product-rich lifestyle. Given that surveys have been of gays and lesbians living only in a few countries it has not been possible to identify which are the main gay and lesbian holiday-generating countries. Despite doubts about the universal applicability of the data it is none the less argued that travel and homosexuality are fundamentally linked in that gay men and lesbians have needed, in the past, to travel in order to be themselves and continue to need to do that. Travel and homosexuality can be considered to be inextricably related in as much as travel and tourism have been, and still are, significant factors in the ability of many gays and lesbians to affirm their identity.

It is apparent that what gay men and lesbians look for in choosing a holiday type or destination is little different from that of the rest of the population. The 'gayness' factor is of significance, however, for an apparently sizeable proportion of those gays and lesbians for whom information is available. Gays and lesbians will seek destinations that are at least as gay-friendly as is the home environment, if not more so. For most, it seems that the existence of gay space at the destination is important, even though this is not the focus of the holiday, as it guarantees the opportunity to be oneself at least for some part of the holiday. Some, a minority, will seek gay-centric holidays which are totally focused on gay space. This may apply especially to gays and lesbians who are not open about their sexuality at home or to those who are particularly keen to engage in sexual encounters. There will be others, perhaps not so often featuring in the surveys, for whom there will be no gayness requirement. This might be the case especially for tourists who believe they can pass as heterosexual or for those for whom the gay scene is of little importance at home anyway.

Holiday profiles and influencing factors relating to lesbians are even less certain than they are for gay men, but it may be inferred that they are less likely to share the same holiday frequency pattern or demand for the same holiday type. The more overtly gay holiday will probably be of less significance than for gay men.

The opportunity to have sex on holiday does not appear to be a particularly significant factor for gay men's holiday or destination choice. It obviously is for some but surveys suggest that even though they be more likely than heterosexuals to have new sexual partners when on holiday, gay men are less likely to have unsafe sex. Some evidence relating to the (minority) pursuit of circuit parties in the USA does give cause for concern, however. There is little to confirm popular perceptions that gay men are the main source of HIV-infection or that travel by gay men has spread the infection, though this community may initially have been the first group to become infected and the first carriers in the USA and Europe.

In the next chapter, the influence of some of these holiday requirements on the choice of destination will be examined.

Destination Choice as Risk Avoidance

4

Introduction

This chapter considers some of the specific issues that might arise in the choice, by gays and lesbians, of holiday destination. This is done in the context of a model of destination choice that suggests that the rejection or discard of some destinations is as significant as is the positive acceptance of others. This is considered to have particular relevance for gays and lesbians given the issues relating to homosexuality and to gay and lesbian tourism that were raised in previous chapters. Disapproval and discrimination experienced by many gays and lesbians suggests that there may well be more inhibitors in the choice process than there are for much of the rest of the population.

It was seen in Chapter 3 that gay-friendliness, gay space or at least the absence of homophobia are important issues for many gays and lesbians when on holiday. These extra dimensions to the holiday mean that choosing a holiday destination carries more risk than that experienced by the rest of the population. 'For gay people . . . even well-trodden paths can be goose-pimply adventure travel, fraught with possible perils' (Van Gelder and Brandt, 1991, p. 8). The desire or need, on the part of gay men and lesbians, for places that are 'safe' and 'comfortable' may be regarded as a need for places where risks of being 'unsafe' or 'uncomfortable' are minimized or eliminated. All holiday decisions are characterized by risk – political, safety, financial, psychological and so on – as holidays are experience products that cannot be tried out beforehand. Considerations of risk are influential, particularly in the avoidance of places, and thus in the discarding of destinations from consideration (Sonmez and Graefe, 1998;

Lawson and Thyne, 2000). The destination choice may even be thought of as being less an optimizing process, in which there is a search for the best possible set of attributes to meet needs, and more a settling for a destination at which risks are reduced given the existence of desirable attributes (Um and Crompton, 1992). There are many potential destinations, but some are excluded because of 'risk' and become part of the 'discard set' ('inept set'). The process can be conceived of as one of exclusion from a range of apparently equally attractive destinations.

For gays and lesbians the choice process itself is no different from that of anyone else, though risks may be high and of a different nature for gays and lesbians. The discard set may be larger than for the rest of the population, leaving fewer destinations in the 'evoked set' ('consideration set').

Risks

In addition to the usual risks, one qualitative study of gay men in Britain has shown how additional risks of 'discomfort, discrimination and physical attack' were especially significant in the destination choice process (Hughes, 2002a, b). These are an extension of the particular risks gays and lesbians may face when not on holiday. There may be a greater 'physical risk' than for other travellers, given the possibility and fear of violent attack (and perhaps sexual assault), theft and mugging. There is also the possibility of being subject to verbal abuse and being the object of anti-social or threatening behaviour, or of simply feeling uncomfortable in the presence of apparently disapproving heterosexuals – 'discomfort' risk. In addition, there is a 'discrimination' risk, whether that discrimination be overt or covert, legal or otherwise. Gay men and lesbians may be denied double rooms in hotels or may be unable to make bookings in some accommodation, they may be refused entry to bars and clubs and they may be given less favourable treatment in public places.

In the study, nearly all gay men reported some adverse occurrence whilst on holiday which was related to their sexuality. This was more often 'verbal abuse rather than instances of outright intolerance or physical attack' (Hughes, 2002b, p. 308). There was also, in some instances, a general unease and self-consciousness about situations which might have suggested 'gayness' to others. This discomfort reflected the possibility of being subject to verbal abuse and of being the object of anti-social or threatening behaviour. In addition, it reflected concern and disquiet arising from perceptions of disapproval (real or otherwise) by heterosexuals. This gave rise to internal tension: not unusual at home but was felt to be particularly frustrating whilst on holiday, which had held out the prospect of 'escape'. There was a similar disappointment associated with the need for behaviour modification and coping mechanisms which had been developed in the home situation but which were also required whilst on holiday. Some sought to conceal their gayness in particular places and situations on holiday and, in extreme cases, throughout the entire holiday. Experiences had caused anxiety and had influenced in the past, or were likely to influence in the future, choice or rejection of holiday destination. In addition, there were strong perceptions of places, although not hitherto visited, that were considered to be unfriendly or hostile to homosexuals. These perceptions arose from many sources, including the media and word-of-mouth.

As a consequence, gay men avoided particular places – individual towns, cities and beach resorts as well as entire countries. Some places, for instance many Mediterranean beach destinations, were seen as having a predominantly heterosexual ambience where gay men would not feel comfortable. In other instances it was a more positive desire to avoid such places arising from a definite fear of adverse reaction (possibly violent) by straight holidaymakers. Large parts of the world were discarded, by some, because of perceptions of anti-gay legislation or strong cultural disapproval. 'Although one may celebrate the ever greater choices available to lesbians and gay men, one must not lose sight of the fact that these are constrained choices' (Binnie, 1997, p. 240).

A further qualitative study suggested that gays and lesbians on holiday might be at higher risk than others, of crime and victimization, because their own behaviour may be relatively perilous (Brophy, 2004). Tourists tend to minimize the possibility of crime whilst on holiday anyway and reduce their guard but, in addition, gay men may frequent gay space (a focus for the attention of homophobes), may regard the holiday as an opportunity to be more out and obviously gay (drawing attention to themselves) and indulge more in drug and alcohol use and in casual sex (associated with risk of assault and theft).

All respondents in Brophy's study had witnessed, been a victim of, or knew of incidents of gays or lesbians experiencing holiday crime or victimization (this latter included verbal abuse, homophobia, discomfort and discrimination). Apart from the discrimination commonly associated with booking double rooms, the most frequently encountered problems had been assaults, verbal abuse and threatening behaviour. It was felt that gays were seen as easy targets and incidents were perceived to be particularly related to the sexuality of the victims. Lesbians were much less likely to experience these incidents. They were not as attracted to gay space and nightlife as were gay men and, because of a gendered heightened awareness of personal safety, moderated their behaviour. There was a reluctance to report serious incidents to police, not only because of embarrassment and a fear of 'outing' but because of a belief that they would not have been taken seriously and may even have been subjected to further harassment. Travel agents and tour operators were criticized for not providing sufficient safety information to gays and lesbians and it was felt that security in popular gay and lesbian destinations could be significantly improved.

Despite the particular issues associated with travel, Cox (2001) suggests that homophobia encountered on holiday was not necessarily 'bad'. In an argument similar to that of Myslik (1996) he posited that holidays provided an opportunity to confront 'oppositional sexual cultures' and offered learning experiences with which to cope at home.

Sources for risk assessment

The risk involved in visiting a destination is assessed in many ways, including past experience, but for first-time travellers there may be more reliance on word-of-mouth and sources such as guidebooks, tour operators' brochures and travel agents' advice. The decision to visit a place will be influenced by visitors' perceptions of how a destination may satisfy their needs. This will be influenced, *inter alia*, by images received from any of several sources categorized as either induced and organic (Gunn, 1988; Gartner, 1993). Induced (or projected) images arise from direct attempts by tourist boards or tour operators to influence the image of a destination, whereas organic images are the outcome of more indirect and underlying sources such as newspapers, television, film, books and personal and social contacts, which are particularly important sources of organic image (Sonmez and Sirakaya, 2002). It has been noted earlier how books written by Burton, Isherwood and Orton could have helped construct images of gay-friendly destinations and impacted on the decisions of gays and lesbians to travel. More recent books such as those about Provincetown (Cunningham, 2004) and Cherry Grove, Fire Island (Newton, 1993) will have helped further the existing favourable images of these as vacation destinations. The image of the city of West Hollywood (part of Greater Los Angeles) that was generated by the press at the time of incorporation in 1984 was mentioned in Chapter 2; this image presented an idealized and positive version of gay and lesbian life that could well have impacted on tourism. The possible influence of Maupin's *Tales of the City* on the image of San Francisco was mentioned in Chapter 3.

Tourists may gain much of their information about potential destinations from more general news reports (television, newspapers, magazines, etc.), either about general matters or about specific gay life and gay rights issues in a particular country or town. Some of the situations relating to gay and lesbian life in different countries described below will have fed through to the destination choice process. News reports of treatment of and attitudes towards gays in Jamaica, Egypt, Zimbabwe and Saudi Arabia may be expected to have negative effects on travel decisions whereas, for instance, the introduction of marriage for gays and lesbians in four countries (and a US state) is likely to have created a positive image of those as tourist destinations.

There are many parts of the world where homosexuality continues to be regarded as a problem. Thomas Roth, President of Community

Marketing (the US gay and lesbian travel marketing research organization) felt strongly that he 'would never recommend a Muslim country to gay people who care how locals are treated, who care about government policies and care about what would happen to them if it were ever discovered they are gay' (Roth and Luongo, 2002, p. 133). Even in The Netherlands, which has enjoyed a reputation for toleration of sexual difference (derived from a tradition of tolerance of dissidents that goes back at least to the 17th century) and has been in the forefront of positive legislation, acceptance of homosexuality may be no more than skin-deep (Hekma, 1999).

Anti-gay Images of Destinations

News reports of attitudes towards and treatment of gays and lesbians can have a particular influence on destination choice. Some relevant reports are discussed here.

In Russia, a 2005 opinion poll showed that 43.5% of the population supported recriminalization of consensual gay sex and nearly three-quarters opposed gay marriage (Anon., 2005b). Jamaica is considered to be a particularly homophobic society where 'violent acts against men who have sex with men are commonplace' (Human Rights Watch, 2004a, p. 2). Buggery is a criminal offence, carrying up to 10 years' imprisonment, and any form of physical intimacy between men up to 2 years' imprisonment. The murder of a prominent gay activist, Brian Williamson, in June 2004 was regarded by police as robbery-related, but others saw it more as a homophobic attack. Williamson himself is quoted as saying 'we who are homosexuals are seen as the devil's own children' (Younge, 2004). Homophobia has characterized the Jamaican popular music scene, including Buju Banton's *Boom Boom Bye Bye*. Concern that homophobic lyrics of a Beenie Man song could incite violence led to cancellation of his concert in London in 2004 (Branigan, 2004a).

Homosexuality is illegal in the Solomon Islands and until 1988 the ban on gross indecency applied only to men. This was held to be unconstitutional but, perversely, the ban was then extended to women (Anon., 2004). Human Rights Watch also reported that the Egyptian government continued to arrest and torture men suspected of homosexual activity (Rodgerson, 2004); homosexual acts are not illegal, but charges of 'debauchery' and 'contempt of religion' can be laid against gay men. In the 'Queen Boat' case in 2001, 53 men were arrested in a Cairo disco on charges arising from sexual relations with other men. There were allegations of torture and 23 were sentenced to 1–5 years' hard labour. In Saudi Arabia over 100 men were sentenced to imprisonment and flogging for 'deviant sexual behaviour' (Human Rights Watch, 2005). The men were arrested at a private party and tried in closed court. An article reporting this in *Gay Times* also referred to the Singapore government's prohibition of an AIDS concert because of proposed performances by gay singers. Reports in the same issue of *Gay Times* (September 2005) that Uganda had passed legislation to prevent marriage of same-sex couples and that Iran had publicly executed two gay teenagers are unlikely to have created a favourable image of these countries.

Although the Republic of South Africa was the first to expressly forbid, in its constitution, discrimination on the grounds of sexual orientation, a high level of homophobia remains (Cock, 2003). A number of positive legislative steps have been taken, such as the ending of workplace discrimination against gays and lesbians, the decriminalization of same-sex acts and the extension of equal partner benefits, but the everyday lives of gays and lesbians have changed little (Rahim, 2000). Elsewhere in the southern part of the African continent, 'many leaders in southern Africa have singled out lesbian, gay, bisexual and transgender people as scapegoats for their countries' problems' (Long, 2003, p. 1). The presidents of Zimbabwe, Namibia and Uganda have all been quoted as expressing strong anti-homosexual views. Botswana, Namibia, Zambia and Zimbabwe all have sodomy laws and have denied legal status to gay and lesbian organizations.

Northern Ireland has been the subject of several adverse news reports with respect to gays and lesbians during 2004/05. A headline in *The Guardian* newspaper stated: 'Gays and lesbians under siege as violence and harassment soar in Northern Ireland' (Chrisafis, 2005, p. 13) and, in another article, the province was referred to as 'the hate crime capital of Europe' (O'Hara, 2005, p. 2). Homophobic attacks in the province reported to the police had risen by 176% between 2003/04 and 2004/05 (and by 300% in Derry). In part, this may have been due to an increased willingness to report incidents, but it may well also have been due to a legacy of violence in the province and the greater conservatism of a society under strong religious influence. Perversely, the easing of political and religious tensions may have resulted in other targets being looked for. The murder of ten men in a gay massage parlour in Cape Town in January 2003, although allegedly not a hate crime, could be expected to create an unfavourable image (however short-term) of this increasingly popular destination.

A travel feature in *Gay Times* focused on 'exotic' destinations and rated them according to the internal situation and homophobia or human rights abuses within the country, rather than identifying situations where tourists, in particular, had faced difficulties (Gregory, 2004). The reviews of Brazil, Cuba, Egypt, India, Jamaica, Malaysia, Mexico, Sri Lanka and Tanzania as tourist destinations identified some of their 'darker sides' as well as obvious tourist attractions. Jamaica, Egypt and Tanzania were bottom of the 'pink ratings' (with scores of zero, one and two out of ten, respectively); the implication seemed to be to take care in and perhaps avoid such destinations. Brazil and Malaysia were top (eight and seven, respectively), which also seemed to suggest a greater degree of gay-friendliness for visitors.

Even Amsterdam, traditionally a liberal and gay-friendly city, has experienced some recent adverse publicity – homophobic attacks and a general waning of tolerance (Minto, 2005).

Locals and Tourists

Risk will be assessed also through knowledge of local population reactions specifically to gay and lesbian tourists as opposed to local views with respect to homosexuality generally. Reactions to gay and lesbian tourists may be from local residents (including particular interest groups) but also from suppliers (such as accommodation or airlines) or even governments. Some local populations may have reacted negatively to such tourists and this may be common knowledge either through word-of-mouth or through reports in the media. There are few, if any, academic studies of local residents' reactions to gay and lesbian tourists, though there is a significant number relating to residents' attitudes towards tourists in general. Most suggest that they hold positive views about the tourist inflow (Andriotis and Vaughan, 2003). There is recognition among residents that tourism does have negative aspects but none the less the reaction is, on balance, a positive one. Positive aspects have included employment and business opportunities, improved architectural standards, enhanced leisure and transport facilities and the stimulation of cultural activities.

Commonly, issues relating to traffic, crime, tourists' behaviour, cultural and social change and impact on the physical environment have given rise to negative attitudes towards tourism. It would appear that there are often small groups who feel particularly strongly one way or the other about tourism, whereas the majority of residents are indifferent or are willing to tolerate even if aware of negative aspects. The reactions within host communities vary according to factors which may be categorized as extrinsic and intrinsic. The latter are those which relate to the individual characteristics and circumstances of the resident such as age and education, spatial proximity to the tourist areas, personal involvement in tourism and nature and extent of contact with tourists. Extrinsic factors are those which relate to tourism itself such as the 'type' of tourist, the cultural distance between tourist and resident and the stage of development of tourism.

Most studies suggest it is factors to do with the nature of the tourism itself that have the greatest effect on attitudes (Brunt and Courtney, 1999). Several also identify, in particular, the factor of stage of tourism development in the destination as a significant influence. Butler's (1980) concept of the tourism area life cycle relates stages of exploration, development and stagnation to number of tourists and it may be that in the course of such a cycle, residents' attitudes alter. Doxey (1975) hypothesized (as the 'Irridex') that residents pass through stages from euphoria to antagonism as tourism development progresses. This largely appears to be a reaction to increased numbers, though Andriotis and Vaughan's (2003) study in Crete suggested that, even in such a 'mature' destination, there were very few negative views about tourism development. Those with a significant economic stake in tourism development may be particularly 'powerful' within host communities, in which case any discontent may not be acknowledged.

Residents may be particularly sensitive in circumstances where there is a considerable cultural distance between themselves and visitors, which can be of such a nature that tension results. Cultural distance can though be positive where visitors and locals appreciate the benefits of interaction and regard acculturation as positive. There is a common belief among residents and visitors that local cultures can be preserved and strengthened by the contact (Besculides *et al.*, 2002).

The nature of particular cultures may be such, however, that tourist–resident interaction is unbalanced and local cultures become distorted and diluted. Acculturation, a process whereby cultures borrow from each other, may, in reality, result in a homogenization where host cultures in some parts of the world take on characteristics of those of the tourist (Berno and Ward, 2005). This may not be welcomed by all locals, especially where it is behaviour that conflicts with a society's religious and moral norms. Some of the acculturation (or 'cultural drift', where change is of a more temporary nature) is due to contacts between locals and tourists, whereas other change is more associated with a demonstration effect – observing the behaviour of tourists. Relatively few locals may come into direct contact with tourists though they may observe or may even be simply aware of presence and activity though media or word of mouth. It is widely recognized that the behaviour of tourists may bear little resemblance to their 'usual' behaviour and, as a consequence, locals may receive a distorted view of the norms of behaviour of the non-locals.

The demonstration effect may cause tension, especially in less developed societies, where locals aspire to own, but are unable to afford, the gadgets and clothes of more affluent tourists (De Kadt, 1979). Also, locals in some restrictive societies may be attracted to particular behaviour patterns of more liberal tourists. Given that tourists may behave in a more flamboyant and less inhibited way on holiday than when at home, host communities may develop distorted views of ways-of-life in tourist-generating countries. Young people may be particularly susceptible to the demonstration effect and wish to mimic clothes and behaviour of tourists. If it proves impossible to achieve the consumption and activity patterns of tourists, discontent may arise. Further issues arise when some do achieve these patterns and others do not, leading to division within local communities.

Locals and Gay and Lesbian Tourists

Although studies of residents' attitudes towards gay and lesbian tourists have not been undertaken, there are reports of locals' reactions in some parts of the world. Sometimes this amounts to isolated instances of tourists being refused accommodation or of being physically abused on the grounds of sexuality and, in other cases, it is a more widespread adverse reaction to a gay and lesbian inflow, a reaction that may be government-led. None of these can be regarded as representative of community views, especially as many are based on newspaper reports. As with all studies of residents' attitudes, it might be expected that there will be mixed views on an inflow of gay and lesbian tourism, with economic issues dominating other aspects. Dimensions such as cultural norms and religious beliefs might be expected to be particularly significant in locals' reactions, though these may well conceal a more fundamental prejudice and intolerance.

Travel guides and promotional magazine articles often point out that locals may be offended by overt gay behaviour and open displays of affection, and advise that travellers should be sensitive to local cultural and religious sensitivities. There is often reference to anti-gay feelings or legislation in particular countries, though there are few reported instances of abuse or prosecution directed at tourists as such. The UK government provides an advisory web site for gays, lesbians, bisexuals and transgender persons travelling abroad (http://fco.gov.uk/knowbeforeyougo). This advises travellers to be aware of local laws and attitudes and to avoid 'an excessive physical show of affection . . . in public' especially outside of 'gay neighbourhoods', in rural areas and in countries where there are strongly held anti-gay religious beliefs. There is also a warning about the reluctance of accommodation providers in some parts of the world to accept bookings from same-sex couples.

There are reports of individual incidents of abuse, such as a French male tourist couple being beaten up in Cape Town in 2002 – apparently because of their public kissing (http://www.uk.gay.com, 2002). The murder of an American resident in Prague was believed to be the outcome of a gay encounter with a male prostitute. This, and an earlier murder of a New Zealander, 'prompted many to question whether the Czech Republic is safe for . . . gay tourists who visit the country every year' (Lavers, 2004). Fiji is one of the few countries to have protection in its constitution against discrimination based on sexual orientation, but an Australian tourist and a Fijian man were sentenced to 2 years' imprisonment for offences 'against the order of nature' and 'gross indecency' under legislation that is a legacy of British colonial rule (Human Rights Watch, 2004b). The magistrate is reported to have described the behaviour as 'something so disgusting that it would make any decent person vomit'. An article in *Gay Times* reflected on the irony of the choice of Fiji for a UK television reality programme that followed the love entanglements of 'celebrity' straight couples but at the same time had such anti-gay legislation (Banks, 2005). Alan Bennett, a well-known UK playwright and author, in an article about his birthdays, recounted how he had been physically assaulted by youths during a one-night stay in a small seaside town near Rome in 1992 (Bennett, 2004). Medical attention was required but police assumed it was an attack provoked by a homosexual advance and therefore required no further investigation: 'Simply by recounting the circumstances of an assault the victim becomes the culprit' (p. 28).

Over one-third of gay and lesbian visitors to one of the largest and most popular gay and lesbian beaches in the USA (in Florida) had, at some time, experienced verbal or physical abuse whilst visiting the area (Philipp, 1999). In the early 1990s the local mayor had stated that gays and lesbians were not welcome and the local tourist development council expressed a desire to promote the town as a place for 'family' vacations.

Accommodation

More common are problems in the area of accommodation bookings in particular. 'Hotels are the worst landmines' (Van Gelder and Brandt, 1991, p. 5). A small (non-academic) study conducted in the UK by a national newspaper showed discrimination against same-sex couples in the booking of accommodation. A gay couple were refused bookings or required to sleep in separate beds by three out of the ten hotels contacted in this small *ad hoc* survey (Tuck, 1998). The newspaper also referred to a Stonewall report which indicated that 17% of gay people had been made to feel unwelcome because of their sexuality when staying in a hotel. A similar nation-wide phone survey undertaken by an Internet magazine also suggested that about 17% of UK hotels outside London would refuse a booking from a gay or lesbian couple. The survey enquirers were open about employment by the magazine and it is conjectured that, as a result, responses were more favourable then would otherwise have been the case (S. Bustin, http://www.queercompany.com, 2000, personal communication). In the UK Mintel study (2000a), 16% of respondents reported having experienced discrimination (unspecified) or homophobia in a hotel or guesthouse; this was especially the case for females.

A lesbian travelling in France with her partner described her feelings about the process of booking a shared hotel room: 'I knew the dreaded question was about to emerge from the woman's immaculately painted French lips – the question that was so simple, so complicated, so well designed to make me feel wrong from head to toe' (Barrington, 1998, p. 59). She and her partner were also verbally abused by a hotel porter in Spain after pushing together two single beds.

The reaction of reception staff to a male couple at a Birmingham (UK) hotel was such as to cause them to seek alternative accommodation.

The hotel manager, whilst anxious to reassure the press of the non-discriminatory policy of the hotel, none the less stated that the hotel 'would never knowingly let a double room to two men but would . . . offer them a room with twin beds'. He claimed that there would not be a problem for two women to book a double room and the policy was justified by reference to complaints received from other guests in the past about a gay motorcycle group (Skinner, 1995). A male couple were refused a double room in a Devon (UK) guesthouse though the tourist board (VisitBritain) accepted that its code of conduct did not cover this discrimination (Rutherford, 2005). Some of these experiences may be more to do with policies adopted by individual managers or owners than by hotel companies; one male couple, denied a double room in Warwickshire (UK), were initially informed that it was company policy to do this, something that the parent company subsequently denied (Anon., 2002). A gay man who had experienced denial of accommodation wrote to *Gay Times* (July 2004, p. 8) about his experience. He and his partner (travelling in the UK with two straight couples) were denied accommodation at a camping park in Skegness (a Lincolnshire seaside resort) on the grounds that same-sex couples were not accepted. A subsequent letter to *Gay Times* (October 2004, p. 8), however, recounted the positive holiday experiences of a male couple (with children) at a Pontins holiday camp in the UK.

A 'mystery-shopper' type of study of a number of hotels (320) in the USA found that, in responses to enquiries for bookings, 'significantly fewer requests were granted to the same-sex couple than to the opposite sex couple' (Jones, 1996, p. 155). This was most evident in the smaller, bed and breakfast type of hotel, and it was conjectured that it might be due to personal prejudice or to a fear of same-sex couples being more conspicuous.

Considerable publicity was generated in 2004 by the case of a male couple who were offered a room with twin beds rather than their preferred double bed when booking accommodation in a Scottish Highlands guesthouse. The proprietor justified this by his not wanting to 'condone your perversion' and expressed his disapproval of 'unnatural acts being performed in my home' (quoted in Blackstock, 2004, p. 6). Needless to say, VisitScotland (the national tourism promotion body) condemned this and sought to reassure potential tourists that it was an isolated incident (Copestake, 2004b). In the following week, a small-scale phone survey by a national newspaper journalist seeking a double room for a male couple failed to turn up similar reactions (Jeffries, 2004). The journalist contacted 50 hotels and guesthouses across Britain and encountered problems on only one occasion (in the Channel Islands). A UK hoteliers' trade paper was very upbeat about the potential of this market and encouraged hoteliers to actively market to the gay and lesbian market (Golding, 2003). It pointed out, though, that one of the main issues that would need to be addressed by hoteliers was 'check-in phobia': an unwelcoming reception or an assumption that either twin beds or separate rooms were required.

Wider Reactions

In addition to accommodation problems there have also been reports of issues arising at a more general level. The 2001 campaign by Cape Town Tourism (a publicly-funded destination promotion organization) to further develop the city as a holiday destination for gays and lesbians stimulated some religious leaders to condemn the strategy (Macgregor, 2001). Whilst claiming to be tolerant of homosexuality, some Muslim and Christian communities considered that tourism strategies should instead emphasize the other attractions of the city. One religious leader was quoted as saying 'several men of God washed their hands after handling this brochure' (a guide to gay Cape Town). He also wrote to the city's mayor: 'we do not believe that a special-interest minority group such as the homosexual movement has the right to hijack the city for their own agenda' (Williams, 2001).

The Greek Mediterranean island of Lesvos has attracted female homosexual tourists for some considerable time, with mixed reactions from locals. The association of lesbians with the island has led to tension between tourists and locals ever since lesbian tourists began to arrive in significant numbers. Initially this took the form a makeshift community of huts and tents established by women themselves that led to continuing open conflict during the 1980s (Kantsa, 2002). There have been pressures within the local community, generated by a desire to promote to a more general market and a recognition of the economic benefits of lesbian tourism but also pressures generated between locals and lesbian tourists, who identify the island as a 'spiritual home'. A newspaper article in 1996 reported how the island was welcoming lesbian tourists despite the earlier anti-lesbian drives. The mayor of Erossos is reported as saying that 'we are very happy to receive lesbians. As long as they don't make love in the square and kiss, because that upsets people, we don't have a problem having them here.' Perhaps, cynically, the article concluded that it was the income generated that was stimulating the positive overtures (Smith, 1996).

One particular package tour (for a group of 26 organized by Sappho Travel) planned for September 2000 seemed, however, to be a catalyst for the vocalization of strong local reactions (Theobald and Howard, 2000). The depiction of Erossos as a lesbian paradise with 'erotic dancing', 'sexy room service' and a 'wet pussy pool party' caused locals, led by the mayor, to appeal for an end to the conjunction of the island with lesbianism and to threaten a court injunction to bar the trip. Once more, whilst claiming an acceptance of the diversity of sexual orientation, views were expressed not only that the lesbian link was damaging to the image of the island but also that some of the behaviour of tourists (especially public displays of affection) was unacceptable. The mayor is quoted as saying 'we want to promote the tourist industry, but for everybody. We don't want this place to be a ghetto for these kind of women' (Anderson, 2000, p. 23). The tour went ahead, minus some of the planned events.

Cruises

Some of the most publicized reactions have been those to cruises. Over 800 gay men (mostly from the USA) were prevented by police from visiting the historic ruins at Ephesus (Turkey) after an Atlantis cruise ship, the *Olympic Voyager*, docked at Kusadasi in September 2000 (Theobald and Howard, 2000). The action was widely believed to be due to the sexuality of the passengers. Local businesspeople expressed their anger at the police action and the local mayor and Turkey's tourism minister later apologized. An Atlantis cruise ship was also prevented by the government from docking in the Cayman Islands in 1998, and an Olivia cruise was met with anti-lesbian demonstrations in Nassau (the Bahamas) in the same year. There were also protests against the visit of the same Atlantis cruise to the Bahamas. Concern was expressed about the tourists' behaviour and about the effects on local youth (http://www.planetout.com, 1998). Olivia cruises had made a number of trouble-free trips previously to the Bahamas, but the 1998 visit was greeted by crowds shouting comments such as 'God made woman for man' and 'keep your perversions in the bedroom' (Stagg Elliott, 1998). A protest organizer considered that foreign tourists would only add to the domestic homosexual 'problem' (http://www.planetout.com, 1998a). Want (2002) recounts a number of similar incidents of governments or tourist boards in places such as Costa Rica, Vanuatu and Queenstown (New Zealand) being unwilling to welcome gay or lesbian tourists.

These adverse reactions are not confined to the past. Passengers on a more recent cruise (July 2004), organized by R Family Vacations, were also faced by protests from a church group in Nassau (Bahamas) chanting 'gay ways are not God's ways' (Laign, 2004). In April 2005, the visit of a cruise ship carrying 2000 gay and lesbian tourists to Turks and Caicos Islands (Caribbean) gave rise to criticism by local politicians. In response, the government's Chief Minister expressed support for civil liberties but also his 'regret' and 'concern' about the exposure of residents to 'the alternative lifestyle of these individuals' (Newman, 2005). It was also reported that, in March 2005, port authorities in St Kitts and Nevis (Caribbean) refused permission for passengers on a gay cruise to land, as organizers were unable to give assurances that the passengers would not indulge in nude bathing (Heyer, 2005).

Destinations

The Gay and Lesbian Day at Walt Disney World (Orlando), held annually since 1991, is not a Disney-organized event but is the outcome of private initiatives that have stimulated the gathering of gays and lesbians each year. Attendance at the Day is estimated to have risen from 2500–3000 in

1991 to 32,000 in 1995 (http://www.gayday.com) and 135,000 in 2004. There are reports that this has caused some potential visitors to avoid visits on the Day, but the greatest reaction has been criticism by the American Family Association (AFA) and the proposed boycott of all Disney enterprises in 1997 by the USA Southern Baptist Convention (which, with 15 million members, is the country's largest Protestant denomination); and subsequently by the Southern Methodist Church and Concerned Women for America (CWA). This boycott was justified by a number of issues which were regarded as 'anti-Christian and anti-family' and which included the Gay and Lesbian Day and the extension by Disney of employee benefits to same-sex couples (Duval Smith, 1997). Signs were posted at entrances by Disney (1993 and 1994) to inform other visitors of the presence of large numbers of gay and lesbian visitors. Despite these moves, the Gay Day has expanded into a weekend of events in June, with local hotels associating themselves with it, acceptance of one of the organizing bodies into the local convention and visitor bureau and sponsorship, including Bud Light and Virgin Megastore. The boycott by the Baptist Convention (and by AFA) ended in 2005, allegedly because of its minimal effect (Bates, 2005b).

Sandals operates 12 all-inclusive resorts in the Caribbean (Jamaica, St Lucia, Antigua and the Bahamas), which were initially targeted at heterosexual couples. Bookings were not accepted for children or from same-sex couples (though they were accepted for the company's Beaches resorts). This was justified on the grounds that 'the concept was introduced to cater for a niche market, predominantly weddings and honeymoons' (quoted in http://www.365gay.com, 2003). The policy attracted criticism and sanctions, including a ban on television adverts, on adverts on the London Underground, the removal of direct links on Yahoo! and the removal of Sandals holidays from Expedia and from US Airways Vacations, AOL and Barclaycard (credit card) promotions. In October 2004, however, the ban on same-sex couples was lifted. This occurred at a time when a UK Member of Parliament was expressing concern and a determination to introduce legislation that prohibited such discrimination in the provision of goods and services (Hencke, 2004).

Even in cities such as Manchester (UK) and Amsterdam (The Netherlands) there has been resistance to drives to promote them to gay and lesbian tourists. A 1992 campaign promoting Amsterdam to US gays was not universally welcomed by tourist interests in the city (Binnie, 1995). Even the city Alderman responsible for gay and lesbian policy commented that 'we have to be careful about promoting Amsterdam as a purely gay destination ... The average family tourist stays away' (Crawford, 1994, p. 11). In Manchester, the gay campaign was but one of several launched at the same time in 1999, but it overshadowed the others and attracted a great deal of publicity in the local and national press (Hughes, 2003). The comments of the chair of the city's Civic

Society were reported in virtually every national newspaper: 'This could alienate other visitors . . . This could trivialise the city. Anywhere can be a gay capital but how many cities have the wealth of history that Manchester has?' This was quoted in several papers, including *The Times* (24 July 1999) and on the front page of the local newspaper. He seems to have based his reservations largely on a concern that the campaign was 'tantamount to marketing the city for sex . . . It is not gay marketing but sex marketing' (Anthony Wilson, 2001, personal communication). A prominent local councillor, Pat Karney (lead councillor for gay men's issues), also expressed reservations. He is reported as saying 'the priority is to market Manchester as a family-friendly city and a place for new business . . . Gay tourism is not our priority' (*Daily Telegraph*, 24 July 1999). The campaign continued, none the less, with full financial support. Financial assistance for WorldPride in Rome (Italy) in 2000 was withdrawn under pressure from the Vatican, despite initially being supported by the mayor (Luongo, 2002).

Places in the USA that have, by now, sizeable resident gay and lesbian populations, initially associated with tourism and which are still popular gay and lesbian holiday destinations, have also experienced anti-gay sentiments from locals in the past. Cherry Grove (Fire Island, NY) may well have been the 'world's first gay dominated town' (Newton, 1993, p. 237) but throughout its 'gay' history from the 1930s onwards, non-local gays were subject to expressions of concern by locals, periodic harassment by police and occasional 'gay-bashing'. The opposition was never very strong, however, especially as the initial influx was of a 'privileged few', relatively well-to-do white gays from the arts community. As the community become one of long-term and seasonal gay and lesbian residents, different tensions emerged: between these established residents on the one hand and, on the other, day-trippers and new generations of gay and lesbian tourists with differing perspectives on the meaning of being 'gay' (Newton, 1993).

On occasion, gay and lesbian activity has been identified as an inevitable and undesirable consequence of tourism. These are similar to the assertions that homosexuality is a Western evil unknown to other civilizations. After the killing of 62 tourists by Islamic 'militants' at Luxor, Egypt, in November 1997, Sheikh Abu Hamsa Misri of the North Central Mosque (London) expressed the view that 'from the Islamic point of view, the tourist industry is not allowed . . . It is unlawful to make tourist money from wine, nudism and homosexuality' (Bhatia, 1997).

Zanzibar, an Indian Ocean island and semi-autonomous region of the east African state of Tanzania, is a popular tourist destination, especially for South African gays, and tourism is its second industry. The Zanzibari government introduced legislation in 2004 that provided for imprisonment for men convicted of gay sex or for participating in 'gay marriage' ceremonies (Vasagar, 2004). The rationale was expressed by the constitutional affairs minister as being that 'Zanzibar is a predominantly

Muslim country and in Islam homosexuality is strictly prohibited' (http://www.gmax.co.za, 2004). There was no indication that the legislation was aimed at tourists. It is widely believed, however, that the legislation was a reaction to the values and behaviour of tourists (both hetero- and homo-sexual) and to the island's popularity with homosexual tourists and, specifically, to a public 'gay marriage' performed at a Zanzibari hotel (http://www.afrol.com, 2004). The legislation may have been introduced more with the aim of prosecuting the local population. In this way, it might have been designed to 'protect' local traditional values from the threat of 'corrupting' influences brought from outside by tourists.

Airlines

Although not the reactions of locals in the form of residents, there have been occasional incidents involving airlines that have been interpreted as being anti-gay. British Airways faced unwelcome publicity from the threat of a South African passenger to sue over allegations that he was asked to stop kissing his boyfriend on a flight to London (Townley, 2004). The resulting exchange led to the passenger's arrest and court appearance in London. A transgender male took out legal proceedings against United Airlines after being removed from a flight to London from the USA and asked to change into male clothes (Verkaik, 2001). United Airlines was also the subject of a boycott in 1997 which, it is claimed, resulted in a sig-nificant fall in the number of gay travellers, after resisting San Francisco's city ordinance requiring employers to introduce same-sex partner benefits (http://www.ethicalmatters.co.uk, 2004).

American Airlines experienced particularly unfavourable publicity in 1993 when an HIV-positive passenger was removed from a flight after refusing to cover up his lesions and stow his intravenous bag (http://www.planetout.com, 1999). In another incident in the same year, a crew member requested a change of passengers' pillows and blankets, pointedly because they had been used by gay passengers (Lukenbill, 1999). Subsequently, the airline has made a point of adopting very posi-tive gay and lesbian policies and, ironically, has subsequently come under attack for these. This has included a commitment to becoming the 'official airline' of gay events and organizations and a dedicated glbt sales market-ing and sales force (the 'Rainbow TeAAm'). It was the first major US air-line to target, in 1997, the gay market and has contributed funds to several equal rights organizations and sponsored gay and lesbian events. It was also the first major US airline to adopt internal employee policies such as same-sex partner benefits, the inclusion of sexual orientation and gender identity in its non-discrimination policies and recognition of a glbt employee group (http://www.usnewswire.com, 2004). The airline was the target of anti-gay complaints in 1997/98 by a number of groups, including CWA and the AFA, about 'the extension of undue privileges in the service of an ideological agenda advanced by militants' and for supporting events allegedly characterized by illicit drug use and promiscuity (http://www.planetout.com, 1997). The airline was also criticized in 2003 by the conservative organizations Americans for Truth and the Culture and the Family Institute for co-sponsoring the North American Conference on Bisexuality and for encouraging 'depravity' and 'homosexual experimentation' (http://www.cnsnews.com, 2003).

Other reactions

Although gay and lesbian tourists may experience some negative reactions from locals, there is little to suggest that they generate similar reactions from other (heterosexual) tourists. Informants in Brophy's (2004) study did, though, comment that many of the adverse reactions they experienced or feared were from other British heterosexual tourists, especially young males. The hostile reactions to the Manchester and Amsterdam tourism campaigns were also justified by reference to the supposedly negative effects on other tourists.

Less frequent are instances of gay tourists expressing concern about other tourists. Rehoboth Beach, a beach town of only 1500 residents in Delaware, USA, has long been popular with gay visitors from Washington, DC, Baltimore and Philadelphia. Since its initial development as a Methodist summer camp in the late 19th century, the town has had a reputation for 'acceptance of all', but concern has been expressed by visitors and local business people that an increasing number of straight family visitors has altered the atmosphere in the town. This is regarded by some as a 'threat' to gays and lesbians but, by others, as an acceptance of gay lifestyles (Anderton, 2004). A more significant issue may actually be the increasing physical development of the town, which may mean it loses its character and intimacy.

Cherry Grove had been the preserve of gay and lesbian tourists (and residents) since the 1930s, but its increased visibility in the 1970s led to an influx of straight visitors (especially day trippers). This led to moves to discourage these visitors, which included the deliberate absence of lifeguards and public toilets on the beaches aimed especially at day-trippers both gay and straight; more a case of residents objecting than tourists objecting, but many were seasonal residents or weekenders (Newton, 1993).

Conclusions

Although it was established in previous chapters that gays and lesbians were often seeking similar holidays to the rest of the population, the gayness element does raise particular issues. Gay space, gay-friendliness and lack of homophobia are important in the holiday choice and it would appear that gay and lesbian tourists do face some additional difficulties when on holiday. These affect the holiday experience and can influence future choices and the choices of others. It is not only personal experience, but also awareness of local reactions through other means, such as news reports, that will influence holiday choice. Some of the additional difficulties include assumptions about sleeping arrangements, acts of verbal and physical aggression and outright opposition from some local communities, or at least parts of them. There are, though, no comprehensive studies of local residents' reactions to gay and lesbian tourists similar to those undertaken in several other studies mentioned earlier. The evidence is disjointed and often drawn from non-academic sources. It is also unclear whether or not the reactions identified here would seriously influence holiday choice; few studies exist on this issue.

Adverse reactions undoubtedly exist and some of those discussed in this chapter are down to an abhorrence of homosexuality or the belief that an inflow of such tourists will corrupt others. In the terminology used earlier, it is the extrinsic factors relating to the type of tourist and their behaviour (actual or anticipated) that are at the root of the reaction. It is, too, other extrinsic factors related to the nature of the host society that is a key issue; societies that do not have well-developed and open gay and lesbian communities are often those that create difficulties for tourists. There is though, in many cases, a willingness to accept gay and lesbian tourism provided it is 'discreet' and that behaviour is 'respectable' in the public sphere. This required discretion extends beyond behaviour to promotional policies on the grounds that other tourists may be dissuaded by overt identification of places with gays and lesbians. Willingness to tolerate would sometimes appear to be the outcome of a tension between personal, deeply felt aversion to homosexuals and a recognition of the economic benefits that may accrue from gay and lesbian tourism. Intrinsic factors (of personal gain) overwhelm extrinsic in such cases.

The destination choice process for gays and lesbians does, then, seem to have some extra dimensions – extra risk elements that feed into the process. There may well be fewer options for consideration as destinations and rather more in the discard set. All tourists face the risk that a holiday is not as anticipated, and gays and lesbians can make misjudgements in the same way as anyone else. It may be, though, that a misjudgement could lead to a particularly poor holiday experience where sexuality has to be concealed or where it results in abuse or discrimination – situations that are avoided at home and which are not anticipated on holiday.

In the following chapters, how these factors have influenced the popularity of destinations and also how 'the industry' has responded will be considered further.

Gay and Lesbian Tourism Destinations

5

Introduction

In previous chapters, particular issues relating to the requirements of gay and lesbian tourists have been discussed. These issues will affect the choice of holiday destination and, in this chapter, an attempt will be made to identify which are the most popular destinations for gay and lesbian tourists. The first part of this chapter will consider the ways in which these destinations can be ascertained. The second part will describe a number of places that are apparently popular with gays and lesbians for holidays.

Destinations are usually thought of as specific geographical areas and can take many forms, including coastal towns dominated by tourism, cities which are multi-functional, countryside, mountain villages and the sea itself. Their ability to attract tourists lies in 'attractions', the nucleus of the system that could serve to meet the needs of tourists, and which are successful in generating tourists through markers (Leiper, 1990). A nucleus becomes a tourist attraction or destination by the influence of markers such as guidebooks, films, books, television programmes and recommendations, and also promotional material generating images of the nucleus (Gunn, 1988). If they relate positively to motivations, these images may generate tourist flow. Tourist places are thus marked or coded as such and the choice of places to visit is influenced by 'place-myth' – the creation of image.

Information about where gays and lesbians go on holiday is as limited as are most other aspects of gay and lesbian tourism, though there is a view that 'the range of destinations offered to gay visitors . . . has been blown wide open and it continues to grow every year' (Mellor, 2002a, p. 13). One tour operator, Mantrav International (based in the UK, the USA and

The Netherlands), believes that 'the hottest gay and lesbian destinations . . . [are] . . . the same destinations that have always drawn people with taste and a sense of adventure throughout the ages. Pyramids along the Nile, Mount Kilimanjaro, Paris after dark' (http://www.mantrav.co.uk). Notwithstanding the sentiment underlying this assertion, it is unlikely that these are the most popular destinations for gays and lesbians. It was noted in Chapter 4 how destination-discard, the rejection of places to visit, may be a particularly significant feature of the destination choice process for gays and lesbians. Particular destinations may never enter into the 'consideration set' because of reputation for, or experience of, gay-unfriendliness. What the destinations of gay and lesbian tourists are is not easily determined, though there is a prevalent consensus about the most popular. In the first part of this chapter, the basis for this consensus is examined.

Surveys

Surveys are one source of information, but these have to be treated cautiously. Clift and Forrest's (1999a) survey of gay men in the UK requested respondents to indicate which of 16 predetermined, mostly international, destinations they had visited in the previous 5 years. These were variously specified as individual cities or resorts, or as countries or sub-continents (e.g. Australia, North Africa). As such, it is difficult to determine what individual places were the most popular, whether gay men have visited one or several of the destinations specified or the frequency of visits to each in that time period. Inevitably, given the general pattern of tourism, European destinations appeared the most popular, with over 40% having visited Paris and Amsterdam, respectively, though 40.7 and 12.3% had visited the USA and Australia, respectively, but with no particular destinations specified in either country.

Other popular European destinations included the coastal destinations of Gran Canaria (31.5%), Ibiza (23.0%), Sitges (14.4%) and Mykonos (8.0%) and the cities of Berlin (9.6%) and Prague (7.1%). The study did not examine the number of holidays in each place taken by respondents, though there was an indication in the survey of the relationship between number of the destinations visited and factors such as income and age. Over 40% of the respondents had visited four or more of the places specified; higher incomes were related to high numbers of destinations visited and although there was some positive relationship with age this was not significant. Only half had visited a 'European gay resort' in the previous 5 years (Clift and Forrest, 1999b). In a related survey it was determined that 'gay' destinations had been the most recent holiday destination for 56% of gay men and 'non-gay' destinations for 44% (Clift *et al.*, 2002a). The UK Stormbreak (2000) survey recorded that the most popular destination for the 'last holiday taken' was Spain (16%) followed by North America (14%) and the UK (10%).

The 2001–2003 surveys of Community Marketing give an indication of the relative popularity of long (four or more nights) holiday destinations for US gay and lesbian travellers. Over 80% had taken at least one long holiday in the USA in the previous year, 37% in Europe, 17% in the Caribbean, 15% in each of Canada or Mexico and 13% in Australia and the Southern Hemisphere (Community Marketing Inc., 2001–2003). Community Marketing also asked US respondents to chose their 'top destination choices . . . for travel in the next year' (Roth and Paisley, 2004, p. 18). In the USA the three most popular were New York (43%), San Francisco (39%) and Hawaii (30%). The Florida destinations of Fort Lauderdale, Key West and Miami, as well as the Californian destinations of Palm Springs and West Hollywood – and Provincetown in Massachusetts – were each chosen by at least 25% of respondents. There were differences between gays and lesbians in the popularity of these places: the three most popular US destinations for lesbians were San Francisco (32%), Provincetown, Massachusetts (30%; 23% of men intended to visit here) and New York (28%). For men the top three were New York (44%), San Francisco (39%) and Palm Springs, California (31%), a place that very few lesbians (9%) intended to visit. Other places popular with gay men, such as Fort Lauderdale and South Beach, Miami, were much less popular with lesbians. Outside the USA, the most popular choices for gays and lesbians were France (20%), Britain (19%), Italy (18%), Australia (16%), Puerto Vallarta (Mexico) (14%) and Puerto Rico (11%). Canada and South Africa were not specified. Lesbians were far less likely to visit any of these destinations than were gay men. These choices referred only to future travel and not to places actually visited, and it is not certain whether this was a 'wish-list' or a definite statement of intent to visit.

In the online survey of gay and lesbian Canadian, US and Australian travellers (http://www.gaytravelguides.info, 2004) the most popular foreign countries visited by Canadians during the previous 5 years had been the USA (88.8%) and Mexico (40.4%); the Caribbean was visited by 30.9% and Europe by 44%. Ten per cent of US glbs polled in another online survey planned to travel to Europe in 2003 for reasons other than business (Witeck-Combs Communications and Harris Interactive, 2003a). The single most popular destination was 'the British Isles' (21%) followed by Germany, Austria and Switzerland (collectively at 13%) and Spain and Portugal (11%). Given this, glbs were apparently more 'adventurous' than heterosexual respondents in that 49% (compared with 24% of heterosexuals) said that they would like to visit 'other' European destinations.

The evidence from such surveys is mixed. Some refer to individual towns and cities and others to whole countries or continents, and they are therefore difficult to compare. Those referring to the past do not indicate frequency of visit and thus popularity in that sense and the time period over which activity is measured varies. It is not clear either whether visits were made to one destination only or to several destinations in the time period. Surveys about the future may refer more to desire than to actual intent.

Indirect Sources

Other sources of information about gay and lesbian destinations are indirect. Ivy identified places that were likely to be popular gay destinations by using the proxy of gay leisure and tourism establishments and assuming that 'the clustering of gay travel services can create an important draw for the gay tourist' (Ivy, 2001, p. 352). The gay travel guide *Spartacus* was used as a source of information for gay facilities (including bars, clubs, restaurants, shops and saunas) and it was concluded that North America (and the USA in particular) accounted for over a third of the world total of such establishments; California accounted for 20.3% and Florida 11.9%. The UK was fourth in the country ranking with 5.5%, and The Netherlands fifth with 3.6%. The presence of these establishments is not, however, necessarily indicative of tourist flows. Facilities, other than hotels and guesthouses, may owe more to local gay cultural development than to tourism and, in the case of tourism, may have relevance to a particular part of the gay and lesbian population only.

Gay and lesbian tourists themselves may utilize a number of sources of information about potential destinations and it is these that are utilized here as indicators of gay and lesbian destinations. The search for information is common to all models of the travel decision process. That information may be from an internal source, such as a person's previous experience or may be an external source, such as advertisements or a tour operator's brochure and is used to reduce uncertainty or risk. Tour operators' brochures may play a decisive role in destination choice given that operators are often regarded as gatekeepers of information (Gartner and Bachri, 1994; Pearce, 2002). Travel guidebooks will also provide an indication of gay and lesbian destinations, as will articles in the press or on television – both gay and straight. Some newspaper and magazine articles are written as a result of familiarization tours organized and financed by tourist boards, tour operators or airlines, with the expectation that comments will be positive. In such cases the commentary may be less than objective. Articles in the media can be about promoting 'new' destinations, which contribute further to reservations about reference to such indirect sources of information as indicators of the places that gays and lesbians actually do visit. Independent guidebooks may be expected to have more objectivity about them, though invariably they too express personal experiences and observations.

Advertisements and Marketing

A primary indicator of gay and lesbian destinations will be advertisements and marketing campaigns by particular places that are aimed at gays and lesbians. Some of these will be for places that are already popular and some will be for places that are hoping to become popular, and there is no obvious way of distinguishing the two. Typically, UK magazines do not feature many advertisements for destinations as such. Exceptions have included Key West ('The fabulous gay and lesbian destination' – see Fig. 5.1), Palm Springs, Philadelphia and Fort Lauderdale (all USA), Lanzarote (Canary Islands), Montreal and Vienna ('Delightfully queer' – see Fig. 2.1). Destinations may also be determined by reference to advertisements for hotels in gay magazines. Amsterdam features heavily: in the case of *Gay Times* (long-established UK monthly magazine) there has been a regular section devoted entirely to listings of the city's accommodation, bars and clubs. Otherwise, places represented in these advertisements for accommodation only include San Francisco and Palm Springs, Cairns and Turtle Cove (Australia), Cape Town, Paris and a number of rural destinations in France, the Algarve, several Spanish destinations and more recently, Budapest and Prague.

Within the UK, accommodation is advertised in most of the popular gay-friendly places such as London, Bournemouth, Brighton, Torquay and Blackpool, as well as less obvious places such as Bristol and Tenby

Fig. 5.1. Press advertisement produced by Florida Keys and Key West Tourism Council.

(South Wales). There is invariably a gay-owned or gay-friendly hotel or guesthouse in most towns and cities and, as a consequence, accommodation is advertised in places that do not necessarily have a gay scene nor are particularly popular with gays and lesbians.

A further indication of 'probable' destinations is the existence of separate or specific gay and lesbian tourist guides produced by towns, cities, regions or countries. Marketing of destinations directly to consumers is relatively uncommon, however, and most efforts are committed to encouraging intermediaries such as travel agents and tour operators to include a destination in their programmes. Cape Town Tourism produced the 'Official Visitors' Guide to Cape Town 2003', which included a two-page gay and lesbian section as well as a separate booklet relating solely to gay and lesbian life and venues. Similarly, Marketing Manchester (UK) has produced a separate dedicated guide entitled 'Manchester: a guide to the UK's hottest LGBT city' (2004–2005), and has a separate gay and lesbian section on its web site. The 2005–2006 version of the guide (see Fig. 5.2) is labelled a 'gay guide' and features a sole male against a background of Canal Street, the heart of the Gay Village.

The official tourism web site for the state of Victoria (Australia) also has a separate gay and lesbian section, with a particular focus on the city of Melbourne: '. . . the sophisticated alternative to Sydney's glitz and glamour' (http://www.visitvictoria.com). Web sites of the destination marketing organizations for Vancouver (Canada) and Vienna (Austria) both have sections devoted to gay and lesbian tourists (http://www.

Fig. 5.2. Front cover page of the 2005 gay guide to Manchester, produced by Marketing Manchester (UK).

tourismvancouver.com and http://www.wien.info). The Vienna Tourist Board directly targets the market through press advertisements and it also publishes a 25-page *Queer Guide to Vienna*, which can be downloaded. The Palm Springs Bureau of Tourism publishes an *Official Gay Visitors Guide*, available online. The gay and lesbian content of the web site for Tourism Australia (Australian Tourist Commission) is under 'special travel needs'; this leads to the Commission's comprehensive gay and lesbian guide to each of the states, a guide that is downloadable. Similarly, the gay and lesbian content of the German National Tourist Office is accessed via 'things to do' or directly through http://www.GayGermany.co.uk (see Fig. 5.3).

Travel Guides

Travel guides, either in the form of guidebooks or web site sources, also provide an indication of the destinations used by gays and lesbians. Some guidebooks are aimed at the gay and lesbian traveller. Some, such as *Spartacus*, have a comprehensive coverage of countries and individual places, but show what is available in respect of gay and lesbian venues in each of these places without an indication of popularity with gay and lesbian travellers (though see Ivy, 2001, above). They are basically listings

Germany is a hot ticket all year round, from Berlin's incredible nightlife to Bavaria's glorious scenery. Ready to be amazed? It's all here.

www.GayGermany.co.uk   Germany

Fig. 5.3. UK gay market campaign by Out Now Consulting for German National Tourist Office, 2005–2006 (for gay marketing information visit www.OutNowConsulting.com).

of hotels, bars, restaurants, saunas and the like, with brief descriptions and some comment about the nature of gay life in the country or town; the 2005 version of *Spartacus* is the 34th edition of this guide.

Damron gay and lesbian guidebooks have been published in the USA since 1964 which, at that time, reflected the personal travel experiences in the US of the eponymous founder. Currently the company publishes an annual 'Men's Travel Guide' with over 12,000 international listings of 'gay-friendly' businesses and a 'Women's Traveller', with over 9000 international listings though both inevitably have a particular focus on the USA. Both also include information about events and festivals and, for men, information on 'cruisy areas'. Damron also publish an international guide devoted specifically to accommodation and a 'City Guide', covering 75 major cities and resort destinations. The emphasis is on the USA (61 destinations) with only one city covered in each of England, France, Germany, The Netherlands, Spain, Czech Republic, South Africa and Australia (http://www.damron.com). Odysseus has been operating in the US gay travel market since 1984 and publishes a similar guide, the 'Gay Travel Planner', covering 116 countries; this was in its 17th edition in 2002–2003 (http://www.odyusa.com). Both Damron and Odysseus also have online listings and the Odysseus guide is available as a cd-rom. Neither organization has entered the travel industry in the form of holiday provision, though Odysseus does offer an online hotel reservation facility.

Gay and lesbian guides are produced as periodic magazines by the Australian publisher 'Gay Travel Guides' – these are also available online (http://www.gayaustraliaguide.com); the longest established is the guide to Australia. More recent additions include several issues relating to America (including articles on West Hollywood, San Francisco, Palm Springs, Fort Lauderdale and Dolly Parton's theme park of Dollywood). The first 'Europe' issue (2003–2004) covered London, Vienna and Amsterdam.

The guidebook written by Van Gelder and Brandt (1991) was as much a travelogue as a pure travel guide, being based on the actual experiences of the two women authors. It covered only a limited number of European destinations (14) that the authors felt would be of particular interest to gays and lesbians. They believed that existing gay travel guides contained insufficient information about gay culture and history in the places covered. They included places commonly considered to be gay destinations such as Brighton, Amsterdam, Sitges and Mykonos, capital cities such as London, Paris and Copenhagen as well as less obvious places such as the Loire Valley (France) and the small town of Llangollen in Wales. This town's claim to homosexual fame lay in it being where two aristocratic Irish ladies set up home together in the late 18th century.

Apart from specific gay and lesbian travel guidebooks, some travel guides aimed at the general public, such as the Rough Guides and the Lonely Planet publications, also include sections designed for gay and lesbian travellers. The *Lonely Planet Guide to Cape Town* (3rd edition 2002), for instance, had a six-page gay and lesbian section (in a book of over 200 pages). The Lonely Planet *Best of Paris* (2004) had a one-page section (out of just over 100 pages) and the *Mini-Rough Guide to New York* (2002) had a nine-page gay and lesbian section (out of nearly 400 pages). The sections usually amounted to listings of gay venues such as bars, clubs and accommodation, but with more comment about each than appeared in some of the more specific listings guides. Fodor's have been US-based publishers of travel guides since 1936, and currently produce over 400 guidebooks. The general guides to destinations do not have gay and lesbian sections of any significance but, in the late 1990s, these included separate guides to parts of North America including San Francisco, Los Angeles, Toronto and New York, as well as a more general *Fodor's Gay Guide to the USA* in 2001.

Thomas Cook, the long-established travel company, publishes a number of specialist guides including one for back-packers, but also an 'Out Around' series catering for gay and lesbian travellers. There are nine books in the series – 'the first totally gay travel guide series' – covering places such as Amsterdam, London, Paris, Miami, New York and Sydney. These, like the guides aimed at the general public, cover the 'usual' tourist attractions and general tourist information, as well as significant sections about gay and lesbian life and facilities.

Tour Operators' Programmes

The brochures and programmes of specialist gay and lesbian tour operators will indicate destinations (and also the type of holiday) that appeal to gay and lesbian tourists. (See Chapter 6 for further discussion of tour operators.) Brochures of specialist operators targeting gays and lesbians self-evidently feature destinations which are believed to be popular with that target market. In 2004, summer holidays offered by both of the largest gay and lesbian UK tour operators (Respect and Sensations) were almost exclusively to the beach destinations of Sitges, Ibiza, Mykonos (all Mediterranean) and Gran Canaria (Canary Islands). Alternative Holidays (with Sensations, part of the Man Around group) has organized gay weeks in individual resorts for several years. It has also, since 1997, arranged a 'European Gay Ski Week'. Both events are exclusively gay holidays with a whole beach complex or hotel reserved for clients with accompanying social programmes.

The Man Around group offers accommodation and event ticket packages to Sydney's Mardi Gras and makes accommodation bookings at recommended hotels in destinations worldwide, including San Francisco, Boston and Montreal in North America, Amsterdam and Prague in Europe and Bangkok, Chiang Mai and Pattaya in Thailand, as well as most parts of Australia. SpainGay holidays was an independent UK travel company whose specialization on Spain reflected an obvious popularity of this country. Beach holidays were offered in the usual popular gay and lesbian destinations of Gran Canaria and Sitges, but also in places such as Alicante and Benidorm; city destinations covered most Spanish cities, including Barcelona and Madrid. The company also offered golfing holidays, heritage tours and honeymoon holidays. As the UK market has developed, a number of UK tour operators are now offering specialist programmes similar to those of US operators. AMRO has, for instance, an 'Inca Highlight' tour, which includes Lima and Machu Picchu and holidays in Marrakech (Morocco). The company also offers trips to the 'usual' gay and lesbian destinations, as well as to places that are less obviously gay-oriented (see Fig. 3.1).

US tour operators

Compared with the UK there is less need in the USA for the inclusive holiday abroad when seeking sun and sea, as there are many domestic destinations that meet that need. Many holidays offered by US tour operators targeting the gay and lesbian market are small-group, special-interest holidays. These are arranged for groups of usually between two and twenty people and cover the 'usual' range of special-interest holidays including cultural, heritage, safari, adventure, activity and sport in the USA, but also in countries such as Vietnam, Nepal, Bolivia, Peru, Tibet and the Pacific islands. The programmes of US tour operators are therefore probably less representative of popular gay and lesbian destinations. Out West Global Adventures, for instance, includes in its programme Grand Canyon rafting, biking in Burgundy, trekking in Nepal and Tibet, Gay Ski Week in Aspen, ranching in Montana and safari in South Africa (http://www.outwestadventures.com). Hanns Ebensten Travel has a programme that includes the Gobi Desert and the Silk Road (China), the Galapagos Islands and Easter Island (Pacific). Many are destination-only packages in that travel (usually air) is left to customers to arrange, though may be arranged by the operator on request.

The largest tour operators in the US are those that offer cruises. Atlantis and Olivia both have programmes of cruises that are aimed primarily at gays and lesbians, respectively. Their itineraries are little different from those of the rest of the cruise market and are chiefly Caribbean-based, typically with departures from Miami and Fort Lauderdale. Alaskan and Mediterranean cruises are also offered, though the latter usually feature a mix of cultural visits such as Florence and Athens and gay destinations such as Ibiza and Mykonos. Atlantis' Mexican coast cruise focuses on Mexico's 'best beaches', including Puerto Vallarta. Both Atlantis and Olivia also feature all-gay or all-lesbian weeks at resorts reserved for exclusive use, usually in the Caribbean or Mexico. Gays and lesbians, at least in the USA, appear to be particularly keen on cruise holidays: 20% of gays and lesbians have taken at least one cruise in the previous 12 months compared with a national average of 2% (Community Marketing, 2003). Most of the larger operators targeting the market operate cruises on an exclusively gay and lesbian basis. Cruises for men have more of a party atmosphere about them than do the women's cruises; up to 80% of Olivia's clients are couples (Trucco, 2004). Romance Voyages targets 'sophisticated couples' who are not interested in the party scene. Most of their cruises are in small ships and have a particular emphasis on excursions to cultural sites. A European cruise in 2004, for instance, included Budapest, Vienna, Cologne and Amsterdam. RSVP claims to be the oldest gay tour operator, having organized its first cruise in 1986. Each of its cruises has between 200 and 2000 (male) clients, with on-board entertainment a particular draw.

Atlantis considers that it is the 'largest gay and lesbian tour operator in the world', though its business is more than just cruises and includes a Kenyan safari and holidays in Las Vegas. In all, it has more than 12,000 clients annually. Its cruise clients are younger than those of RSVP – mostly male – and cruises typically include theme pool parties and night-time entertainment, as well as shore excursions. A west coast cruise to the 'best of Mexico' focused on visits to five Pacific beaches, including Puerto Vallarta. Their January–February 2005 Caribbean cruise was advertised as 'the largest gay cruise in history' on the world's largest cruise ship: they intended to carry 3200 passengers. Part of Atlantis' product offer is a full programme at the 2005 Sydney Mardi Gras of accommodation, tickets for parties and grandstand seats for the parade, not including airfares. It also operates Club Atlantis resorts: an entire beach resort is taken over for a week for an exclusively gay vacation, including accommodation, meals, drinks, nightly entertainment, parties and optional sports such as snorkelling, windsurfing and sailing with instruction. In 2005, it was held at a resort (Mexico's 'hottest vacation destination') just south of Cancún (Mexico). This concept has been replicated by the UK operator, Alternative Holidays.

The cruise operator Olivia, which focuses on the lesbian market, also offers a programme of activity holidays including biking, walking, rafting, kayaking and hiking in places such as the Grand Canyon, Yellowstone and the Rockies. Whilst Atlantis and Olivia charter cruise ships for the exclusive use of gays and lesbians, Pied Piper (USA) organizes luxury cruises for gay groups on existing cruises, most of which have been on the QE2. They include a welcome party, private dining tables and private group excursions.

R Family Vacations is a recent addition (2004) to the cruise scene. This organization was established to offer vacations for gay and lesbian families with children, with a particular object of facilitating children meeting other children in similar family units. The first cruise (in 2004) had 1700 clients and was considered a success, despite being met by a church group protest in Nassau. For the future, small tours, ski vacations, fishing trips and safaris are planned. Olivia also introduced a family vacation in the form of a resort vacation at Club Med near west Palm Beach in 2003.

Lesbian tour programmes

Given the limited number of tour operators targeting the lesbian market, it is not possible to get a picture of popular destinations in the same way as can be done for gay men (however limited that might be). The handful of holidays offered to UK lesbians by tour operators do focus, though, on Lesvos. AMRO has extended its programme to the lesbian market by offering inclusive packages to women's resorts in the USA (see Fig. 5.4).

Holidays elsewhere are often advertised on a different basis – that of accommodation only in rural or coastal locations – with an emphasis on privacy. There are a handful of small organizations that target the lesbian market, with operators advertising in gay and lesbian newspapers and magazines (such as *Diva*, a UK national lesbian magazine). They include Sappho Travel, who describe themselves as 'specialists in travel to Greece and her islands' and Madison Travel (a travel agent), offering women-only holidays in Lesvos as well as in other European beach destinations popular

Fig. 5.4. Press advertisement produced by AMRO Holidays (UK) showing holidays for women in the USA.

with both gays and lesbians. Other businesses offering holiday products to the UK lesbian market are providers such as Wild Rose Holidays and Walking Women, which offer walking and special-interest holidays including skiing and photography (domestic and overseas but accommodation-only). South Sea Mermaid Tours, based in New Zealand, offer tours in that country or abroad that are 'cultural', with a particular focus on meeting local women in the destinations. There may well be a latent demand from gays and lesbians with children that is currently largely unrecognized.

Gay Magazines and Web Sites

Travel articles and guides in gay magazines and web sites often focus on gay-friendly destinations which are popular with gays and lesbians. Some articles, however, can be about promoting 'new' destinations and cannot be taken as indicators of current popularity with gays and lesbians. Some articles are difficult to separate from advertising features in as much as the writer may well have been invited on a familiarization tour at the operator's or marketing organization's expense. Descriptions of destinations, hotels and attractions may well be less than objective in such cases, accentuating the positive at the expense of the negative aspects. In 2002–2004, destinations such as Boston, Montreal, Rio de Janeiro, Munich, Berlin, Copenhagen, Oslo, Madrid and Seville have featured in separate travel articles in *Gay Times*. The articles are not obviously suggesting that these cities are gay centres as such, but do usually make some passing reference to gay and lesbian venues and events.

Winter destinations suggested in a 'winter warmers' feature in *Gay Times* included 'the usual' places such as Gran Canaria, Sydney, Rio de Janeiro, Florida, Thailand, Palm Springs and Cape Town (Copestake, 2004a). Less familiar destinations – 'the unusual' – were represented by places such as Tasmania (Australia), Puerto Vallarta and Cancún in Mexico, New Orleans and San Diego (USA), Bali and the Canary Islands other than Gran Canaria.

Apart from the regular travel pages in the magazine, *Gay Times* published a travel supplement in 2004 distributed with a monthly issue. This described a different destination for each month of the coming year. Tallinn (Estonia) was deemed to be perfect for romantic weekends, though it was admitted that gay venues weren't easy to find. Buenos Aires (Argentina) was described as fast emerging as the new, hip gay tourist destination in Latin America, but Cyprus, although included, was not considered as an obvious destination for gay travellers because of its rather illiberal attitudes. Other places covered included Reykjavik (Iceland), Galapagos, Barcelona ('coolest city in the world'), Hawaii and Japan.

Several gay and lesbian travel web sites exist which cover most of the destinations mentioned previously. *Gay Times* launched a travel web

site in 2005 offering 'impartial online travel advice' about destinations
(http://www.gaytimestravel.co.uk). Destinations described include
Arizona, Berlin, Bratislava, Malmo, Palm Springs and Zurich. *Out &*
About is offered both as hard copy (a newsletter of 16 pages published ten
times a year) and as a web site resource (http://www.outandabout.com).
The web site's 'top twenty destinations' (criteria unspecified) include
New York, Atlanta, Miami, Paris, London and Montreal. *Out & About* also
makes available, as online subscription services, their 'Travel Guides'
relating to individual destinations (which include Amsterdam, Athens,
Rome and Vienna) and 'Travel Guides Plus', focusing on particular
areas or topics such as solo travel, 'bear' travel, gay couples and
adventure travel. Other similar gay and lesbian online travel magazines
include http://www.navigaytion.com and http://www.qtmagazine.
com. Access to web sites with information on gay venues in over 200
cities and towns across the world can also be found at http://www.
pinkpassport.com.

Many general gay and lesbian web sites also have travel sections
within them (see, for instance, http://www.uk.gay.com and http://www.
planetout.com). The content is similar to that of travel pages of newspapers
or magazines rather than listings. US-based http://www.lesbianlife.about.
com provides sponsored links to web sites of lesbian-friendly holiday
destinations and travel operators. Lesbian Nation, the 'leading online
community dedicated to lesbian culture and identity' also includes travel
articles which cover destinations identical to those for gay men mentioned
above (http://www.lesbianation.com).

Non-gay press

Travel articles in the general press also, on occasion, refer to or focus on
destinations that are supposedly popular with gays and lesbians. *The*
Times (UK) national newspaper identified 'the best holiday destinations in
which to spend your pink pound' (Miles, 2000, p. 12) as being Queensland
(Australia), Ibiza, Sitges (Spain), Paris, French Polynesia, Hawaii,
Mykonos, Cape Town, Lesbos, Crete and Fire Island (New York) as well
as cruises. Not all of these are necessarily popular destinations, given that
French Polynesia was described as 'not yet well known as a gay destination . . . [and] . . . you may well find yourself the only gay couple in your
resort' (Miles, 2000, p. 12).

The regular travel supplement in the *Observer* (UK national Sunday
newspaper) was dedicated to gay travel in early 2002 and identified destinations that were 'the places to be' in that year (Mellor, 2002a). They
included Cape Town, Russian River (California), Fort Lauderdale
(Florida), Costa Rica, Budapest, the Algarve (Portugal), Vieques (Puerto
Rico), Vancouver, Queensland, Phuket (Thailand), Tel Aviv (Israel) and

Mumbai (India). These places embrace not only destinations that are already popular with gay and lesbian tourists and those which have potential, but also those in which the gay scene and gay life are limited. Copenhagen was, in the same supplement, described as 'the fashionable Amsterdam for many lesbians and gays; it is not as crowded and it has a compelling stylishness somehow missing from the Dutch city' (Summerskill, 2002, p. 6). Puerto Vallarta, a Mexican coastal destination very popular with North American 'sun-swallows', was also featured as being of possible interest to gays in the UK (Tatchell, 2002).

In 2002–2004, destinations such as Paris and Gran Canaria have featured as gay and lesbian destinations in articles in the *Guardian* (Mowbray, 2003; Wells, 2002) and Sitges in the *Observer*. Interestingly, Sitges has featured in at least two straight media representations. An article in the *Observer* referred to a heterosexual family who chose this coastal town for a holiday, in part, because of its reputation as a gay resort. This suggested an atmosphere that was less loud and tasteless than that in several other Spanish resorts (Hogan, 2003). The town was also included in the regular BBC *Holiday* television programme in April 2003, with an emphasis on its popularity as a gay destination.

The emphasis in many of these sources is destinations associated with beach holidays and city breaks, but gay and lesbians are, presumably, as likely to participate in other types of holiday as are the rest of the population. The *Observer* supplement mentioned earlier included an article on the Are Gay Days in Sweden (Mellor, 2002b). This was a 4-day ski and snowboard event which attracted about 2000 people, most of whom were transported on a specially chartered train from Stockholm. Other gay ski events mentioned were Swiss Gay Ski Week in Davos, the sixth annual Austrian Gay Ski Week, a Gay Ski Week in Queenstown (New Zealand), the Aspen (Colorado) Gay and Lesbian Ski Week, which, with over 5000 participants, is the biggest US gay ski festival, Altitude, (the 10th Whistler, Canada, Gay and Lesbian Ski Week) and the European Gay Ski Week (held that year in Italy). Many of these weeks include extensive programmes of evening parties such that they are another dimension of the 'circuit party' (see Chapter 6).

Conclusion

Gays and lesbians apparently choose to holiday in many of the same places as do the rest of the population. Some places, however, appear to have a particular attraction and have become synonymous with gay and lesbian holidays. The basis for this assertion is not, however, any rigorous study but a number of sources which, together, point to particular places as being the most attractive and most likely to attract and experience high numbers of gay and lesbian tourists. In addition, there is little that confirms which (if any) of the destinations that are popular with the rest of the population it is that gays and lesbians avoid.

It is important to note, however, that the places that are apparently the most popular may well only apply to a proportion of the gay and lesbian population. Those noted here are primarily those promoted to 'the market'. Many of the most popular destinations for gays and lesbians may not be those promoted in guidebooks, in tour operators' programmes or even those mentioned in surveys. These may only be relevant to a particular section of the gay and lesbian population. Many may well not contribute to surveys, may not seek out particularly gay-friendly or gay-promoted destinations or book with specialist operators.

The remaining part of this chapter will describe some of the places in the world that are commonly believed to be popular with gay and lesbian tourists.

Some 'Popular' Gay and Lesbian Tourist Destinations

Given that the most popular destinations cannot be known with any certainty, the following destinations are those that are frequently referred to as being 'popular'. It is not an exhaustive list of destinations, nor is it necessarily representative of destinations that are the most popular. The purpose is to describe the destinations and indicate some of the key issues relating to their supposed popularity. It is not, either, a full description or analysis of each, as there is reference to these destinations throughout the book which provides further detail and identifies other issues.

Amsterdam

With a population of about 800,000, it is the largest city in The Netherlands. It is a port city but has become a particularly popular tourist destination. The attractions are the conventional ones of its heritage of buildings and canals, and the less conventional ones associated with a liberal attitude towards sex (and heterosexual prostitution) and drug use. It has a reputation for being a city of great cultural diversity, and considerable tolerance has been extended to alternative lifestyles. This has included homosexuality and led to its great popularity with foreign visitors who experience less freedom in their home countries. Gay and lesbian life is very open and there are numerous visible gay and lesbian venues in several distinct clusters scattered throughout the city. They include bars, restaurants, hotels, saunas and dance as well as sex clubs. Its tolerance may be no more than skin-deep, however, given the restrictive policies of government and the reluctance of the tourist board to market to gays and lesbian in recent years, along with an apparent rise in 'gay-bashing'.

Argentina

A South American country with a population of 39 million. It is bordered by the South Atlantic and has a temperate climate. Its capital city, Buenos Aires, is alleged to have become the gay Mecca of South America, rivalling Rio as the 'traditional' gay destination for gays from the USA and Europe (Goni, 2004). This is, in part, attributed to its cosmopolitan feel and European lifestyle, as well as a favourable exchange rate. It is believed that some of the current tourist boom is associated with sex tourism.

Brazil

This is the largest country in South America and has a population of 186 million. Its climate is mostly tropical. Homosexuality is legal in Brazil and there are gay scenes in most cities. Despite this, homophobia is still deeply rooted and homophobic attacks common, especially in smaller towns.

Rio de Janeiro, one-time capital of Brazil, has a population of about eight million and is a popular tourist destination despite extensive poverty and shanty towns. Gay life centres on Ipanema and Copacabana beaches rather than on its night-life, which is allegedly better in São Paulo (Egginton, 2004). The tourist highlight of the year is Rio's Carnival, held annually over 4 days in February. Gays have played an important part in the Carnival since the 1930s.

Cairns (Australia)

A tourist town of 120,000 inhabitants on the coast of North Queensland in Australia. It has a tropical climate and is the third most popular tourist destination in the country after Sydney and Brisbane, with over one million visitors annually. Its beaches are a significant attraction, along with the Great Barrier Reef and the inland tropical rainforests.

It is also the second most popular gay and lesbian destination in Australia. The Queensland state government and tourist board actively promote to the gay and lesbian market. It is particularly popular pre- and post-Mardi Gras in Sydney. There are several gay and lesbian resorts and hotels around Cairns: Turtle Cove Resort, with a private gay beach is widely advertised to the gay market. The Liberty resort was reported to be remarketing itself (in 2004) to straight tourists because it had failed to fill a third of its rooms since opening in 2002 (Fickling, 2004).

Cape Town (South Africa)

This is the legislative centre of the Republic of South Africa; it is a coastal city of three million inhabitants of whom 32% are 'Black African' and 48% are 'Coloured'. It lies at the southern tip of Africa and is bordered by the Atlantic and Indian Oceans and has a temperate climate. The Republic of South Africa has experienced majority rule since 1994, when government by the white minority population ended. The principle of non-discrimination enshrined in the 1996 constitution includes that on grounds of sexual orientation.

Since majority rule, Cape Town has become a popular destination for gay tourists from Europe and the USA; it is 'the new Sydney' (Mellor, 2002a). Tourism is based on city-break holidays, shopping, beaches, the surrounding winelands and scenery. It now has a well-established gay scene of bars, clubs, saunas and hotels and guesthouses, as well as regular, high-profile gay and lesbian events such as Mother City Queer Project and Cape Town Pride.

The Caribbean

Countries in the Caribbean Sea do not have a particularly good reputation with regard to gay-friendliness. Jamaica, the 'cultural heart' of the Caribbean, has a population of three million and a tropical climate and is possibly the most homophobic of the islands (Gregory, 2004). Homosexuality is illegal and verbal abuse, violence and even murder of gays is common. Homosexuality was decriminalized in Cuba in 1979 but it is still illegal if 'publicly manifested', with a penalty of up to one year in prison (Gregory, 2004). The gay scene takes place in private clubs.

St Kitts was singled out, however, in one UK gay paper as offering a 'warm welcome' despite not having a thriving gay scene (Miles, 2003). Similarly, Puerto Rico was promoted as 'one of the only destinations in the Caribbean truly considered as gay-friendly' (Czyzselska, 2003, p. 20). This tropical island has a population of about four million and despite being self-governing remains a 'commonwealth associated with the US' following a period of US ownership. It has the most developed gay and lesbian infrastructure within the Caribbean of bars and clubs, gay-popular beaches and hotels. Most gay life for tourists is centred on the capital city of San Juan, which is a cruise port and also a UNESCO World Heritage site.

Costa Rica

Central American country bordered by the Caribbean Sea and the Pacific Ocean, located between Nicaragua to the north and Panama to the south.

It has a tropical and subtropical climate; inland topography is rugged mountains, including over 100 volcanic cones, of which several are major volcanoes. It has a population of four million of whom three-quarters are Roman Catholic. The country is politically stable, has a reputation for tolerance and has laws against sexual-orientation discrimination.

Its tourism is based on beach holidays, but also increasingly on ecotourism and adventure tourism associated with its mountains, rain forests, rivers and 'extraordinary panoply of wildlife, flora and fauna' (Copestake, undated). The (inland) capital of San José has a significant gay scene and there are gay beaches on the Pacific coast in particular.

Fire Island (USA)

A 32-mile-long island on the southern edge of Long Island, about 45 miles east of New York City. Its unspoilt beaches are protected by the National Park Service. There are two centres of gay and lesbian life on the island, Cherry Grove and Pines. The Grove developed as a gay resort in the 1920s and 1930s, catering for an 'artistic' set of visitors from New York, and by the 1960s it was 'a kind of informally organized gay theme park' (Newton, 1993, p. 110). The Pines resort was developed in the early 1950s and became established as a place for 'the party crowd', who were considered to be less of a community than in the Grove. Pines is for 'snooty-gayboys-with-good-bodies' (Theobald, 2002) and for the 'modern and muscly' (Miles, 2000) and has, over the years, earned a reputation for beach parties, drugs and wild sex. Conversely, the Grove has become associated more with 'less trendy' gays and with lesbians. Both the Grove and Pines are popular for day visits and hotel accommodation is limited. The Grove is characterized by small, owner-occupied cottages but at Pines, in particular, there are many large, multiple-share houses which are let on a weekly, monthly or seasonal basis.

Fort Lauderdale (Florida, USA)

A town of 1.8 million on the Atlantic coast of Southern Florida, it long had a reputation as a place for student 'Spring Break' which, in turn, was associated with rowdy behaviour. It has turned itself around, however, during the 1980s and 1990s into a beach destination for families, international travellers and, noticeably, gay and lesbian visitors. It has an extensive gay scene, including a gay beach and numerous gay-owned and gay-friendly hotels, bars and clubs. It is also close to Orlando, Miami and the Keys. It 'now bears more resemblance to Monte Carlo or St Tropez' and its appeal seems to be for those who have 'little in common with the pill-popping, disco-crazed queens' (Roach, http://www.gaytimestravel.

co.uk). The Greater Fort Lauderdale VCB has deliberately targeted the gay and lesbian market and claims that they 'have been nationally recognized as one of the pioneers in the gay–lesbian marketing effort' (Michael Kenney of Greater Fort Lauderdale VCB, quoted in Van Drake, 2003).

Gran Canaria (Canary Islands)

Gran Canaria is one of the seven Canary Islands in the Atlantic Ocean, located off the north-western coast of Africa; they are part of Spain. Other islands in the group include Tenerife and Lanzarote. Their location means they have a year-round semi-tropical climate and the larger islands are major tourist destinations. Gran Canaria is a year-round destination with a local population of about 800,000. It is the single most popular desti- nation sold by UK gay and lesbian tour operators.

The attractions of the island are many, including its scenery, watersports and adventure tourism, but the attractions for most gay and lesbian tourists are the sandy beaches and dunes of Maspalomas (with gay sections) and the gay nightlife of Playa del Ingles which, together, comprise the biggest gay resort town in Europe (Walker, 2000). The Yumbo Centre in Playa del Ingles is a shopping mall by day, which also houses about 60 gay bars and discos which, when they open at night, transform the Centre. The Centre offers clear attractions for any gays or lesbians who experience no or a limited gay scene at home, though it 'must be one of the most God-despairing, architecturally arrested holes on the planet' (Davis, 2004, p. 139). Playa del Ingles is also a popular tourist destination for non-gays and there is no evident conflict with the gay and lesbian visitors; there is little reported homophobia or violence.

Ibiza (Mediterranean Sea)

Ibiza is one of the Spanish Balearic Islands (which include Mallorca) in the western Mediterranean Sea. The islands are major tourist destinations. Ibiza became a major centre of tourism during the 1950s and 1960s, when it attracted an alternative culture that included hippies, artists and gays. Since that time it has become a popular destination for families but retains its appeal to others, including younger singles attracted by the club nightlife. It has had a considerable reputation as the clubbers' capital, a centre for dance music lovers. Although there a number of signifi- cant resort towns on the island (the biggest being San Antonio) which cater particularly for straights, the most popular with gays are Ibiza Town and the surrounding towns such as Figueretas – which is the main area for gay hotels. Most of the gay nightlife takes place in or around Ibiza Town.

Key West (Florida, USA)

Key West is a two-by-four-mile island located at the tip of the Florida Keys, a chain of small coral islands, largely consisting of nature reserves or parks. The islands are linked to one another and the mainland by a causeway, and Key West is a 3-hour drive from Miami. Notable past literary Key West residents include Ernest Hemingway, Tennessee Williams and Truman Capote. As it declined as a seaport town in the 1970s, Key West was transformed and regenerated as a holiday destination by and for gays and lesbians. Victorian houses were restored and refurbished as upmarket guesthouses and restaurants; most gay accommodation is in this historic district, close to restaurants and gay bars. There are a number of well-established, men-only resorts, many of which are clothing-optional and cruisy. It has, for some time, been a predominantly gay and lesbian holiday town but, more recently, it has catered for a wider range of visitors.

Lesvos (Mediterranean Sea)

Lesvos is a Greek island in the Aegean Sea (eastern part of the Mediterranean), close to the Turkish coastline. The island has an appeal for families seeking more than just a beach and bar, as its attractions include historical sites, museums, Roman ruins, hot springs, walking and bird-watching (Macleod, 2003). Skala Eressos is a small village on the western coast which, as the alleged birthplace and home of Sappho, has a particular significance for lesbians. Women-only guesthouses and hotels are common, the beach has a women-only nude sunbathing area and many bars restaurants, bookstores and gift shops are run by lesbians. This popularity has created some tension with local residents at times, especially as other tourist markets have been targeted. It has become increasingly popular with families and with heterosexual honeymooning couples.

Manchester (UK)

This is an old industrial city in the north-west of England, whose initial prosperity as a manufacturing and commercial centre for cotton has declined. Like many other such cities, it has endeavoured to re-invent itself, at least in part, as a tourist destination and as a vibrant, cultural centre of consumption. The city has a population of about half a million but is the centre of a conurbation of 2.5 million people. It lacks specific individual tourist icons but has based its tourist appeal on a number of features targeted at specific markets, as well as a more general targeting based on the combination of those features.

The targeting of the gay and lesbian market has focused on the existing gay space of the 'Gay Village', located in the city-centre. This is a gay space of bars and clubs, saunas, bookshop and restaurants, which has a concentration and coherence not apparent in any other UK city. This gay space is an open, tolerant, relatively safe area where, in summer in particular, there is an appropriation of the Village streets. It featured in a national UK television series *Queer as Folk* in 1999. The city has a long-established gay and lesbian festival and, in 2003, hosted the Europride festival. The gay space has not featured in the marketing in isolation, but along with the usual attractions of a large urban area – theatres, shopping, eating out and sport, as well as easy access to rural parts of England and Wales.

Mexico

Mexico is a country of 106 million people that borders the USA – the states of California, Arizona, New Mexico and Texas in particular. Discrimination is forbidden by the Mexican constitution. There is a lively gay scene in many cities and towns, though homosexuality is not universally tolerated in the more rural areas. Mexico City contains one of the largest gay populations in the world, but its gay scene is limited. Acapulco (on the Pacific coast) had a famous international gay scene with openly gay spaces before they appeared in Mexico City (Sanchez-Crispin and Lopez-Lopez, 1997).

Puerto Vallarta, on the Pacific coast, dubbed the 'San Francisco of Mexico', has developed as Mexico's premier gay resort (Tatchell, 2002). It has a modern marina and is also a cruise ship port. It is a town (of over 300,000 inhabitants) which is a popular holiday destination for Mexican families and, also – mainly US and Canadian – gay men. It has a gay scene of hotels and resorts as well as bars, clubs and a gay beach on the main shore.

Cancún, on the Caribbean coast, is a purpose-built holiday town on an island connected to the mainland by two bridges. It is an Americanized beach destination with upscale resorts and hotels, clubs and malls. There is no gay resort or hotel accommodation as such, but it is a gay-friendly destination with gay bars and clubs and a gay strip on the beach (Ferber, 2001).

Miami Beach (Florida, USA)

This is the beach holiday part of Miami connected to downtown by a number of causeways. The part that has been most popular with gays and lesbians is South Beach, an area characterized by 1920s and 1930s Art Deco buildings, including hotels and guesthouses that were renovated in the 1980s (see Fig. 5.5). Prior to this it had become a particularly run-down part of Miami. Gays and lesbians were instrumental in some of the regeneration and the area acquired its own large resident gay community. There are number of gay bars and clubs, though the scene is not as large or as hectic as in Fort Lauderdale. It is renowned also for circuit parties such as the White Party (November), when gay life typically dominates South Beach.

Mykonos (Mediterranean Sea)

Mykonos is a Greek island in the Aegean Sea (eastern part of the Mediterranean) with a population of about 6000. It is one of the most cosmopolitan of the Greek islands and has long attracted intellectuals and artists (Miles, 2000). It is not a particularly scenic island, but its attraction lies in its beaches and nightlife. It is popular with an upscale Greek market, but also has become particularly popular with international gay tourists so that it has probably the gayest scene of Greece. Gay nightlife is concentrated in Mykonos town but beaches are out of town and are reached by bus or boat. The island of Delos, a short boat journey away, includes the sanctuary of Dionysus with its two pillars supporting large, stone phalluses (see Fig. 5.6).

Fig. 5.5.   An art deco hotel, Ocean Drive, Miami South Beach, Florida, USA.

Fig. 5.6. Sanctuary of Dionysus, Island of Delos, eastern Mediterranean.

Palm Springs (California, USA)

This small town is about 100 miles east of Los Angeles on the edge of the Californian deserts. As such, it has a warm and clear year-round climate and has grown into an exclusive retreat and retirement centre. There are a large number of second homes in Palm Springs, the permanent population of which is 44,000, with another 27,000–30,000 people living there in the winter. Despite the proximity to the deserts it is a particularly lush green oasis in which there are over 100 golf courses and 600 tennis courts. Temperatures can reach into the upper 30s Celsius, though the surrounding mountain ranges (up to 11,000 feet) with a cooler environment are accessible by way of an Aerial Tramway. The town is characterized by mid-20th century modernist architecture, which itself is part of its tourist resource.

It is a major draw in California, after San Francisco and Los Angeles, for gay and lesbian visitors and, although it has little by way of nightlife or gay hotels, it has numerous gay resorts, many of which are clothing-optional and some themed (leather or S&M). It is also home to renowned circuit parties for men (White Party at Easter) and for women (Dinah Shore). It has been described as 'Gran Canaria without the vulgarity . . . Mykonos minus the pretty whitewashed houses' (Copestake, undated). It is also particularly popular as a weekend destination for gay and lesbian Californians.

Provincetown (Massachusetts, USA)

This small town with a population of about 4000 lies at the tip of the Cape Cod peninsula in Massachusetts; the nearest large city is Boston, which is a 90-minute ferry boat trip away. Its historical claim to fame is as the first landing of the Pilgrim fathers on American soil, from the *Mayflower*, in 1620. Its growth was associated with whaling but subsequently it became an 'artists' colony' in the late 19th century. By the 1960s it had become a tourist town renowned for a particularly liberal attitude to alternative life-styles – including hippies in the 1970s. It has been portrayed as an idyllic coastal vacation destination 'where those who live unconventionally seem to outnumber those who live within the prescribed boundaries of home and licensed marriage' (Cunningham, 2004, p. 64). Now, a large propor-tion of the permanent and visitor population is lesbian or gay, and gays and lesbians own most of the businesses and real estate. It is a very popu-lar summer destination for gay and lesbian tourists, many of whom are day trippers. There has been little anti-gay sentiment, probably because of its initial small local population, relative geographical isolation and its attractiveness for 'refugees, rebels and visionaries for almost 400 years' (Cunningham, 2004, p. 64).

Russian River (California, USA)

Russian River is a rural area in Sonoma County, California, about a 90-minute drive north of San Francisco. Its importance lay initially in forestry, and its redwood forests attracted visitors in the 19th century. Its economy is now very much dependent on tourism and day trippers, who come to experience the forests, vineyards, farms, orchards and wineries and engage in activities such as riding, hiking, camping, fishing, biking and canoeing.

Guerneville is one of the largest of the Russian River villages (though only 3000 population) and has become the centre for gay and lesbian visitors to the region. It has gay bars and gay resorts and is 'a rustic paradise of hiking, hot tubs, cute cabins and laid-back, clothing-optional sunbathing areas' (Mellor, 2002a, p. 14). Its 'notorious' 3-day alfresco Sundance Party in mid-August attracts about 4000 gays, mainly from San Francisco and the Bay area. The Women's Weekend held in May has been a tradition for over 20 years; another is held in September.

San Francisco (California, USA)

One of the USA's most compact cities with a population of about three-quarters of a million, located on the Pacific coast. Its growth owes much to the discovery of gold in California in the late 1840s and to its development as a west coast port. It has had a reputation as a 'frontier town' and as a place of non-conformity, with permanent and transient populations of prospectors, sailors and immigrants from Asia in particular and military personnel. Its reputation in the 1950s and 1960s as the home of the 'beats', of hippies and the 'love generation' has been an important factor in its image as a particularly liberal, tolerant city. This and its iconic Golden Gate Bridge, the prison of Alcatraz and its cable-cars have contributed to making it one of the most popular tourist destinations in the USA, attracting about 17 million visitors a year.

The city has had a particular resonance for gays and lesbians, especially in view of the existence of the predominantly gay neighbourhood of the Castro. This central part of San Francisco had been in decline but, through a process of regeneration and gentrification in the 1970s by gays and lesbians, became a part of the city where homosexual residents have come to outnumber non-gays. San Francisco has had a noticeably high-profile and politically powerful gay and lesbian community and it had been dubbed the 'gay capital of the USA' by *Life* magazine as early as 1964. There is also an extensive gay scene in the city which is not confined to the Castro.

Sitges (Spain)

This small town is on the northern Mediterranean coast of Spain just south of Barcelona (population of over three million), which is a 25-minute train ride away. Sitges has been an artistic and 'bohemian' resort since the 19th century and has been a planned tourist town since the early 20th century. It has avoided the worst excesses of much of the tourism development on the Spanish Mediterranean coast, so that high-rise and high-density apartment and hotel building and cheap mass tourism do not characterize Sitges. It is largely unspoilt and upmarket and attracts Spanish families, especially at weekends, from Barcelona.

It is a very popular destination for many European gays and lesbians. There are more gay bars than in Barcelona itself, numerous gay clubs, gay fashion shops and gay beaches, one of which is centrally located. An 'unbelievably open and matter-of-fact way gayness meshes with the very traditional family-oriented culture of this town' (Van Gelder and Brandt, 1991, p. 254).

Sydney (Australia)

This city (population of nearly four million) is in the state of New South Wales in the south-east of Australia. It is the oldest and largest city in the country and over half of all international visitors to Australia come to the city. It has a number of iconic landmarks, including the Opera House and the Harbour Bridge. Its beaches, especially Bondi, are particularly well known.

Despite its distance from the USA and Europe, it is becoming a popular destination for gays and lesbians. There is an extensive and open gay scene of bars, clubs, hotels, sex clubs and saunas, as well as the renowned Mardi Gras festival held annually in February.

Thailand (South-east Asia)

A country of 65 million people, with a tropical climate and a coastline on both the South China Sea and the Indian Ocean. It has had a reputation for sex tourism, mainly heterosexual men seeking sex with Thai women, though also with a homosexual angle. The country has been anxious to shed this image and move the emphasis to holidays focused on its heritage, scenery and wildlife – as well as family-oriented holidays based on the numerous tropical beaches.

It remains an attractive destination for gay men in particular. Homosexual behaviour between consenting adults is not a criminal offence and Thailand has one of the world's more liberal sexual cultures in terms of tolerance of homosexuals, though public displays of affection are not advisable. There are large gay scenes in Bangkok, Phuket, Pattaya and Chiang Mai. Bangkok, the country's capital city, has an extensive gay scene; many venues are cruisy but highly commercial, and frequented by Thai men and boys willing to engage in relationships with tourists for money. Pattaya (on the south-eastern coast) is a well-developed and flamboyant destination which has been popular with gay visitors for many years. Phuket (an island off the western coast) has a number of beaches including Patong Beach, which is particularly popular with gays. Chiang Mai, an ancient inland walled city and university town of about half a million inhabitants, has a more relaxed though still commercial gay scene.

Vancouver (British Columbia, Canada)

Toronto and Montreal in eastern Canada may have a particular popularity with gay and lesbian travellers, but Vancouver on the Pacific coast has emerged as a significant destination. It is the third largest city in Canada, with half a million inhabitants, and is Canada's largest port. It is also a major tourist destination partly due to its population links with the UK, but also because of its location between mountains and sea, its proximity to the Rockies and because it has one of the mildest climates in Canada.

British Columbia was one of the first Canadian provinces, along with Ontario and Quebec, to legalize same-sex marriage in 2003 before the national legalization in 2005. The city, a 'laid-back, open city' (Townsend, 2004), has the largest gay and lesbian population in western Canada and has two well-established gay and lesbian residential areas. There is an extensive gay scene of bars, shops, restaurants and clubs. It hosted the third Gay Games in 1990. The annual gay and lesbian ski week, Altitude, is held in Whistler (Rockies) and starts with the 'Avalanche' party, in Vancouver. Salt Spring Island, off the east coast of Vancouver, has a community of about 10,000 people, many of whom are artists, sculptors and musicians and is a popular destination for lesbians (Mellor, 2002a).

Conclusions

This listing is by no means comprehensive. Destinations such as Vienna (Austria), Prague (Czech Republic), Barcelona (Spain), Berlin (Germany) New York, West Hollywood and Hawaii (USA), Toronto and Montreal (Canada) and London and Brighton (UK) are not included, though their inclusion is as justifiable as is that of those listed. It is clear, however, that destinations cover the 'usual' range and include cities and coastal destinations. In many cases destinations are in countries that have well-developed local gay and lesbian communities or in places that are at least prepared to tolerate gay and lesbian tourists. The reasons for that toleration have been discussed in previous chapters.

Some of the largest cities have had an attraction as centres of gay life and of anonymity and confidentiality; some of the smaller communities, which have often been away from the main centres of population, have developed as centres of 'unconventional', often artistic, life in many forms. They have been perceived as a 'haven' and attracted gays and lesbians as a consequence. Gays and lesbians (local and others) have often played a significant role in the development of such destinations. Other places may not have grown organically as gay and lesbian holiday destinations, but have set out to target that market or have been identified by tour operators as having the potential to meet the needs of gay and lesbian travellers, and have been promoted as such. Still other places might be perceived to be 'exploitive development', in as much as popularity has resulted more through external pressures and demands for tourism opportunities than through indigenous advancement.

Intermediaries, Accommodation and Attractions   **6**

Introduction

This chapter will consider the supply side of gay and lesbian tourism. This covers organizations that provide inclusive tours (package holidays), accommodation, transport and 'attractions' that gays and lesbian may wish to visit, and other intermediaries such as travel agents that facilitate the booking of holidays with the others. 'Attractions' will include those that appeal to tourists other than gays and lesbians, but in this chapter consideration will be given to some particularly gay and lesbian attractions such as pride festivals, circuit parties and sport.

In previous chapters, the propensity and intensity of gay and lesbian holiday-taking has been examined and holiday destinations determined as best the existing studies and material would allow. It has been apparent that the nature of the holidays has been similar to those of the rest of the population and destinations have been similar, though apparently with some limitations and some particular spatial concentrations of demand. It was noted too how there was a requirement for gay-friendliness or gay space and for avoiding places where homophobia might be evident. As a consequence, it might be expected that tour operators, travel agents, carriers and accommodation providers would be tailoring their services to meet these requirements. Service providers who target the heterosexual population may also target gays and lesbians and, given the perception of this market, it might be expected that 'travel agents, tour operators and related industries bend over backwards to accommodate this high-spending, frequently flying and adventurous group' (Mellor, 2002a, p. 13).

Tour Operators

There will be those, especially in the UK, who use tour operators to provide an inclusive holiday for them if travelling to a foreign destination. This has usually meant a package holiday of both transport and accommodation. The tourism distribution channel is conventionally considered to be made up of producers, wholesalers (tour operators), retailers (travel agents) and clients (Pearce, 2002). The channel acts as a source of information but also as a mechanism for purchasing the product. The tour operators and the travel agents are intermediaries in the channel, facilitating contact between 'producers' (destinations, accommodation, etc.) and the holidaymaker. It is evident that not all information or purchasing follows that particular model, as direct-sell between tour operator and client exists as does a model where both tour operator and travel agent are absent and clients seek information from and purchase directly from the producers, including accommodation and transport. The Internet has undoubtedly facilitated these particular models (Buhalis, 1998; Lang, 2000).

There has been a commonly held view that tour operators wield significant influence in this distribution channel (Klemm and Parkinson, 2001; Richards, 2001). The decision of tour operators to offer holidays in a destination may be decisive in the development of that destination, especially in the early stages of the lifecycle (Lumsdon and Swift, 1999; Tapper, 2001). Tour operators may, though, have limited allegiance to any particular destination (Klemm and Parkinson, 2001) and this may especially be the case for the mass-market tour operators. For them and for clients, individual destinations may be highly substitutable in the sea and sun market. Other operators, such as those who deal in special interest tourism products, may be more concerned about destination difference and encourage the longer-term sustainability of those destinations (Carey *et al.*, 1997). Although gay and lesbian tourism may not, strictly speaking, be special interest tourism, tour operators may be similarly concerned about destination difference and maintaining loyalty to particular destinations identified as gay-friendly.

The UK inclusive tour market is characterized by domination by the 'big four' tour operators (Thomson, Thomas Cook, MyTravel and First Choice), with a large (but imprecise) number of smaller operators – sometimes referred to as 'independents' (Evans, 2001; Klemm and Parkinson, 2001). The big four dominate the mass sea and sun market, whereas the independents tend to specialise in niche, non-competing markets. The big four have, none the less, entered these niche markets by means of sub-brands, often through acquisition of smaller or independent firms (Cope, 2002).

One of the most important tools that tour operators have is the brochure, whether conventional print copy or Internet version. Given that the holiday is an experience product, the brochure acts as a 'surrogate for the actual product' (Ioannides, 1998, p. 146). The brochure performs the dual role of information source and image-generator, regardless of customer uptake. High-risk and infrequent purchases such as holidays are often associated with a greater information search than are other purchases. The brochure is invariably an important source of information relating specifically to the operators' product offers including content, availability, price and quality. In addition to being a source of information, 'destination brochures play a particularly vital role in this image-building process' (Pritchard and Morgan, 1997, p. 347). The 'hard copy' brochure is displaced to some extent by online brochures – that of the UK gay operator, Throb, is available only online – and by interrogating web sites of accommodation and transport providers. None the less, the printed brochure retains a significance for many travellers, including those who may subsequently book with tour operators online or make arrangements other than through tour operators, such as direct bookings.

In the UK, mainstream tour operators have made some efforts to target the gay and lesbian market, though attempts in recent years have not always been successful (Summerskill, 2001). A number of mainstream travel agents have also endeavoured to target the market: Going Places (travel agency arm of MyTravel) set up Travel Unlimited as a gay division of its telesales service in 2000 and was the first mainstream company to target the gay and lesbian market (Walker, 2000). Thomas Cook was selling Respect holidays through its travel agency branches in 2002, the only mainstream agency to do so (Wells, 2002). As some gays and lesbians may not feel comfortable arranging their holidays in high street travel agents, the UK's first call centre travel agency exclusively for gays and lesbians (http://www.gayplaces4u.com, part of United Cooperatives) was launched in 2004. A similar service was offered by http://www.friendsofdot.com, part of Co-op Travel.

The UK Mintel survey (2000a) did show that most of the gays and lesbians surveyed used mainstream operators and agents and only 3% of respondents booked through gay travel agents or tour operators. None the less, specialist tour operators have developed. Gays and lesbians may well find it difficult to ask mainstream tour operators or travel agents about the issues that are important to them as travellers. Apart from this unease factor, mainstream operators may not have the knowledge about destinations and accommodation that specialist operators have (Rob Harkavy, Respect Holidays, London, 2004, personal communication). Mainstream operators and their travel agencies have perhaps not given sufficient recognition to the needs of gays and lesbians for gay-friendliness and lack of homophobia, and there may be a perception that they are not particularly interested in this market. In addition, mainstream providers will not regard it as making economic sense to provide for the needs of those gay and lesbian tourists (a minority) who are looking for gay-specific or gay-centric holidays.

Mainstream operators may also be regarded as irrelevant by gays and lesbians because of the perceived targeting of the heterosexual market through use of heterosexual imagery, including that of 'traditional' families. This 'invisibility' of gays and lesbians may also serve to alienate them and turn them away in search of other provision, such as that of specialist tour operators.

Despite these issues that help explain the rise and survival of the specialist operator, there is nothing inevitable about a shift of gays and lesbians away from mainstream. It is becoming increasingly possible for potential tourists to research destinations and accommodation though many sources such as guide books and the Internet (including web sites of specialist operators) and then to book with mainstream operators through the High Street or through mainstream online travel companies. Such personal research also facilitates direct bookings with carriers and accommodation.

US specialist tour operators

There are numerous small operators targeting the gay and lesbian market in the USA. Many offer special-interest holidays rather than the sun and sea holiday primarily associated with UK tour operators. Most are not wholly inclusive, in that transport to the location or tour starting point is not included in the price, though arrangements can be made. Many are small, 'upmarket' and offer special-interest holidays and reflect the market research image of gay men, in particular – upmarket, cultured and seeking more than sea and sun or sex. Some target a more 'caring' clientele wishing to relate closely to their destinations and cultures and many offer tour programmes that individual clients will experience as part of a small and exclusively gay (or lesbian) group.

One US company, 'David Tours', offered five-star customized holiday tours to southern Africa, central Europe, India and Scandinavia, in particular with the opportunity to meet local gays (Wells, 2001). Tour parties were typically six to twenty individuals, many of whom were couples. It also traded on its reputation as 'a queer eye for the straight traveller' by targeting straight customers. 'Hanns Ebensten', regarded by some as the first tour operator to cater for gay travellers, has operated since 1972. Tours are again for small groups, typically to exotic and extraordinary places, but with comfort (see Chapter 5). 'Footprints', based in Toronto, offers small group tours to destinations such as Thailand, Vietnam, Nepal, Tibet, Turkey and Bolivia. 'Zoom' has taken groups ranging in size from two to 100 to destinations worldwide: their clients 'typically seek a deeper physical, cultural and emotional bond with the people, places, sights and entertainment choice of featured destinations yet demand the highest level of comfort, service and value'.

There is a significant segment of the industry that caters to a demand for adventure holidays. 'OutWest Global Adventures', founded in 1995, claims to offer the same high level of quality as mainstream companies at similar prices (see Chapter 5). Accommodation is upscale, most clients are in their 30s to 50s and most are singles. 'Toto Tours', founded in 1990, also offers small-group adventure travel for gay men and seek 'to promote understanding and acceptance through interaction with fellow travellers and other cultures around the world'.

Cruises are a significant part of the US gay and lesbian tourism market and cruise organizers operate on a larger scale than most of the rest of the 'dedicated' industry (see Chapter 5).

UK specialist tour operators and travel agents

UK tour operators offer programmes that are more sea and sun-oriented than are those of US operators. This is despite the fact that they may not be able to compete price-wise (or otherwise) with the mainstream sun and sea inclusive package holiday operators. Their prices for this form of holiday may well be higher, because of lower sales volume, than those of mainstream operators, though Respect was founded in 1998 to provide affordable holidays for gays and lesbians out of a conviction that others were charging a premium (Rob Harkavy, Respect Holidays, London, 2004, personal communication). The specialist market in the UK is dominated by Respect and Man Around, the latter also trading as Sensations and Alternative Holidays. Most of the product offer of Respect and Sensations is inclusive holidays (usually accommodation and air transport) to beach holiday destinations in Europe. They, and other tour operators, offer a range of accommodation, all of which is designated as, at least, gay-friendly. Some accommodation, especially apartments, is exclusively gay or lesbian. Respect offers holidays in their own all-gay 'resort' in Gran Canaria which, for a week in June 2005, was exclusively all-lesbian. This Women's Week had been organized by two of the few lesbian bars in the UK, the Candy Bar in London and Vanilla in Manchester. In addition to inclusive holidays, Respect and the others also offer the flexibility of accommodation-only and flight-only bookings.

Man Around, which merged with Sensations in 1999, offered destinations in 2005 that included Bangkok, Phuket, Pattaya and Chiang Mai in Thailand. It is also the sole UK agent for the Sydney Mardi Gras and for the OutGames 2006 (see later). Sensations focuses on the European beach holiday market and, like Respect, has its own exclusive gay resort (Club Tucanes) on Gran Canaria. Alternative Holidays was founded 1997, created the first European Ski Week and became part of Man Around in 2001. About 400 gays and lesbians attended the 2003 ski week in the French Alps. The UK gay and lesbian ski market is also targeted by Dream Waves, whose annual ski week is operated in connection with Mark Warner, a large, mainstream ski holiday specialist operator. Alternative also organizes exclusive resort holidays on the Atlantis model. This was held in Sicily in 2003 and in Sardinia in 2004 and attracted between 600 and 650 clients, mostly men. The week-long holidays include a programme of sport and pool and dance parties; the atmosphere has been described in a gay newspaper as 'a happy combination of social and sexy' (Tatchell, 2003, p. 25). Notwithstanding this, the 2004 week was featured on the national BBC TV *Holiday* programme.

AMRO is a relative newcomer (founded in 2002) and has a focus on long-haul holidays that others had previously not provided. The inability to compete with mainstream sun and sea operators explains, in part, the decision to focus on a programme similar to that provided by US operators. Group holidays are offered but most holidays are tailored to individual requirements and specific needs of the market, a particular strength of the specialist operator (Andrew Roberts, Amro Holidays, Borehamwood, UK, 2004, personal communication). The programme offered includes 'Inca Highlights' and 'Gay Marrakech'; the most popular destinations include the USA, Latin America, Hong Kong and Australia. AMRO have also given prominence to lesbian holiday opportunities: in particular, they have marketed all-women accommodation in the USA, including resorts in New Hampshire, Key West, Palm Springs and Russian River.

Other UK specialist tour operators include Away Gay, which also tailors holidays to individual requirements, mainly to South Africa, New Zealand and Australia. As with other gay and lesbian specialists, they offer reassurance that all accommodation has been vetted for gay-friendliness, but also assure that 'all of our travel documents, ticket wallets, luggage labels, etc. are subtle and tasteful' as if, by implication, others are not. Gay Boats is a small operator catering for a particular niche market – canal boat holidays in the UK (see Fig. 6.1). This grew from a personal interest of the founders and a belief that gays and lesbians would appreciate a wider choice of holiday type than is currently on offer (Michael Gibberd, Exclusively Gay Cruising Company, Ilkeston, UK, 2004, personal communication).

Rainbow Holidays, part of Superbreak Mini Holidays, the UK market leader for short breaks, has a programme of short breaks throughout the UK that are specifically designed for same-sex couples. Initially, in 2002, they followed a policy of ensuring that all hotels used were 'gay-friendly', but this is no longer the case as, according to the web site, 'we have identified [that] most hotels make every effort to be welcoming to all visitors' (http://www.rainbowholidays.com). This may be optimistic, though hotels in their programme are usually (though not always) part of national or international chains.

There are few gay and lesbian travel agencies as such, though undoubtedly there are individual agents who are sympathetic to the

Fig. 6.1. Press advertisement produced by The Exclusively Gay Cruising Company (UK).

requirements of this market either because of own sexuality or because of awareness of market potential. Village Travel was established in 2005 in premises in Manchester's Gay Village as a walk-in and call centre travel agency, targeted solely at the gay and lesbian market. They deal with both mainstream and gay tour operators and consider that one of their particular strengths is the ability to inform clients of the gay-friendliness of destinations, accommodation and the like (Tony Bloomfield, Village Travel, 2005, personal communication). The range of holidays offered is illustrated in the advertisement shown in Fig. 6.2.

Lesbian tour operators

Lesbian-specific tour operators are few compared with the gay men's market: lesbians looking for targeted holidays may find it more difficult than do gay men. It may be that there is an untapped lesbian holiday market but lesbian-specific destinations or venues in gay and lesbian brochures are few compared with the male gay scene. It is observable from the content of brochures that the major tour operators aiming at the gay and lesbian market in the UK focus primarily on the male segment. It is possible that lesbians are as much alienated by the lack of female imagery as both gays and lesbians are likely to be by the heterosexual imagery of mainstream brochures and advertisements. Advertisements are occasionally altered to show either women or men together according

Fig. 6.2. Press advertisement produced by Village Travel, Manchester (UK).

to the publication in which they are placed, though the copy is unchanged (e.g. Away Gay – see Figs 6.3 and 6.4).

Images of women have barely featured in the past in brochures of, for instance, two major UK operators, Respect and Sensations, which are clearly aimed at a male audience – the male image on the front cover, for instance, of Respect's brochure conveys an obvious indication of this (see Fig. 6.5). For 2005, however, Respect offered a 'Women's Week' in Gran Canaria and the Sensations 2005 brochure carried pictures of women together on several pages. Its separate Gran Canaria brochure also gives more prominence to women. AMRO does promote 'exclusive women's resorts', usually in the USA (see Fig. 5.4) and about 40% of its customers are lesbian (Andrew Roberts, Amro Holidays, Borehamwood, UK, 2004, personal communication).

There is a more obvious provision for lesbians in the USA, where the market is larger and more developed. Some US circuit parties (see later), hotels, weekend camps and the like are specifically targeted at lesbians. Some of the resorts (e.g. in Key West) and circuit parties (e.g. in Palm Springs) mirror gay men's provision but often the focus is different, with holidays in small guest houses in 'quiet' places other than the popular destinations associated with gay men's travel. One of the few exceptions is the promotion of holidays in Lesvos by several UK operators. Apart from this, holidays in the UK lesbian press are usually offered by small

Fig. 6.3. Press advertisement produced by Away Gay Holidays (UK).

Fig. 6.4. Press advertisement produced by Away Gay Holidays (UK).

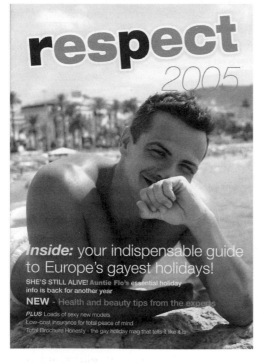

Fig. 6.5. Front cover page of the 2005 summer brochure for Respect Holidays (UK).

operators who emphasize privacy and seclusion in guest houses or small hotels. There is also a noticeable provision of special-interest holidays such as walking, heritage or cultural. Advertisements and promotional material for these holidays usually avoid reference to the word 'lesbian' and use terms such as 'women-only' instead.

Online travel companies

Travel web sites such as Expedia offer the facility to book accommodation and transport, bypassing the traditional tour operator or travel agent, and are of increasing importance. They offer the obvious advantages of flexibility in planning a holiday programme compared with the pre-packaged programmes of many tour operators, and are also able to compete favourably price-wise. As with the traditional intermediaries however, not all will be gay-friendly in that there is no facility for obtaining advice about destinations or accommodation. Some of these travel sites, such as the US-based Orbitz, do have dedicated gay and lesbian micro-sites featuring, for instance, gay-friendly hotels. Orbitz was set up originally by several US airlines in 2000–2001, and is the third largest US online travel site. It is now part of the Cendant Corporation, which also includes ebookers and Octopus Travel. This latter, a UK organization, also established a gay and lesbian micro-site in 2005 (http://www.Octopustravel-gay.com). The success of such sites will depend on their ability to offer something that other travel sites do not: gay and lesbian-specific knowledge and advice and assurances of gay-friendly products.

Trade associations

The International Gay and Lesbian Travel Association (IGLTA) is a US-based trade association of organizations with an interest in the gay and lesbian travel market. It existence and continuing membership growth (over 900 members in 2005 from five in 1983) is indicative of the growth of the market and the increased awareness of market potential (http://www.iglta.org). Its members include tour operators, travel agents, cruise lines (such as Atlantis), accommodation providers, airlines (such as United and American) and visitor bureaus. Most of its members are in the USA, but it does have an international membership that includes airlines such as QANTAS, Virgin Atlantic and visitor bureaus such as Marketing Manchester (UK), Vienna Tourist Board and Tourism New South Wales. It provides a networking opportunity through regular newsletters, symposia and conventions, but it also seeks to promote professionalism and a dedication to serving the needs of gay and lesbian travellers. As part of this it provides an educational programme and it awards IGLTA-accreditation.

Similar networking organizations exist at other levels, for instance, Gay and Lesbian Tourism Australia (GALTA). New Zealand Gay and Lesbian Tourism (NZGLTA) aims to develop gay and lesbian tourism further in NZ both through service provision and promotion. It also operates an accreditation scheme (Rainbow Tourism Accreditation) which requires a commitment beyond 'gay-friendliness'.

Accommodation

It has already been noted that accommodation can be a particularly difficult issue for gay and lesbian travellers. A number of hoteliers and other accommodation providers have recognized this and have taken steps to make the situation easier by emphasizing 'gay-friendliness' or 'gay-exclusive'. In Figs 6.6 and 6.7, for instance, the Bondi Hotel is advertised as 'exclusively gay' and Gabrielle's as 'exclusively lesbian'. Trades Hotel (Fig. 6.8) is also direct but in another way – a hotel for 'men seeking men'. In an ingenious twist, the New Amsterdam Hotel uses the strapline 'straight friendly' (see Fig. 6.9).

Some hotels and resorts indicate a women-only policy. The consortium 'Women Innkeepers of Provincetown' (Fig. 6.10) is made up of nine inns owned by women, and guests are invited to 'express your feelings in Provincetown'. Pearls' Rainbow, a Key West resort exclusively for women, is described as a 'testosterone-free zone' and Highlands Inn (New Hampshire) states it has served the lesbian community since 1983. The web site http://www.womenstaynewzealand.com advertises a range of homestays, guest houses and inns in that country that are woman-friendly and lesbian-friendly. From some accommodation web sites, it would appear that 'women-only' does not always mean 'exclusively lesbian'.

The US-based Travel Alternatives Group (TAG) operates a scheme of 'approved accommodation', which are claimed to be genuinely gay-welcoming properties. Over 700 properties worldwide are TAG-accredited. In addition, TAG organizes seminars to encourage 'best practices' in targeting and promoting to this market. It does also accredit travel agents and organizes educational programmes and familiarization tours for them.

The provision of exclusively gay or lesbian apartments by some tour operators offers the security and privacy that some may require. An unusual instance is the Coyote Moon Health Resort and Spa (Tucson, Arizona), which opened in October 2004, as 'the only health resort and spa to offer [a] range of holistic health, spa, fitness, lectures, daytrips (hiking, biking, horse trail rides, etc.) and entertainment programs tailored specifically to needs of gays and lesbians' (http://www.qtmagazine.com, 2004). Individual hotels may also promote themselves as gay- or lesbian-friendly

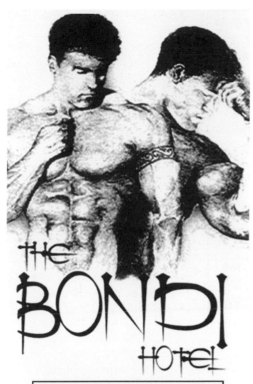

THE

BONDI

HOTEL

EXCLUSIVELY GAY
43, ST. MICHAELS RD,
BOURNEMOUTH,
DORSET, BH2 5DP.
TEL/FAX
(01202) 554893
email: thebondi@hotmail.com
www.thebondi.co.uk

Fig. 6.6.   Press advertisement produced by Bondi Hotel, Bournemouth (UK).

or as women-only. An indication of gay or lesbian ownership may also offer reassurance (see also Chapter 7). Pinkotel is a central hotel reservation agency, launched in the UK in 2005, which made a particular selling point of avoiding hotels that claimed to be gay-friendly. This was on the grounds that many did not fulfil their promise and therefore it would offer only hotels that were gay-run and provided accommodation specifically for gays and lesbians (http://www.pinkotel.com). Accommodation included Turtle Cove resort in Cairns and the Glen Boutique Hotel in Cape Town.

   Mainstream hotel companies have targeted the gay and lesbian market by, for instance, advertising in gay and lesbian magazines. A full-page

Fig. 6.7. Press advertisement produced by Gabrielle's Hotel, Blackpool (UK).

Fig. 6.8. Press advertisement produced by Trades and Rainbows Hotels, Blackpool (UK).

Fig. 6.9.   Press advertisement produced by Hotel New Amsterdam, Herengracht, Amsterdam, The Netherlands.

Fig. 6.10.   Press advertisement produced by Women Innkeepers of Provincetown, Massachusetts, USA.

advertisement for Holiday Inn, Intercontinental and Crowne Plaza hotels in *Gay Times* (UK), May 2001, showed a picture of two men, one with his arm around the other's shoulder. A full-page advertisement for Moat House Hotels (May 2005) featured a picture of a semi-naked man (alone) in bed with the strapline 'it might not be long but it feels good'. In the USA, Seattle Days Inn and La Jolia, California, Hyatt, ran gay print ads as early as 1994, and in 2000 Hyatt ran corporate campaigns in gay magazines. In 2003, the MGM Mirage properties, Borgata (Atlantic City) and New York–New York (Las Vegas), entered the gay market as did the group's Luxor resort (Las Vegas), with an advertisement showing two men hugging (Wilke, 2004). Also in the USA, 'while individual hotels have been seeking gays for years, Wyndham International and Westin hotels and Resorts are the latest chains to open their doors to the gay market' (Wilke, 2004). Wyndham ran a gay-specific print campaign in 2004 which included an advertisement referring to a male partner, promoting Wyndham's 'ByRequest' programme in which members get customized room amenities including snacks, drinks, pillows and bathrobes. This programme is also aimed, though tailored differently, at other niche markets including women, Latinos, seniors and Afro-Americans.

W Hotels (Starwood's 'chic boutique' mini-chain), which has five hotels in New York and 19 elsewhere (including Mexico and Seoul), ran an advertisement in *OUT* in 1998 (Wilke, 2004). In 2003, its advertisement featured two men in bed and it emphasized that its front desk and other staff were trained to expect same-sex couples. 'Pride 365' was a year-long W Hotels weekend package that celebrated the gay and lesbian community. The package included 'Dirty Linens' pillowcases (inspired by Tom of Finland) and CD, as well as special room rates. The Red Carnation hotel group also trains employees to ensure that gay and lesbian guests receive the same level of service as all other guests, e.g. front desk staff not to assume that same-sex couples want twin beds and concierges to hold information about local gay nightlife (Steele, 2004).

Individual hotels may join in joint efforts to target the gay and lesbian market. As with other hotel consortia, this is seen as a way of gaining the critical mass to compete in marketing with chain hotels – for instance, the 'Women Innkeepers of Provincetown' consortium mentioned earlier. The consortium 'World's Foremost Gay and Lesbian Hotels' has a membership of 'upmarket' hotels that concentrate solely on the gay and lesbian market (see Fig. 6.11). In October 2004 there were 21 members, most of whom were in the USA, but also in Mexico, Canada and Australia. Locations included the 'popular' destinations of Puerto Vallarta, Toronto, Hawaii, Palm Springs (4), Fort Lauderdale (3), Key West (4), Provincetown (4), San Francisco, New Hampshire and Cairns. A similar approach is adopted by gay-friendly hotels, resorts and apartments participating in a destination promotion, e.g. the Fort Lauderdale joint advertisement covering several resorts and guest houses. Brighton in the UK has used a

Fig. 6.11.   Press advertisement produced by World's Foremost Gay and Lesbian Hotels.

similar advertisement (see Fig. 6.12). A number of hotels, guest houses and apartments in the seaside town of Blackpool (the largest in the UK) have joined to form the marketing consortium of 'Blackpool Accommodation for Gays' (BAGs). This association of over 60 establishments offers

Fig. 6.12. Press advertisement produced by Gaydealsbrighton.co.uk, Brighton (UK).

assurances of gay-ownership, produces a leaflet and operates its own web site (http://www.bagsblackpool.com).

The Pink Route in South Africa is a similar collection of gay-owned or gay-friendly lodges, hotels and guest houses including several in Cape Town (http://www.pinkroute.co.za). It also includes accommodation in the winelands, eastern Cape, the Garden Route, Johannesburg and a game lodge close to Kruger National Park.

Not all gay and lesbian travellers will be seeking hotel, resort or apartment accommodation. The Freedom Club (UK) is a gay caravanning and camping club that organizes 'meets' in the UK and across Europe (http://www.freedomclub.co.uk). It uses sites, however, that are also used by heterosexuals and it asks its members to behave in such a way so as to not draw attention to gayness or to cause offence. A desire for 'freedom' and privacy is particularly indicated by 'Lezzie Camp'. This is a low-cost, collective cooperative venture which has operated since the early 1990s, offering camping holidays (in tents) to lesbians, including those with children, in a secluded rural part of the UK (http://www.lezziecamp.co.uk).

Others have identified alternative accommodation that might be particularly suited to the needs of gays and lesbians. Home exchange through an organization such as 'Home Around the World' (UK) arranges stays with other gay people on a reciprocal arrangement basis. It is promoted as avoiding the hassle encountered in hotels and as offering the opportunity to make new friends. The Lesbian and Gay Hospitality Exchange International (Berlin-based), founded 1991, is a network of gays and lesbians in over 30 countries that offers free hospitality to other members at no charge for up to 2 nights at a time.

'Attractions'

When tourists travel, they may see or visit a particular 'tourist sight' such as the Eiffel Tower (Paris) or the Empire State Building (New York), or an event such as the Olympic Games. There is a great variety of 'sights' and events – tourist attractions – and they may either be particularly influential in the decision to travel or they may be incidental to the main purpose. Gay and lesbian tourists will undoubtedly visit the same tourist sights as do other tourists but there may also be other attractions which have a particular appeal to this market. Gay and lesbian sporting events such as the Gay Games, and parades and festivals such as the Sydney Mardi Gras, can be expected to act as particular stimuli to travel. The circuit parties that have characterized the US gay scene in particular are also believed to be a significant feature in travel decisions. (See, for instance, AMRO holidays offered to the Key West Pride and to the Disneyworld circuit party – Fig. 6.13.) These will be considered in the rest of this chapter, as will the rather different factor of same-sex marriage and partnerships. These are available in only a few places and, as such, may be an increasingly important reason for travel.

It is possible that some tourists may have a particular interest in gay and lesbian heritage, even if only as part of a wider vacation trip: the site of the Stonewall 'riots' in Greenwich Village (New York) may be a place of

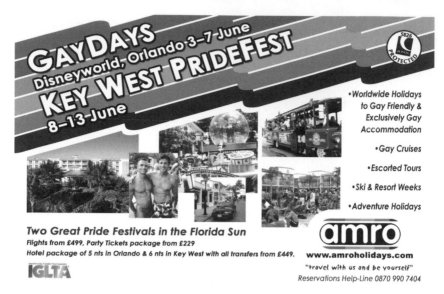

Fig. 6.13.   Press advertisement produced by AMRO Holidays (UK).

Fig. 6.14.   'Gay Liberation' by George Segal, Stonewall Place, New York, USA.

pilgrimage for some. 'Gay Liberation' is a sculpture in Stonewall Place outside the reconstructed Stonewall Inn (Fig. 6.14). The 'homomonument' in Amsterdam may have similar significance. This is a composition in the form of three large, horizontal, granite triangles which commemorates

Fig. 6.15. Homomonument by Karin Daan, Westermarkt and Keizergracht, Amsterdam, The Netherlands.

Nazi persecution of gays and lesbians, but which has become a symbol of a more general world-wide discrimination. The monument dates from 1987 and is located on a prominent canal-side site close to the Anne Frank House (see Fig. 6.15). The AIDS memorial in Company's Garden, Cape Town (Fig. 6.16) has a particular poignancy in a country where such a large proportion of the population is HIV-positive.

A lesbian and gay heritage trail has been developed in Manchester (UK), with places of significance marked by rainbow tiles set into the pavement. The trail takes in the memorial to Alan Turing, a pioneer of computer development who committed suicide in 1954 following a prosecution for homosexual activity. It also includes the Beacon of Hope, the UK's only HIV/AIDS memorial. Oscar Wilde has a particular significance for many gays and lesbians, if only because of his famed trial and subsequent imprisonment for gross indecency in 1895. Silver Cane Tours offer a variety of London walking tours, including one entitled 'Oscar Wilde's West End'. This includes the Savoy Hotel, where Wilde and Lord Alfred Douglas stayed for 3 weeks, the Café Royale and Vine Street Police Station, where the warrant for Wilde's arrest was issued (http://www.uk. gay.com).

Marriage and Partnerships

The gradual legalization of marriage and of partnerships between same-sex couple in several parts of the world has created a new market in

Fig. 6.16.   AIDS memorial at Company's Garden, Cape Town, South Africa.

ceremonies comparable to that for heterosexual weddings and celebrations. The extension of legalized same-sex marriage throughout Canada would, it was believed, encourage visits for the purpose of marriage, but would also contribute further to the gay-friendly image of the country (Johnston, 2004). It was reported that in Toronto nearly half of the 2000 marriage licences issued since 2003 had been to couples from the USA and from elsewhere outside Canada. Toronto may well have an advantage in this respect as there is no minimum residence requirement, whereas in Quebec there is a 30-day waiting period. The Gay Toronto Tourism Guild web site has a section devoted to same-sex marriage and how to arrange it, along with details of 'wedding packages'. Over 800 same-sex couples from the USA were married in British Columbia (Canada) in 2003 (Shenker, 2005) and within a year of same-sex marriage being legalized in Massachusetts, 'tourism in Provincetown has exploded with same-sex couples rushing to the resort town for licences' (van Metzke, 2005). About half of international respondents to an online gay travel survey felt that the ability to get married was, to them, an attraction to visit Canada, though only 14% planned to visit to get married (http://www.gaytravelguides. info, 2004).

A study of the implications of same-sex marriage for California's state finances concluded that there could be a boost to tourism and consequent increased sales tax revenue of between US$4 and US$6.9 million per year during the first 3 years (Sears and Badgett, 2004). This represented up to 27% of all savings on the state budget that could arise from same-sex marriages. The short-lived issue of marriage certificates in San Francisco attracted couples from 46 states and eight countries to get married. The gay and lesbian travel campaign launched by Boston and Cambridge (Massachusetts) in 2005 was, in part, based on positioning the state in the market for gay weddings (Johnson, 2005b).

The registration of same-sex partnerships recognized in law has been permitted in the UK from December 2005. The city of Liverpool has been styling itself as the leading British city for same-sex commitment ceremonies for some time prior to this, when registration without legal significance was being offered by several cities including London, Manchester and Brighton (Herbert, 2005). It is one of only a few that did not have a residency requirement and was the first city to make a gay couple the focus of its civil ceremony publicity material, by featuring two men on the cover of its main brochure (a non-marriage ceremony available to both homo and hetero couples). The first ceremony was in 2002, since which time 24 male and 31 female ceremonies have taken place and many of the couples were from outside the city. One enterprising UK company (White Sands Commitments) has been offering commitment ceremonies in New York, Las Vegas and Hawaii.

There are obviously opportunities for individual hotels or hotel groups to take advantage of these changes. It has, in recent years in the UK, become possible to have civil heterosexual marriage ceremonies in a number of locations other than registry offices. These alternative locations include hotels, which are evidently well-placed to offer not only venues for ceremonies but also 'packages' of accommodation and catering. As civil partnership ceremonies for same-sex couples become legal in the UK these locations are likely to experience demand from gays and lesbians. The Crowne Plaza hotel in London's Dockland, for instance, advertised in the May 2005 edition of *Gay Times* in anticipation of the legalization later that year.

Sport

Others will have a particular interest in sport. In the USA, in particular, a large number of gay and lesbian sporting teams and leagues exist and these, like all sporting events, attract spectators (Pitts, 1999). Teams and individual competitors will be tourists when competing in away fixtures and there has been such an increase in the number of events that there are sports travel packages targeted at this participant market. In addition, about half of the travel companies listed in gay and lesbian travel guides (US) mention or specialize in sports activity travel products such as archery, hang-gliding, swimming, soccer, golf, sailing, hiking, rafting and trekking. The Gay and Lesbian Tennis Alliance was formed 1991 and there are over 39 annual GLTA-sanctioned tournaments, mostly in the USA but also The Netherlands, Switzerland and the UK. They attract about 5000 players each year, though tend to be male-dominated. The PINKster Tennis Tournament (Amsterdam) is unusual in that participants are about 50 : 50 male : female, and over 300 international participants were expected in 2005. It has been alleged that the annual Eastbourne (UK) women's tennis festival attracts a large number of lesbian spectators (Lee, 2000). Gay rodeos are popular in the USA and are likely to have tourism potential. They are held throughout North America and have attracted sponsors such as Bud Light and American Airlines. The International Gay Rodeo Association fosters rodeo and Country and Western activities.

The Bulgarian Rainbow Sport Festival was promoted to US and Western European participants as the 'first international gay tournament in the Balkans' in 2005. It was organized by a gay and lesbian sports club in Sofia and held at a Black Sea resort. Sports included badminton, volleyball, running, soccer, swimming and tennis.

Gay Games

The sporting event that is believed to have the greatest tourism potential is the Gay Games. These have been held every 4 years since the first in San Francisco in 1982. The purpose has been to foster and augment self-respect of lesbians and gay men and to engender the respect and understanding of the non-gay world (http://www.gaygames.com). Initially the Games were held in the USA and Canada, though moved to Amsterdam in 1998. The number of visitors to each of the Games is not known with certainty but the organizing committee has claimed that the Amsterdam Games were attended by 'a quarter of a million visitors from all over the world'. Participants have undoubtedly been international (from 40 countries at the 1994 New York games) and the numbers have grown from 1350 in 1982 to 11,000–13,000 in 1998 and 2002. The latest was held in Sydney in 2002 using Olympic facilities. The number of athletes was 13,000 (about 10,000 from outside Australia) and the opening ceremony (featuring k d lang and Jimmy Somerville) had an audience of 25,000. The organizing company subsequently reported a £500,000 loss. The Australian Tourist Commission estimated that AUS$100,000 would be generated for the New South Wales economy and it capitalized on the opportunity by launching the web site http://www.Gay.Australia.com, aimed especially at the US market. Like many such mega-events, the Gay Games have been accompanied by a cultural programme, but this has been a major contribution to the overall deficits incurred on each occasion since the 1990 Games in Vancouver (Federation of Gay Games, 2003).

The 2006 Games were to be held in Montreal on the site of the 1976 Olympics, but a dispute between the Federation of Gay Games and Montreal over scale and finance meant that they were to be moved to Chicago. The Montreal event, however, is to go ahead regardless, and will be known as the Outgames: 16,000 competitors are expected. The Chicago Gay Games were planning for 12,000 athletes from over 100 countries. The magnitude of these Games can be judged by the fact that 20,000 rooms were reserved at nine downtown hotels in the city in 2004 by the organizers, with a further 20,000 to be added later (http://www.qtmagaazine.com). The Hilton Chicago and Palmer House Hilton are to be the Games' 'Hub Hotels'.

The EuroGames have had similar aims to those of the Gay Games: to fight against discrimination in sport and to stimulate integration. They were first staged in The Netherlands in 1992 (300 participants) and then in Paris in 1997 (2000 participants from 17 countries). The award of the 1999 Games to the city of Manchester (UK) was withdrawn as there was insufficient evidence of commitment and planning on the part of the local organizing committee and the city council. Zurich hosted the 2000 EuroGames and attracted 4300 athletes; Munich in 2004 expected 5300 participants and 20,000 visitors. A 'large' EuroGames is now held every 4 years (2 years after each Gay Games) with a 'smaller' games in the odd years, limited to 1500 participants.

Circuit Parties

These are particularly associated with the gay and lesbian scene in the USA, though do also exist elsewhere. They have been described as 'weekend-long, erotically-charged, drug-fuelled gay dance events held in resorts across the country' (Ghaziani, 2005). They typically are annual events of discos, parties, pool parties, club nights, dinners, concerts and entertainment, in different venues held over several days in resort towns or major cities. There are well over 100 of these in the USA, the largest and most well-known of which are probably the White Party for men and Dinah Shore Weekend for women – both in Palm Springs (in the spring), the White Party (Miami, November), the Winter Party Festival (Miami, March), the Black and Blue Festival (Montreal), Gay Days (Orlando, June) and Sydney's Mardi Gras.

Circuit parties are not confined to beach-related holidays or to cities, but also include holidays such as Ski Weeks. Ostensibly these offer opportunities for skiing with other gays and lesbians but they also usually include evening parties in their programmes. The party-goers often attend every year but also attend several of the parties in any one year – hence the 'circuit'. In a San Francisco survey of the sexual health of male circuit party-goers, 32% of the respondents had attended one circuit party outside the city in the previous year and 40% had attended two or more such parties (Mansergh *et al.*, 2001). Circuit party-goers are typically young, affluent professionals: in the San Francisco survey most were under 35, white and had an annual income of over US$40,000 per year.

The parties, though often focusing on one large themed dance event, are usually multi-event (eight parties in 4 days at Palm Springs in 2004), many of which occur on the same night, in a range of different venues including hotels, clubs and beaches. The Miami Winter Party 2005 included social and cultural events in museums and galleries. Some of the events are organized by professional commercial operators such as the Jeffrey Sanker Agency at Palm Springs and Orlando and Club Skirts at Dinah Shore, Palm Springs, and nearly all of the larger ones make some financial contribution to gay and lesbian or related charities. The Miami Winter Festival is a 5-day event and, according to the organizers, attracts about 10,000 international participants. It is produced by the National Gay and Lesbian Task Force (NGLTF, founded in 1973 as the first national lgbt civil rights organization in the USA) and two-thirds of proceeds go to the South Florida lgbt community and the rest to NGLTF. The White Party in the same city (about 15,000 participants) was started in 1985 and is now the largest source of funds for the local HIV/AIDS charity. The Montreal Black and Blue Fest gives financial support to HIV organizations and lgbt community groups. Aqua Girl is a not-for-profit women's weekend in Miami: proceeds go to the Women's Community Fund which promotes equality, health and visibility of lgbt women in South Florida. A golf tournament at the Russian River Women's Weekend raises money for breast cancer and women's health services.

The main reasons given by gay men for going to circuit parties were, according to the San Francisco survey, 'music and dance' (98% of respondents), 'to be with friends' (97%) and 'to be around beautiful men' (78%). Drugs and sex were low on list of reasons, at 57 and 30%, respectively (Mansergh *et al.*, 2001). The opportunity to renew acquaintance with friends at every party or every year seems to be an attraction, too, reinforcing the feeling of an international community (Brown, 2004).

There is little evidence of where circuit party participants have travelled from but there are frequent assertions in the party organizers' publicity and in the press that the participants are 'from around the world' and it seems that these parties are significant tourist 'attractions'. The 15th annual White Party in Palm Springs (2004) was believed to have attracted 20,000 men (Brown, 2004). The Black and Blue Festival (Montreal), which started in 1991 was, by 2002, a 7-day event with 80,000 attending. The 3-day alfresco Sundance Party at Guerneville (Russian River, California) in mid-August is on a more limited scale and attracts about 4000 gays, mainly from San Francisco and the surrounding area (Mellor, 2002a). The economic impact of the larger parties is believed to be sizeable: Black and Blue brings in US$12 million to hotels alone; the Palm Springs White Party 2004 added US$4 million to city revenues (hotel and sales taxes) and was one of the city's highest revenue-generating events (Brown, 2004). Many now also attract significant sponsors such as Finlandia Vodka, Bacardi Smirnoff Vodka, Bud Light, Orbitz, *Advocate* (national US gay and lesbian magazine) and Delta. Southern Decadence, an annual event over Labor Day weekend in New Orleans since 1972, is claimed to attract over 120,000 participants and to generate almost US$100m in 'tourist revenue'.

'Gay Days' at Orlando is believed to inject about US$100m into the local economy. A Gay and Lesbian Day has been held annually (in June) at Walt Disney World (Orlando) since 1991 and since then a long weekend of events has developed around it, yet neither the Day nor the weekend are official Disney events. Initially an informal initiative for gays and lesbians to meet at Disney World, it has become a circuit party weekend, the first White Party having been held in 1996. In 2005 the Wyndham Palace Resort and Spa (1000 rooms) in Walt Disney World Resort was the official Welcome Center and sponsors included Bud Light and Virgin Megastore. The popularity of the weekend is such that it has resulted in the publication of specific gay and lesbian travel guides such as *Queens in the Kingdom* by J. Epstein and E. Shapiro (2003) and *A Walt Disney World Resort Outing* (see also Chapter 4).

Lesbian circuit parties were generally later additions to the scene than were those of gay men, though the Women's Weekend at Russian River (California) originated in the 1980s. The May weekend is characterized by a golf tournament and events such as kayaking, horseback riding and garden tours during the day, with discos and parties at night. Aqua Girl started in 1999 and, in 2000, attracted 2000 participants, about 30% of whom were from outside Miami (Miller, 2002). Dinah Shore Weekend has been organized at Palm Springs since 1991 and attracts about 8000 women (Miller, 2002). It coincides with the ladies' professional golf championship. The tournament, started in 1972 by Dinah Shore, attracted a large lesbian following and, progressively, lesbian events grew around it (though not acknowledged by the Ladies' Professional Golf Association). Participants at lesbian circuit parties are, as in the men's parties, believed to be mostly upscale and aged under 35. One newspaper commentator observed that Dinah Shore, for instance, was all about the body beautiful, with much expensive jewellery and make-up in sight (Lee, 2002).

Some of the parties have, however, earned a reputation for 'excess' especially related to casual and unsafe sex, use of illicit drugs and alcohol abuse; some health organizations have stopped sponsoring circuit parties because of drug use (Brown, 2004). 'Drug use is incorporated into the setting as an integral part of circuit culture' (Ghaziani, 2005, p. 3). Gay Men's Health Crisis (NY) discontinued its relationship with Fire Island

Morning Party in 1999 due to publicity over drug overdose and a death at the 1998 party (Miller, 2002).

Parades and Festivals

Gay and lesbian parades and festivals are also undoubtedly elements of gay tourism: 'the innumerable Gay Pride events which now take place all over the world provide their own impetus for international gay travel' (Russell, 2001, p. 51). (LGBT events encompassing marches, parades and festivals are often referred to generically as Pride events.) Contemporary gay parades are commonly regarded as owing their origin to the Stonewall incident (variously referred to as 'riots' or 'rebellion') in New York in June 1969. The 'riots' took on iconic status and were commemorated in a gay march through New York and in other US cities on the first anniversary in 1970. Many of the earliest Pride marches and festivals were to commemorate Stonewall and to demand equal rights for gays and lesbians.

Protest parades have, however, become more festive and carnivalesque and, in the process, have generated a wider audience than as purely political events. The original parades may well have been associated with a desire to protest publicly about perceived injustices but both parades and festivals, whether directly political or festive, are often adjudged to have more subtle impacts. They occur in public space, they challenge its heteronormative nature in comparative safety and as such they are empowering (Brickell, 2000). They are a public display of sexuality and they create visibility and indicate presence, all of which can enhance self-esteem for gays and lesbians (Heckert, 2000).

They act too to generate a sense of inclusion and create group identity (Davis, 1995; Markwell, 2002): 'perhaps more than any other event in the city [of San Francisco], the Pride parade serves to consolidate and elaborate queer identity' (Howe, 2001, p. 42). It is believed that many spectators at Pride events are heterosexual (Johnston, 2001) and there is a frequently hoped-for positive influence on those spectators. Through awareness, understanding and tolerance may result. Of those who attended the 2004 Pride in Brighton (UK), 29% were heterosexual (Browne *et al.*, 2005), though this reflects only those who were at the Pride 'party' in the park and not those who watched the parade beforehand.

Many Pride festivals do maintain political campaigning missions. The Equality Forum in Philadelphia (previously PrideFest) claims to be more political than party and seeks to promote understanding of the effect of homophobia and to advance lgbt equality. In 2005 it marked what it referred to as the 40th anniversary of the lgbt civil rights movement. It is claimed that one of the first demonstrations for gay and lesbian rights was held in Philadelphia in 1965, 4 years before Stonewall.

Parades and festivals and tourism

There are a large number of Pride events worldwide: in 2001, events were planned by over 150 organizations in 23 countries. Some, such as those in Sydney, New York, Toronto and San Francisco were 'mega-events', whereas others were on a much smaller scale (http://www.interpride.org). Most have become accompanied by festivals and now expect to attract tourists. The annual Europride is the largest gay festival in Europe; the Europride in Cologne in 2002 is believed to have attracted 1.3 million visitors (Zarra and Ward, 2003). Worldwide, Pride events are believed to have drawn a combined attendance of 15–20 million in 2000 (http://www.interpride.org).

The Christopher Street Party (Berlin) claims to attract about half a million gays and lesbians, the São Paulo (Brazil) Pride parade in 2005 attracted two million people and the Heritage Pride parade (NY) along Fifth Avenue was watched by 350,000 spectators in 2004. Cape Town Pride features as part of the city's long-term tourism strategy and has been held in February, at least in part, to coincide with foreign tourism months (capetown.tv, 2004). A similar justification explained the shift of Sydney Mardi Gras to the same month in 1981. 'Pink Loerie', a much smaller-scale gay and lesbian festival in South Africa, was developed in 2001 to stimulate the fortunes of the coastal holiday town of Knysna; 5000 'visitors' were expected in 2003. EuroPride, an annual event, the first of which was in London in 1992, is due to be held in that city once more in 2006. It is predicted that it will give a £1billion boost to the tourist industry. Crowds on Canal Street, Manchester (UK) after the Pride parade are shown in Fig. 6.17.

A study of the 2004 Brighton Pride (UK) was one of the few to give detail relating to its tourism dimensions. The study showed that 78% of all lgbts (and 69% of all respondents) who were at the event were 'visitors', i.e. from outside Brighton and Hove (Browne *et al.*, 2005). Just under half were staying visitors and, of these, nearly three-quarters stayed at least two nights in the area. Pride was cited as the main reason for the visit by 74% of the staying visitors and by 95% of the day visitors. The most popular place to stay was with friends and relatives (44%), with a further 19% staying in hotels and 8% in bed and breakfast accommodation. It was estimated that Pride was responsible for an extra £3.1 million of visitor expenditure in the local economy.

London's Pride events have had a chequered history, especially recently, with different organizations competing to organize the festival element. Public protests were organized by the Gay Liberation Front in London in 1970 and 1971, leading to the first London 'Gay Pride' in July 1972, organized by the Campaign for Homosexual Equality; at that time it was still predominantly a 'political' event. The London Pride has gone through several transformations since, in respect of organization, focus and name: the term 'Pride' was dropped for the 1999 event, following a

Fig. 6.17. Canal Street, Manchester (UK), during Pride Weekend.

change of organizer, to be replaced by 'London Mardi Gras', with a subsequent return to 'Pride'. Unlike many other events such as that in Sydney, it was a 1-day event of march and festival. There has been ongoing debate about the commercialization of the festival and of the principle of a free festival (Field, 1995). Organizers, who have included consortia of London gay businesses, have been criticized 'for turning a free community event into a depoliticised and over-commercialised festival' (Smith, 2002, p. 41). By 2003, however, there were attempts by the organizers to restore its political edge; in that year it is estimated that 50,000 attended 'Pride in the Park' held in Hyde Park (Reid-Smith, 2003). Estimates of attendance at the 2004 Pride were between 30,000 and 100,000.

Some gay and lesbian festivals are less to do with overt political campaigning and more to do with celebration or showcasing gay and lesbian 'culture'. The Mother City Queer Project in Cape Town (December), for instance, aims to bring 'homosexuals and heterosexuals together in celebratory unifying way proving that differences of sexual orientation are simply part of any city's valuable cultural richness'. It is seen as a 'showcase for queer culture' and, according to the organizers, 'attracts thousands of visitors . . . International travel agents are chartering planes and planning trips for posses of pink playmates'. It started in 1994 and in 2000 it is estimated to have attracted 8000 people – many of whom were believed to be foreigners – and generated £4 million for the local economy (Macgregor, 2001). Two Australian festivals, Feast in Adelaide (since 1997) and Midsumma Melbourne (since 1989) are lgbt arts and cultural festivals of theatre, film, live music, cabaret, literature and visual arts, as well as sporting, social and political forums. The Melbourne festival is attended by over 100,000 people each year, and it is claimed by the organizers that by celebrating the pride and diversity of the local lgbt communities it identifies Melbourne as a culturally sophisticated city.

Sydney Mardi Gras

The Sydney Mardi Gras probably exhibits the greatest tension between the festive and tourism aspect of Pride and the political aspect. It has been one of the more successful as a tourist event but has always been characterized by concern over its direction (Ryan and Hall, 2001). Its origins lie in a 1978 protest march to commemorate Stonewall and to demonstrate for equality of human rights. The name Mardi Gras was adopted in 1979 and the event moved to summer (February) in 1981, partly to facilitate tourists (the term Mardi Gras has been adopted by some lgbt festivals as a generic term for festival and carnival, despite the original application of the term to pre-Lenten, non-gay-related celebrations). Pre- and post-parade parties and arts programmes were a feature of Sydney's festival within 4 years. It has become a month-long festival covering a range of cultural events culminating in the Parade and Mardi Gras Party. Its impact has been confined to building general public awareness rather than pursuing a particular political cause, and it has succeeded in forcing gay and lesbian issues (not least the existence of the parade itself) into the political arena (Marsh and Galbraith, 1995).

The 1998 festival was estimated to have had an impact of AUS$99 million on the city (http://www.mardigras.com.au). The festival features prominently in the programmes of tour operators, such as Atlantis, targeting the gay market; the UK operator Man Around labels it 'the greatest show on earth'. It is generally reckoned to attract more tourists to Australia than any other special event and to be a major tourist attraction in the country's tourist calendar, as well as defining Sydney as an international gay and lesbian city (Markwell, 2002). Sydney's Mardi Gras is used by the national tourism authority to promote tourism to Australia. An Australian Tourist Commission advertisement in a UK mainstream Sunday newspaper (*Observer Magazine*, 13 February 2005) highlighted Australian nightlife. This was illustrated by a picture of a person who appears to be a 'drag' participant at Sydney Mardi Gras. None of this is explicit, though there is reference to Mardi Gras in the text.

The bankruptcy of the Sydney Mardi Gras organizing company in August 2002 led to criticisms such as: 'it's grown too big and too commercialised . . . the event has lost its political edge' (Marks, 2002, p. 17). The new organizers, New Mardi Gras Ltd (NMGL) sought to re-examine the purpose of the event. They claimed that Mardi Gras had always been political but 'every year there are demands that the Parade be more political . . . and in the same year, complaints that it is too political and should be more glamorous' (NMGL, 2002, p. 1). It was claimed that the fun and celebration had contributed to the breakdown of barriers and to acceptance. The fundamental objects, it was suggested, should remain (amongst others) the pursuit of equal rights, increased visibility, education of the public and to 'affirm identity of GLBT people and enhance self-esteem' (NMGL, 2003). A commentator on the 2003 Mardi Gras none the less claimed that it is 'firmly in bed with corporate sponsors' (Fickling, 2003, p. 23).

Still political?

Notwithstanding the festival character of Pride events, there is still a strong belief that these are still primarily human rights events. Interpride, the international coordinating body of individual Prides, claims that 'together they represent the strength and commitment of people . . . who are determined to achieve, maintain and expand the rights of GLBT people' (http://www.interpride.org). For as long as there is a view that lgbt people are denied equality of human rights, Pride marches and festivals will undoubtedly continue. The first WorldPride (a title licensed by Interpride) was held in Rome in 2000 as a particular gesture against the Vatican's Millennium celebrations, as well as to campaign against discrimination affecting the Italian lgbt community (Graham, 2002; http://www.interpride.org). It is estimated that over one million people participated, mostly from North America and Western Europe (Luongo, 2002). The second WorldPride was due to be held in Jerusalem in 2005 but was postponed to the following year.

Given their festive qualities, it seems unlikely that Pride events would disappear even should equality be achieved. In addition, equality under the law will not necessarily remove societal disapproval or the desire to celebrate or to accentuate difference. The fact that Interpride registered events in only 23 countries suggests that there may be more Prides yet to emerge. Human rights continue to be denied to LGBT people in many countries. The political campaigning element of gay and lesbian parades remains strongest in those countries where the rights of gays and lesbians continue to be unrecognized under the law and where cultural attitudes are hostile. There has been no Pride event at all in Prague (the Czech Republic) nor Moscow, though Budapest (Hungary) staged its first in 1997 and Riga (Latvia) in 2005. In Poland there has been continuing opposition to the staging of the Equality Parade in Warsaw since it was first mooted in 1998. It was refused permission that year but was staged in 2003 when 3000 people took part, but was banned again in both 2004 and 2005. The grounds were fears of clashes with anti-gay demonstrators and concern for the religious feelings of others. A similar march in Krakow (Poland) in 2004 was attacked by right-wing demonstrators resulting in over 100 people being injured. In Croatia, the 300 marchers on the first Pride parade (Zagreb, 2002) were nearly equalled in number by the police escort. Despite the presence of the Minister of the Interior and the Prime Minister's wife on the march, violence broke out and 27 arrests made (Predrag *et al.*, 2002). The 2004 Pride passed off uneventfully and included a film festival, concerts and parties (Galliano, 2004). The first Pride march in Romania (in 2005) took place only after intervention by the country's President (Ridgeway, 2005, p. 79).

An Observation on 'Statistics'

The number of participants at circuit parties, parades and festivals and at sporting events has to be treated with some caution. This is especially the case for spectators at parades where there is no accurate way of determining numbers. Reservations about accuracy will arise, in part, because figures are often provided by the 'parent' organizations which may have a vested interest in quoting high numbers of both participants and spectators. Where there are no ticket sales, such as parades, there is no accurate way of determining numbers of spectators. Even if events are not free the number of admissions or tickets sold is not identical to the number of people attending, as some may buy tickets for more than one event over the duration of a festival.

Numbers of 'visitors' are often referred to without further qualification. There is no distinction made between participants and spectators, and none between those who are locals and those who are tourists who are staying overnight. In addition, in the particular case of tourists, it is dubious to claim that all who were at an event as spectators, in particular, were at a destination because of that event. They may have been there anyway or may have brought forward a planned visit, in which case there is no real inflow of tourism that is attributable to the event. It is possible too that any tourists that are present for a particular event have 'displaced' others who have been unable to or have been dissuaded from visiting; there may therefore be little net benefit to a destination.

'Impact' is sometimes quoted imprecisely. The impact of locals in terms of expenditure is quite different from that of tourists. In the former case it is a redistribution within a local economy, unless diverted from expenditure outside the area, whereas in the latter it is usually a net addition. In addition, it is not clear whether figures quoted refer to expenditure or income, which have significantly different values. Some expenditure estimates are also questionable, e.g. on its official web site it is estimated that Southern Decadence (New Orleans) generates US$100 million of 'tourist revenue'; this is calculated as number of 'revellers' (locals and visitors) × average spend of US$800 per person. Some criticisms of this include the point that figures of expenditure are notoriously difficult to determine with accuracy; it is unknown how the number of revellers is calculated and the expenditure of locals can, for the most part, be disregarded.

Conclusions

In terms of the supply side of gay and lesbian tourism, it is clear that there are organizations that are aware of and are seeking to satisfy the particular needs of the market. There is a recognizable demand expressed by many gays and lesbians for gay-friendliness at destinations and accommodation. In choosing these, tourists may consult many information and advice sources and, in some cases, they may feel that mainstream organizations, whether tour operators or travel agents, are not sympathetic enough to those needs. Most do continue to use these mainstream businesses but there has, none the less, been an emergence of specialist companies that satisfy the need of some for more sensitive relationships. In the UK, the more dominant specialist tour operators serve the traditional sun and sea market, though there are now a few companies offering a more varied programme. The US market is characterized by a large number of small specialist operators offering cultural and adventure holidays. The cruise market is also significant in the USA and is dominated by large operators such as Atlantis. Many accommodation providers are also emphasizing gay- and lesbian-friendliness in order to attract this market. Some of the larger hotel chains have recognized the potential and have developed targeted marketing campaigns.

In addition to all of the usual tourist attractions of the world, there are a number of 'sights' and events that may have a particular appeal to gays and lesbians. Heritage, in terms of the 'struggle' for gay and lesbian equality, may be particularly important for some tourists and some sites associated with that struggle have become popular 'sights'. There is, especially in the USA, a large number of gay or lesbian sporting teams and these create their own tourism through travelling for fixtures. There is also the spectator aspect associated especially with the Gay Games (and OutGames) which can generate further substantial tourism flows. The Games were established, at least in part, as a statement of being 'out and proud' rather than as tourist attractions.

Similarly, gay and lesbian parades and festivals usually had some political objective, originally associated with the movement for equality, but many of these too apparently generate significant numbers of tourists. Some of these visitors will be gays and lesbians who wish to share in the political statement of the parade and festival but others will be attracted by the party atmosphere that many undoubtedly now have. Further issues arising from the party/politics dichotomy are considered in Chapter 8.

Circuit parties, particularly associated with North America, have not had a political dimension, though have frequently been associated with fund-raising for gay and lesbian charities and organizations. Their role has been the satisfaction of the more hedonistic pursuits of dancing and partying. They have had an unfortunate reputation, in some circles, of excessive drug and alcohol consumption and an apparently high incidence of unsafe sex.

As a final note of caution, it has to be acknowledged that the tourism dimension of these events and sights, and their influence in the decision to visit a destination, have not been demonstrated clearly. Many of the assertions about the tourism effect are speculative.

Marketing, Segments, Surveys and Identity

7

Introduction

There is undoubted interest by tour operators, travel agents, accommodation providers, airlines and destinations in a 'gay and lesbian holiday market' (Penaloza, 1996). The 'gay marketing moment' exists and many firms consider it appropriate to target a gay market (more so than a lesbian market). Firms have considered gays and lesbians to be a market segment (or segments) worth targeting. Some parts of this chapter are of a general nature, though the general issues raised and considered do have relevance to the more specific issue of holidays and marketing. The first part of this chapter examines whether or not there is adequate justification for the belief that there is such a market segment, though it has been assumed throughout most of this book so far that there is such a segment. The information sources on which this belief is based, especially relating to holidays, are examined further and some reservations expressed about their validity.

It is also suggested that gay identity (as initially discussed in Chapter 1) has a dimension that is fundamentally related to the concept of the market segment. Gay identify has come to be expressed through consumption of goods and services such as holidays rather than primarily through sexuality.

Finally, on a more practical level, some of the more significant issues to be addressed when targeting the gay and lesbian holiday markets are discussed. In particular, the view that a 'dedicated' specific approach needs to be adopted will be considered.

Market Segmentation

Market segmentation is the process of dividing consumers into distinct groups who might require separate products or marketing mixes. Once such a segment is identified, an organization may choose to target it, if considered profitable to do so. Further, decisions will need to be made about the positioning of products; products are perceived by consumers in different ways and it may be that a variety of product-positioning techniques may be necessary for different market segments through appropriate marketing mixes (including promotion and price).

The usual bases for market segmentation have been socio-economic and demographic factors such as age, sex, family life-cycle, income, occupation, and class or geography – where people live. More recently, psychographics – people's attitudes, beliefs and opinions – and behavioural factors such as purchasing patterns have been utilized for segmenting markets. Is, however, sexual orientation sufficient to justify a distinct market segment? Does it dominate other criteria or is it just another influence equal to or dominated by age, location, attitude, etc.? If it is influential, for how many of those who could be categorized as gay or lesbian?

The reluctance of some advertisers to target gay and lesbian markets may be due to a perception that they are not a market segment – that they are fragmented or not profitable. It may be more fundamental in that they are not aware either of the needs or of the potential of these markets. Fugate (1993) concluded, after evaluating gays and lesbians against criteria considered necessary for effective market segmentation, that a viable segment did not exist. Stuber (2002), however, believed that 'the gay and lesbian segment fulfils commonly used criteria for identifying target groups' (p. 99). There are a number of criteria adopted for determining the existence of distinct market segments (whatever the basis used) but they can usually be consolidated as identifiability, sufficiency, stability and accessibility. By the first is meant whether market needs can be determined and are distinctive and measurable; sufficient refers to the numbers in the segment and their purchasing power, whereas stability relates to whether the distinctive characteristics will persist long enough to allow for generation of 'sufficient' profit. The final criterion of accessibility relates to whether or not the segment can be reached through the marketing media.

The four criteria

With respect to the first of these criteria, 'identifiability', there are issues to do with definition of gays and lesbians and to do with the representative nature of surveys, both general market and specific tourist, that have been undertaken (see later). These surveys do suggest, though, that sexual orientation can influence purchasing pattern with respect to holidays. There is undoubtedly a 'group' of people (men more than women) to whom the profile can be applied. It would be simplistic and reductive to assume that sexual orientation would by itself be sufficient to identify this market segment, and the gay and lesbian market is not homogenous (Fugate, 1993; Field, 1995; Stuber, 2002). 'Sexuality is cross-cut by class, race and gender in complex ways which the prevailing myths of the affluent gay consumer in the pink economy invisibilise' (Bell and Binnie, 2000, p. 100) and is characterized by 'a host of sub-segments defined by demographic, attitudinal and ideological factors' (Pritchard and Morgan, 1997, p. 16). Even so, the identifiable and measurable aspect cannot justifiably be applied to all who are 'homosexual', if only because of the problematic nature of this concept.

A similar problem arises with respect to the second criterion, 'sufficiency'; the size of this segment is virtually impossible to determine accurately. The UK government estimate of lesbians, gays and bisexuals as comprising 5% of the population would mean a potential market of nearly three million. This, if an accurate estimate, is a large market but it is not, of course, a uniform market and what proportion of that three million would comprise a gay and lesbian market segment is unknown.

Whatever its size and characteristics, there is some agreement that this segment is likely to be stable. The numbers are unlikely to diminish and, if anything, may rise as homosexuality becomes more accepted and individuals are more willing to 'come out' (Fugate, 1993; Stuber, 2002). The more accepted homosexuality becomes, then the 'need' for holidays with a gay or lesbian angle is likely to diminish. Paradoxically, it is possible to conceive of a situation (however unlikely) where the market disappears through assimilation of gays and lesbians into mainstream society.

With respect to the final criterion, accessibility, there has been a significant growth in the number of magazines, newspapers and lifestyle web sites in the UK targeted at gays and lesbians. The Internet has undoubtedly opened up significant new ways of reaching this market. The development of gay spaces of bars, clubs and shops means that gays and lesbians are more physically accessible too for direct billboard or in-venue advertising, for flyer distribution or for community involvement by organizations targeting this market (Stuber, 2002). Accessibility will be discussed further below.

Gays and lesbians may well, therefore, be considered a 'market segment', though with less precision than might be applied to others. There is widespread belief that a viable market segment of gays and lesbians (however 'unrepresentative') does exist (Hughes, 2004).

Surveys

General population surveys

Information about the 'market characteristics' of gays and lesbians and of their holiday profile is usually drawn from surveys of various kinds.

Alongside any usual reservations about survey data there are additional issues that have to be addressed when considering gay and lesbian data. There is the obvious problem of obtaining a representative sample through random sampling of the whole population, as failure to disclose sexual orientation or to self-identify as gay or lesbian creates an immediate problem. The Yankelovitch Monitor (1994) claimed to be one of the most comprehensive and reliable surveys of gays and lesbians in the USA, as it was a random, home-based, sample of the general population which asked respondents to confidentially identify sexual orientation (Lukenbill, 1999). This did not include questions relating to tourism.

Similar US surveys which did ask about aspects of tourism include the Witeck-Combs surveys: these were online general population surveys of 2000–3500 respondents in which 5–7% identified as gay, lesbian or bisexual (Witeck-Combs Communications and Harris Interactive, 2003a,b, 2004, 2005). It was acknowledged that these were not a probability sample and that comparisons should be made with caution given the small glb sample size.

Roy Morgan research was based on a random sample of the Australian population (over 56,000 respondents in 2003), in which 2% of the respondents agreed with the statement 'I consider myself a homosexual' (Roy Morgan Research, 2003). The Forrester survey was, similarly, a general US population survey with over 60,000 respondents in 2003, in which 5% of men and 2% of women identified as glb (Kolko, 2003). Such general population surveys do make it possible to compare gays and lesbians with the rest of the population with some degree of confidence, if only because the same questions are asked to all. The relatively small proportion of the samples that identify as gay or lesbian, however, make comparisons with the rest of the population of limited validity, especially given that the accuracy of the proportion of the population that identifies as glb is unknown.

Specific gay and lesbian surveys

Other surveys target only the gay and lesbian population, rather than the general population. The GL Census is such a source of information about market characteristics, though its free-access material does not relate to tourism. It is an Internet survey of individuals in the USA who identify as gay, lesbian or transgender which, in 2005, had 8000 respondents. It is claimed that 'the consistency between the data sets is one of our key findings . . . The similarity in results means we are getting a clear picture of what this community is like' (GL Census, 2002). In the UK, regular surveys have been undertaken of the sexual behaviour of gay men since 1993 (Reid *et al.*, 2004). The purpose of these Sigma surveys has been to collect information about gay men's sexual behaviour and HIV issues. Questionnaires have been distributed by gay and HIV health promotion agencies and (since 2001) have been available online (publicized by http://www.gaydar.co.uk and http://www.uk.gay.com). In 2003, 14,551 questionnaires were analysed (10,801 online and 3,750 as booklet). The survey covered only men who had had sex with men in the previous year or who intended to do so in the future. This is a large response but the information derived from the survey is unlikely to be 'representative' of homosexual men.

With respect to the UK, the report by Market Assessment Publications (MAPS, 1998) attempted to identify a number of dimensions of the 'pink pound', including holidays. MAPS set out to collect original data through its own national opinion polls, as well as pulling together data from existing sources such as surveys in the *Pink Paper*. Their own survey was of just over 1000 gays and lesbians contacted directly through an intermediary; the response was only 162, with no indication of the male/female breakdown. Despite this, MAPS felt that it did represent a random cross-section of the gay community.

Clift and Forrest's surveys of gay men's holiday patterns were undertaken with a primary aim of determining sexual behaviour. They were amongst the first to attempt to identify 'holiday motivations' of gay men and to determine the more popular destinations by actually asking gay men. Their surveys, in 1996, were directed at men (only) in Brighton (UK) through bar and club questionnaires and also through questionnaires in local gay magazines (to be returned by post). This resulted in a total of 562 usable responses. The researchers were aware of the limitations attached to this sampling method, though they considered that it did represent a 'broader cross-section of gay men than is the case in previous related studies' (Clift and Forrest, 1999a, p. 618), a reference to sexual behaviour surveys rather than tourism surveys. A follow-up survey based on the Brighton survey was carried out at public gay and lesbian travel fairs in London in 1997 and 1998 (Clift *et al.*, 2002a). This self-completion questionnaire was returned by 295 men and it was acknowledged that this sample was not representative.

Community Marketing has, since the early 1990s, regularly published an influential survey of US gay and lesbian travellers. Their 7th annual survey (2001) was based on 3000 respondents accessed through e-mail newsletters and web site links, and the 8th survey (2002–2003) on 1500 respondents. The organization acknowledged (in its 8th survey) that the results could not be assumed to be representative and were representative only of 'active consumers', but had been validated by the fact that they had been carried out for a number of years (Roth and Luongo, 2002; Community Marketing Inc., 2003). They did acknowledge too that there was not one gay market but several. Community Marketing considered that the 8th survey was the first where they could differentiate the responses of gay men and lesbians: 74% of their respondents were gay men and 21% were lesbians.

An online survey of gay and lesbian Canadian tourists and visitors to Canada (total of 870 questionnaires) identified 85% of the respondents as gay and 10% as lesbian, though the data presented were not differentiated by sex (http://www.gaytravelguides.info, 2004). Most respondents were from the USA (38%), with a further 31% from Canada and 20% from Australia. It was recognized that the number of completed questionnaires from each of three separate questionnaires was inadequate for drawing meaningful conclusions, but it was none the less felt that it was 'acceptable' and 'valuable results' could be derived.

Event surveys

The Mintel survey (2000a) was one of the first surveys to offer comprehensive information about the UK gay travel market and was undertaken at the London Mardi Gras festival in July 2000 (this is a 'Pride' event aimed at gay, lesbian, bisexual and transgendered people). The data was derived from a sample of just under 1000 people who attended the festival. Some of the data were differentiated by sex in presentation. Mintel considered that those attending the festival were likely to be a more representative cross-section of the gay population than would be offered by sampling in bars and clubs. The survey was considered to be as 'robust' as possible under the circumstances. Compared with the UK population as a whole, the survey respondents were over-represented in the 20–34 age group and in the AB and C1 socio-economic groups.

A survey of participants at Brighton Pride (UK) in 2004 was carried out at the one-day 'Pride Party in the Park'. The purpose was to determine profile and views of attendees at Pride and the economic and cultural significance of the event and, as such, included tourism data (Browne *et al.*, 2005). In order to have confidence in the results researchers aimed to survey between 5 and 10% (i.e. 4000–10,000) of expected attendees; over 7000 questionnaires were completed. One-third of respondents identified as gay men, 30% as lesbians and 29% as heterosexuals, the majority of whom were women.

The Stormbreak survey (2000) was conducted at a gay lifestyle exhibition in London and the questionnaire was completed by 283 persons, of whom two-thirds were gay men and one-third were lesbians. Separate responses from men and women were identified for some questions but not for those relating to holidays.

Issues

Most studies present data relating solely to gays and lesbians and do not make comparisons with the rest of the population. In such isolation the significance of the data is muted. A few, however, do make such comparisons even though the surveys related only to gays and lesbians (MAPS, 1998; Mintel, 2000a; Community Marketing Inc., 2003). The issue that arises here is that like is not being compared with like. Sample surveys of the population as a whole, if appropriately undertaken, are more likely to be representative than are surveys of gays or lesbians. To make direct comparisons may well, therefore, not be justifiable.

The issue of how representative surveys are is clearly important for effective and economic marketing. Most studies recognize the limitations of their sources. Despite Cox's assertion that gay and lesbian tourism studies are 'guilty of an over-reliance on market research reports, often failing to seriously challenge the veracity of the data they impart' (Cox, 2001, p. 12), there is a considerable uniformity about their findings and there would seem to be a 'market segment' of gay men (and lesbians?), which, admittedly, may not be typical of all, which can afford to and does travel and is believed to be worth targeting.

One observer, in acknowledging the limited reliability and availability of information about the buying patterns of gays and lesbians, considered that they would be reached anyway through campaigns targeted at the 'alpha consumer' (Hanna, 2005b).

Market Segments and Gay Identity

Despite this, it has to be recognized that there is view that market segments exist only in so far as marketers create them (Sender, 2004). Marketers create segments by grouping together people according to arbitrary criteria, determined by them in order to construct a viable market to justify targeting. According to this argument, marketers have determined the gay identity and what it means to be gay. Marketing and gay publications have created the illusion that there is a single gay or lesbian market or lifestyle. Market research reliance on limited samples has resulted in restricted images of gays and lesbians. In order to get advertisers, the gay press has presented gays as 'respectable' and (at least in the USA) has played down sexual content and political coverage of magazines. It has been in the interests of the gay press, and of many individual gays and lesbians and their organizations, to be portrayed as highly educated, high-earning, employed, trend-setting, free of financial burdens and little different from the mainstream. A particular image of the gay consumer, at least in the USA, has been that of male, white, professional, affluent, good-looking and youthful, trend-setting and well-educated (Field, 1995; Penaloza, 1996; Gluckman and Reed, 1997b). Sender (2004) argued that gay marketing has produced images of 'model minority' stereotypes and a market that is unthreatening. These characteristics have been acknowledged by and drawn on by other, non-US commentators and confirmed, to a large extent, by later UK surveys, though the marketing attention has been limited compared with that in the USA.

The identity created has, however, removed the diversity that characterizes 'queerness' (Sender, 2004). Marketing may have contributed significantly to the creation of gay and lesbian identity, but it has also served to distort that identity. Marketing has fostered a particular 'respectable', aspirational vision of gay lifestyles which, in effect, has rendered sexuality as secondary and has been reductive of diversity. Marketing addressed to the gay and lesbian segments does not recognize the diversity of that population (Community Closet Association, 2003). Kolko (2003), though, suggested that the population could be treated as a single audience and also that one approach would usually suffice for both gays and lesbians.

Lesbians have been subject to marketing and image-distortion less than have gay males, as 'the idea of a specifically lesbian market remains remarkably underdeveloped' (Sender, 2004, p. 178). They are considered to be more difficult to reach as they are less concentrated in cities, less likely to socialize in gay bars or events and are more oriented towards private social activity and entertainment. Lesbians have not been considered economically powerful or visible and have not been targeted as a separate consumer group (Clark, 1993). There has been a perception of lesbians (associated, in part, with an anti-capitalist feminism) as being less interested in fashion and beauty. This is not the case for all and 'lifestyle' or 'lipstick' lesbians have broken from this mould to embrace materialism as much as the stereotypical gay male: 'lesbian chic', a more feminine and less political lesbianism, more interested in shopping (Esterberg, 1997).

Other segments of the lgbt population – working-class people, older gays and lesbians, bisexuals and transgendered, gay couples, gay parents and ethnic minority gays – have also been rendered invisible by this segmenting and targeting of the gay market. Not only might they feel alienated but this can also be viewed as missed marketing opportunities (GLAAD, 2002). In the USA, for instance, it is estimated that by 2020 25% of the gay community will be aged 50 or older (Witeck-Combs Communications and Harris Interactive, 2004). Advances based on purchasing power are also precarious, as the gay market could be neglected as readily as it has been adopted, should economic circumstances alter.

None the less, in so far as the 'marketing moment' exists (and it may well currently be more a phenomenon in the USA than elsewhere), it can be regarded as a legitimization of gays and lesbians as members of society and as distinctive people. Gays and lesbians may well respond positively to being targeted and acknowledged in this way and it may have served to raise self-esteem. It has increased their visibility and raised the level of acceptance by heterosexuals (Sender, 2004). Being gay or lesbian has, through marketing attention, shifted from a negative criterion of being marginalized to a more positive assertion. In addition, gays and lesbians may have self-images, generated through marketing, which are less as a marginalized sector of society and more akin to the mainstream. It is possible, too, that the images created by marketers have been such as to construct a more 'acceptable' perception of gays and lesbians amongst the rest of the population.

Aspects of Marketing to Gay and Lesbian Tourists

In this section some of the more popular assertions about marketing to this market are considered. Most relate to the promotional rather than to other aspects of marketing. There are an increasing number of sources (especially market research companies) offering advice about how best to market to this segment, however 'realistic' or representative it might be. There are common themes to this advice about 'best practice' with regard to marketing to gays and lesbians. Most of the recommendations are not obviously supported by research and are probably more firmly held, 'commonsense' beliefs than demonstrable reality. The most obvious recommendation is to engage in market research among gays and lesbians in order to determine their requirements (Community Closet Association, 2003; Roth and Paisley, 2004). Subsequently, the approach may differ according to whether general-appeal or specific-appeal products (goods and services) are being marketed.

General-appeal products

In the first case of goods and services that have an appeal regardless of the sexuality of the purchaser, there is an option of doing nothing special. It is highly probable that unmodified mainstream advertisements in mainstream media will be successful in attracting gay and lesbian customers for goods and services such as furniture, food, cars, CDs, housing, theatre tickets or air transport, where sexuality is not likely to be an issue. These products are not designed to suit a particular market based on sexuality, but may be marketed to all consumers regardless of sexuality or of any other characteristics such as ethnicity or religion.

It may be, however, that producers deliberately target such market segments to encourage them to buy these general-appeal products out of a belief that it will produce more sales than if they had not been targeted. In addition, there may be particular aspects of these products that are deemed to have an appeal to gays and lesbians – perhaps CDs by a particular performer or housing in a particular area. There is a commonly expressed, though not universal, view that such targeting and commitment to gays and lesbians can be successful in the case of most goods and services. Though it is possible that some gays and lesbians will regard dedicated marketing as inappropriate (Stuber, 2002), there are consistent reports that gays and lesbians are more likely to buy from companies that are 'gay-friendly' (however defined) and in response to (mainstream) advertisements placed in gay and lesbian media or to dedicated campaigns that feature gay or lesbian images (Pritchard and Morgan, 1997; Wood, 1999; Mintel, 2000a; GLAAD, 2002). Placing unmodified mainstream advertising in gay and lesbian media or, for instance, undertaking promotions at a gay Pride event will signal interest in both the market and gay-friendliness and, hopefully, will generate consumer loyalty. Regular unmodified advertisements in UK gay magazines such as *Attitude* and *Gay Times* have recently included those of Ford, Land Rover, Diesel, Gillette, Courvoisier, Calvin Klein, Opera North, Smile (online bank) HMV and Virgin. Gay-friendly can mean simply placing mainstream advertisements in gay and lesbian media.

Destinations for holiday visits can be considered as general-appeal products in as much as they usually seek the expenditure of many market segments. In order to attract gays and lesbians, though, they may need to target that market – by placing advertisements in the gay media as above or, because of the special needs of this market, by some modification of the marketing campaign (see later).

Dedicated campaigns

Stuber (2002) suggests that, if campaigns are not 'dedicated', companies may be seen as uncommitted and they may not succeed in attracting some gays and lesbians. It may be felt appropriate, therefore, to modify an advertisement or to have a completely different one if it is believed that this would have a more direct appeal to gays and lesbians. It is claimed that gays and lesbians respond favourably to clear, dedicated messages and to advertisements with gay imagery (Ricker and Witeck, 2003; Oakenfull and Greenlee, 2004). Community Closet Association is a US-based organization that monitors 'gay advertising' and promotes good practice in marketing to gays and lesbians. It considers that gay-themed advertising gets a disproportionate response from gays and lesbians because they are not used to seeing themselves represented in this aspect of marketing. According to the Association, some of the earliest mainstream companies to target the gay and lesbian market included American Airlines and American Express, as well as brands such as Absolut Vodka and Johnnie Walker and, more recently, Ford and Avis. Companies such as MTV, Unilever, VW, Virgin, Levis and Coca-Cola have also included gay and lesbian themes in their marketing. It is suggested that, as gays and lesbians often experience discrimination and marginalization, they will be especially responsive to those who target and recognize them (especially through positive portrayals) in specific marketing strategies (Stuber, 2002).

Gay-specific advertisements can take many forms, ranging from individual models of the same sex as the target audience or same-sex couples (such as in IKEA and Miller Brewing adverts) to those with more subtle signifiers (such as coding, gestures, clothing, environment) through to 'dual marketing'. An act as simple as placing a picture of a single male in an advertisement may be sufficient, such as in recent advertisements in *Gay Times* (September 2005) for such general services as estate agents (realtors) and even the Battersea Dogs and Cats Home. It was noted in an earlier chapter how a hotel company placed an advertisement in a gay magazine which featured a same-sex couple but without an overt gay connection. Recognizing the role that sexual imagery plays in many forms of mainstream advertising, it might be expected that this would feature also in gay- and lesbian-specific advertising. This might be curtailed in some instances, though, given the possibility of arousing the opposition of some sections of the non-gay population.

An Orbitz television advertisement for its gay travel micro-site (in 2003) featured marionettes rather than humans: one 'male' was interested in booking in a potential hotel because of the sight of another, lounging pool-side. Modifications may be minor, by including iconography such as a pink triangle or rainbow flag and expressions such as diversity, gay-friendly or 'all are welcome' (Penaloza, 1996; Stuber, 2002). An advert for Delta Airlines in the (UK) *Gay Times* (February 2005) highlighted Atlanta (Georgia) as 'one of the great gay destinations in the US'. This was obviously targeted at the gay market, though the visual images were subtle and consisted only of two intertwined arms (indistinct sex) and three rainbow-coloured wispy lines. Gay-friendliness, in the case of London Zoo, took the form of an 'authorized Gay Sunday' (in September 2005) advertised in the gay press. Presenting a voucher at the zoo entitled gay and lesbian visitors to an entry fee discount and a free drink.

It seems almost a truism that it is recommended that marketing, especially imagery in adverts, should be sensitive and avoid confirming stereotypes of gays and lesbians (Community Closet Association, 2003). Realistic representations of gay and lesbian lives in advertisements are more likely to be successful than are one-dimensional stereotypical images, especially those of gay men in drag (Hanna, 2005a; Johnson, undated).

Dual marketing (or 'gay window advertising') may be appropriate when advertising in mainstream media; it is when advertisements have a particular appeal to gays and lesbians but also to heterosexuals (Clark, 1993). The gay and lesbian angle is not obvious to others, as the advertisements are open to different interpretations. Such advertisements may well be more cost-effective than dedicated adverts. Physical proximity or subtle touching between two people may be sufficient. Calvin Klein underwear or Abercrombie and Fitch menswear advertisements have often been considered to be in this category. Recent UK advertisements for Gillette shaving systems have included photographs of good-looking, bare-chested football or rugby players (David Beckham and Jason Robinson) placed in mainstream and gay publications. Attractive male models may appeal not only to the gay male market but also to the non-gay female and possibly, subliminally, to the non-gay male market and 'today, gay lifestyle is firmly in the mainstream with homoerotic imagery used by everyone from footballers to perfume manufacturers' (Wells, 2004, p. 9). Lukenbill (1999) also considered that overt gay and lesbian imagery was becoming a more regular part of mainstream advertising and coding was less necessary. Even though not targeting the gay and lesbian market, (US) advertisers use gay themes to 'stand out, find coolness and sometimes to be inclusive' (Wilke, 2005).

Other aspects

Gays and lesbians may also be attracted by indications of gay-friendliness other than through targeted advertising. Companies have been advised to become involved with the gay and lesbian community by, for instance, joining social and community groups, by donating to charities and by sponsoring and marketing at gay and lesbian events (Lukenbill, 1999; Stuber, 2002; Roth and Paisley, 2004). Rather idealistically it has been claimed that 'the gay and lesbian community cannot be bought. But [sic] it can be engaged through sound business and marketing practices that result in social change' (Lukenbill, 1999, p. 118). Donations to charity could be referred to in advertisements (Stuber, 2002). In 2005, Olivia Cruises sponsored Martina Navratilova at a tennis tournament in Eastbourne (UK), the first time that she had had a gay sponsor (Swift, 2005a). American Airlines has been particularly active in sponsorship of and being the 'preferred airline' for many gay events, including the International Gay Rodeo Association and organizations such as World's Foremost Gay and Lesbian Hotels (Trucco, 2004). Other sponsorships and marketing linkages such as 'suppliers' to events have been mentioned in earlier chapters.

It has been recommended also that employment policies should be, and should be seen to be, inclusive and non-discriminatory (Lukenbill, 1999). In addition, ensuring front-line staff are 'gay-friendly' by way of appropriate training may be beneficial; this can be signalled in advertising or in the display of relevant symbols (Roth and Paisley, 2004). Stuber (2002) has suggested that staffing tour operators, travel agents and airlines by both gays and straights would give a message of inclusiveness. The contribution of gay employees in designing marketing strategies is featured as a recommendation too (Kolko, 2003).

Specific-appeal products

All of these approaches – targeting via gay and lesbian media, gay-themed advertising and gay-friendliness – become particularly significant where producers of goods and services seek only, or mainly, gay or lesbian consumers. Producers may do this because they consider that their product meets particular needs of gay and lesbians and not those of heterosexuals. These needs will arise where sexuality is an issue, such as where social needs are to be met, where products are significant for gay identity-formation and identity-confirmation and where confidentiality or minimization of risk are considered important (Stuber, 2002). This may include a variety of personal services including legal advice, insurance, financial or health services as well as leisure services of bars and clubs and holidays. None the less, not every product or service aimed at gays and lesbians succeeds (Hill, 2002). The G&L Bank (UK) opened in 1999 as the only Internet bank serving gays and lesbians, but collapsed in 2002 largely because it had too few customers; service and costs were not competitive and being 'pink' was insufficient.

For such a market segment with particular needs, tailored products may be provided. Tour operators may arrange holidays targeted at gays and lesbians that are focused on gay venues or holidays with other gay or lesbian travellers; resorts and hotels may position themselves as exclusively gay or lesbian. It has seen in earlier chapters that specialist tour operators and travel agents targeting gays and lesbians do exist, as do hotels and resorts. These latter will usually promote themselves as gay-friendly or gay-exclusive (see Figs 6.5–6.8). In addition, a specific-appeal product can take the form not so much of distinct products as of providing 'mainstream' travel services sold with sensitivity to gay and lesbian needs. This includes the targeting of gays and lesbians by destinations and by mainstream tour operators, travel agents, hotels and resorts.

Destinations may endeavour to position themselves as gay and lesbian products, though rarely exclusively. Destinations are a little like general-appeal product in as much as they often seek to attract a range of visitors and are targeted at all. Therefore, a destination could put a mainstream advert in gay or lesbian media. It is unlikely, however, that unmodified marketing campaigns would succeed, given the need of many gays and lesbians for gay space, gay-friendliness or lack of homophobia. Gays and lesbians seek attributes of a destination and aspects of the services of tour operators, travel agents and hotels that differ from those of other market segments. Dedicated marketing would therefore be more appropriate when targeting these markets. Gay-themed advertising, use of gay and lesbian media and gay-friendliness emphasized in the marketing and, where appropriate, the ability to advise accordingly will inevitably feature significantly in such cases.

It was seen in Figs 6.5–6.8 how hotels can be explicit about their gay or lesbian friendliness or exclusivity in their promotional material. The advertisement placed in the gay press by the Village Lodge (Cape Town),

the village lodge

49 napier street,
de waterkant,
cape town 8001

t. +27 (0)21 421 1106
f. +27 (0)21 421 8488

reservations@thevillagelodge.com
www.thevillagelodge.com

Fig. 7.1. Press advertisement produced by Village Lodge, De Waterkant 'Village', Cape Town, South Africa.

however, is no more than a picture of a front door plus location and contact detail (see Fig. 7.1). This understated advert covers a number of guest houses and cottages located in the gay 'village' district of Cape Town.

Several advertisers use male or female imagery in their advertisements or brochures as represented by, for instance, Vienna (Fig. 2.1), Manchester (Fig. 5.2) and Germany (Fig. 5.3), Away Gay Holidays (Figs 6.3 and 6.4), Respect Holidays (Fig. 6.5) and Bondi Hotel (Fig. 6.6). The term 'rainbow' features on occasion, e.g. rainbow flag in the Vienna advert, the name of Gabrielle's Hotel is printed in rainbow colours (Fig. 6.7) and another Blackpool hotel is named Rainbows (Fig. 6.8). The Women Innkeepers of Provincetown advertisement uses female imagery without recourse to the term 'lesbian', though the picture is of two women apparently in an embrace (see Fig. 6.10). Both male imagery and the term 'gay' are used in the Desert Paradise Resort Hotel (Palm Springs) (see Fig. 7.2). The male imagery used in the German advert is accompanied by a phrase in German which is suggestive of sexual activity.

The advertisements for Key West have retained the strapline 'the fabulous gay and lesbian destination', but are subject to frequent change. Invariably the theme is quite subtle, but none the less striking; in Fig. 5.1, for instance, the dominant colour of the photo is pink, which, along with the use of the word 'pink', encapsulates the atmosphere of the town. No human imagery is used in the advertisement shown in Fig. 7.3, though the ingenious use of two male dolls once more conveys a clear message. A Key West advertisement aimed at the lesbian market (Fig. 7.4) simply shows a road with a strapline 'You go girl!', conveying a message of freedom.

Fig. 7.2. Press advertisement produced by Desert Paradise Resort Hotel, Palm Springs, California, USA.

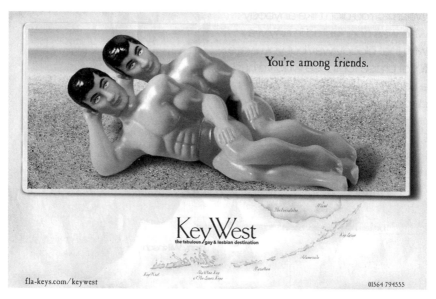

Fig. 7.3. Press advertisement produced by Florida Keys and Key West Tourism Council.

Gay-friendliness

There is an emphasis by many commentators that any involvement with the gay and lesbian market, whether through advertising or sponsorship, etc. should be sincere and be seen as such and not opportunistic. Insincere, misdirected and misinformed attempts to cultivate this market are

Fig. 7.4. Press advertisement produced by Florida Keys and Key West Tourism Council Key West.

predicted to fail and respect, reassurance and stimulation of positive inclusive self-images are considered key factors (Russell, 2001). It is advised that suppliers demonstrate their long-term steady commitment to this market. Community Closet Association (2003) has entreated companies to be consistent and not withdraw or modify their approach in the face of criticism. A commitment to advertising over a long period of time rather than simply as a one-off (or equivalent) is considered to be a productive policy, as it demonstrates loyalty to the market.

A number of surveys suggest that gays and lesbians claim to take note of 'gay-friendliness'. Over three-quarters of gays and lesbians in a

US survey claimed to have switched brands to companies with a positive stance towards gays and lesbians (Witeck-Combs Communications and Harris Interactive, 2003b). Over 70% were influenced by advertising in the gay media, by 'giving back to the community' or by having progressive employee policies, but gay images in advertisements were important to only 50%. Whether this preference for gay-friendly companies applies to all types of product is not clear. Commercial Closet Association reported that a 2002 study had established that purchases by lgbts were more likely than were those of heterosexuals to be influenced by a company's diversity policy (47% compared with 18%). In the GL Census, 70% of (US) respondents claimed they were more likely to be persuaded by advertisements that featured gay themes than by those that did not, and nearly half tried to find out if a company was gay-friendly before buying from it (GL Census Partners, 2004–2005). Over 70% of gays and lesbians at the 2004 (UK) Brighton Pride festival had bought from a company because it was gay-friendly (Browne *et al.*, 2005). It is also believed that if companies are perceived to be homophobic in some way or resistant to gay and lesbian 'progress', then gays and lesbians will be less favourably disposed towards them and will not buy their products (Lukenbill, 1999). The UK Stormbreak survey (2000) showed that three-quarters of respondents would avoid buying from companies with a reputation for being homophobic. Whether or not such positive and negative attitudes translate into purchase action is not always clear, however. The Community Closet Association points out that companies do not share information about this, but the fact that so many do target the market would seem to suggest that it is worthwhile. In the case of non-gay friendly organizations, it is reported that United Airlines experienced a 2-year boycott by gays and lesbians from 1997 following the airline's initial failure to extend benefits to same-sex partners of employees. Similarly the Bank of Scotland (UK) dropped a proposed business link with the US evangelist Pat Robertson after protests by gays and lesbians in 1998 (Burrows, 2004).

Tourism and gay-friendliness

The issue of gay-friendliness in tourism has been discussed previously (Chapters 3 and 6). In the case of tourism, 86.8% of respondents to an international survey of gay travellers were more likely to support a tourism business if it was gay-friendly and 78.6% were more likely to support such a business if it advertised directly to lgbts (http://www.gaytravelguides.info, 2004). Nearly 90% of US travellers stated they preferred to do business with companies which 'give back' to the gay and lesbian community (Community Marketing, 2001). In the UK, over a third of gays and lesbians were 'more inclined' to book holidays with gay-friendly companies and 43% believed that it was important to stay in a gay-friendly hotel (Mintel, 2000a). The Wyndham Palace Resort and Spa in Walt Disney World Resort was chosen as the official Welcome Center for Gay Days at Orlando in 2005 – because of its high score on the Human Rights Campaign Index for diversity issues and the company's positive marketing to the lgbt community.

When choosing an airline or a hotel, US gays and lesbians were more likely than others to rate 'equal treatment of all its employees' as an important factor: rated by 28–34% of gays and lesbian compared to 6–7% of others (Witeck-Combs Communications and Harris Interactive, 2004). Targeted media advertising was also considered important in affecting choice of airline and hotel chain by US gays and lesbians (14 and 13%, respectively) (Witeck-Combs Communications and Harris Interactive, 2004). These were not the most important factors though: 'convenience' and 'friendly and welcoming customer service' were the most important reasons for both gays and heterosexuals in airline and hotel choice. Boston's (Massachusetts) gay tourism campaign in 2005 was based, in part, on the belief that gays and lesbians will support destinations that show understanding and acceptance of the lgbt community (Johnson, 2005b).

Backlash

Targeting gay and lesbian consumers may, however, lead to criticism from some in the rest of the population and to a backlash in the form of sanctions, such as boycotting of purchases. As a consequence, advertisers of general-appeal products may be reluctant to target gay and lesbian consumers. A number of hotels have indicated to the US travel company, Orbitz, that they did not want to be listed as gay-friendly (Trucco, 2004). Adverse consumer reactions may simply be due to the fact that gays and lesbian are being targeted regardless of the nature of the advertising; further criticism arises, though, of gay-themed advertisements. Outwardly gay or lesbian characters and the portrayal of gay and lesbian lifestyles in advertisements may alienate the non-gay market. A Guinness advertisement of 1995 featuring domestic scenes of two men was withdrawn before showing; allegedly because of the feared reaction by the general public (http://www.commercialcloset.org/portrayals). Advertisements for the Italian men's clothing range, Ra-Re, which included one featuring a man clutching at the crotch of another, gave rise to considerable opposition in Italy (McMahon, 2005). In the USA, organizations such as the American Family Association and Focus on the Family have condemned various advertisers for targeting the gay and lesbian markets.

It has been noted in earlier chapters how gay and lesbian tourism and promotional campaigns have given rise to conflict and boycotts. Marketers walk a 'narrow line between making gayness visible and making it too visible in ways that alienate people' (Sender, 2004, p. 123). Some images generated may also displease gays and lesbians themselves (Phillips, 2003). In one study, five advertisements with gay or lesbian imagery created positive feeling amongst only 21% of heterosexuals (Ricker and Witeck, 2003). It was not obvious that this would cause them to move away from the product but it was concluded that more subtle representations of gayness might be appropriate. A further study suggested that the use of 'subtle lesbian imagery' might be a more successful approach (Oakenfull and Greenlee, 2004, p. 1284). Heterosexual consumers (especially male) generally have a more negative attitude towards imagery of gay males than towards that of lesbians. The Commercial Closet Association, none the less, reported in a 2004 study that 81% of US heterosexual respondents felt it would not matter to them if a company whose product they bought also targeted the gay and lesbian market. Nearly 40% would feel better about that company, though a much higher proportion would feel better about a company that supported breast cancer research. Gay- or lesbian-themed advertisements are less likely to be contentious if confined to the gay and lesbian press or cable television. Some papers and magazines may, though, have put off potential advertisers by their sexual content (Fugate, 1993; Wood, 1999).

Regardless of backlash, however, there is a view that companies are increasingly willing to ignore its effect – actual or potential – as 'the profits to be reaped from treating gays and lesbians as a trend-setting consumer group finally outweigh the financial risks of inflaming right-wing hate' (Gluckman and Reed, 1997b, p. 3). Apart from the obvious appeal of such a supposedly lucrative market, the inclusion of diversity themes in marketing may be undertaken by companies as much to demonstrate their liberalism to the community as a whole as to directly target gay or lesbian markets. In this way they may appeal to particular segments of the non-gay population.

Where to Place Advertisements?

Magazines and newspapers

The placing of advertisements in the media, whether newspapers, magazines, television or on web sites, is a common approach to reaching target market segments. It has been suggested that companies targeting the gay and lesbian markets should advertise in the mainstream media in order to capture a wider number, especially those who do not read the gay or lesbian press or access gay and lesbian web sites (Roth and Luongo, 2002). The Commercial Closet Association reported that mainstream news magazines were read frequently or occasionally by 60% of US gays and lesbians (compared with 45% of heterosexuals) and lifestyle and design magazines by 41% (compared with 30% of heterosexuals). According to Witeck-Combs Communications and Harris Interactive (2003b), 87% of US gays and lesbians had read a non-sports magazine in the previous month (compared with 76% of heterosexuals). As 'intensive' readers, it would appear appropriate to use the 'straight' printed media as one way of reaching gays and lesbians.

With respect to gay and lesbian magazines, however, there seems to be some doubt about readership. More than half of the US gay and lesbian population does not access gay media of any kind and an advertisement in *OUT* or *Advocate* (the two most widely circulated gay magazines in the USA) have been estimated to reach only 3% of the gay and lesbian population at most; their circulations are approximately 100,000 each (Oakenfull and Greenlee, 2004). By comparison, magazines with the highest US circulations in 2004 included *Reader's Digest* at 10 million, *National Geographic* at 5 million and *Good Housekeeping* at 4.6 million (http://www.magazine.org). The Commercial Closet Association, however, report that one-third of US gays read national gay magazines frequently or occasionally. The circulation of monthly gay magazines in the UK is between 40,000 and 60,000; the monthly lesbian magazine *Diva* has a circulation of about 35,000 (http://www.axm-mag.com; http://www.gaytimes.co.uk/diva; http://www.gaytimes.co.uk/gt). Readership for each is estimated to be at least three times as great – between 100,000 and 200,000. The UK (heterosexual) men's lifestyle magazines *Nuts* and *FHM* had circulations of 300,000 and 500,000, respectively, in 2005 (http://www.abc.org.uk). There are few UK gay or lesbian newspapers as such, though the *Pink Paper* is a free fortnightly with a national circulation of 40,000 (http://www.pinkpaper.com). Typical readers of the magazines and paper are aged under 40 and are in professional and white-collar occupations with above-average earnings. This apparently upscale profile of the market may be sufficient to outweigh the disproportionate cost of advertising in such 'low-circulation' or expensive media (Stuber, 2002; Hanna, 2005b).

Television and radio

Television marketing may be too expensive to justify advertising to such a relatively small market segment, though gay-themed channels may be attractive. To date, this has not been the case as many have been short-lived and have had a particular association with pornography. It is believed that gays and lesbians are more likely to watch cable television (Commercial Closet Association) and a high proportion of gays and lesbians (65 and 61%, respectively) watch gay-oriented television programmes weekly (GL Census, 2004–2005). NBC's Bravo channel (USA) is not gay-oriented but is believed to have a particular appeal to that market segment. It has also screened programmes such *as Queer Eye for the Straight Guy*. Orbitz experienced a 50% increase in traffic on its web site after it aired its television commercial targeting gays on Bravo (Bess, 2004). MTV Networks (VH1 and MTV) launched a gay-themed 24-hour cable channel 'Logo' in June 2005 into 13 million US households. It is a channel of documentaries, series, films, music and news to which Orbitz has signed up (Bess, 2004). Key West and Philadelphia have also placed dedicated gay advertisements on Logo.

Radio has a limited appeal, though in the UK Gaydar Radio (launched in 2001) broadcasts over the Internet and digital radio in London and the south-east. It attracts a 90% upmarket male listenership (Gibson, 2004). JOY FM is an lgbt community radio station which has broadcast in Melbourne (Australia) since 1993 (Johnson, 2005c) and, it is claimed, sponsors can reach an audience of between 100,000 and 120,000 listeners. Direct mail appears to be a greater possibility in the USA than elsewhere. There is less availability of such lists in Europe (Stuber, 2002).

Internet

The Internet is becoming more significant as both an information source and a booking means for holidays generally (Buhalis, 1998; Lang, 2000). It probably has a greater significance for marketing to the gay and lesbian market than to others. The attractions of the Internet for gays and lesbians lie, to some extent, in its risk-minimization and its ability to ensure anonymity and confidentiality (Kolko, 2003). These issues may be particularly important in accessing information about homosexuality generally, gay lifestyles and the gay scene, as well as in finding a partner. Half of male gay Internet users surveyed in London used it to find casual sexual partners (www.city.ac.uk). These particular attributes of the Internet can also be particularly important in seeking information about holidays. A UK survey showed that gays and lesbians were more able to obtain information about gay space, for instance, than they could from travel agents or tour operators, and also to identify destinations and accommodation that suited their needs (Poria and Taylor, 2001). Not only might the usual intermediaries not have access to such information, but gays and lesbians also felt reluctant to seek it from them.

There is a high level of ownership of personal computers and of online access among gays: 77% compared with a national average of 26% in the UK (Mintel, 2000a). Similarly, a higher proportion of (US) gays and lesbians than of heterosexuals are online: 80% of gays and 76% of lesbians compared with 70% of straight men and 69% of women (Kolko, 2003). They are also more likely to have made a purchase online in the previous 3 months: 63% compared with 53% of heterosexuals. They are more intensive users of the Internet, too: over 25% of (US) gays and lesbians use the

Internet more than 21 hours per week compared with 18% of the rest of the population (Ricker and Witeck, 2003).

Gay and lesbian web sites are some of the most popular of all in both the UK and USA. Gaydar (launched November 1999) is a contact service which has grown from a membership of 78,000 in 2000 to 1.2 million (500,000 in the UK) in 2003. It is now the fifth most popular web site in the UK, just behind Google and ahead of http://www.bbc.co.uk (Smith, 2004b). The number one web site in the USA to reach single men with incomes of over US$75,000 is http://www.gay.com; its UK satellite is http://www.uk.gay.com (Lillington, 2003). Nearly half of gay men and one-quarter of lesbians visit gay-oriented US web sites daily (GL Census Partners, 2004–2005).

Several destination web sites created by destination marketing organizations have gay and lesbian sections. Monthly visits to Philadelphia's gay web site are reported to have risen from 400 to over 8000 since their gay and lesbian visitor campaign began (Trucco, 2004). In addition, there are numerous gay and lesbian online magazines that have travel sections and it is rare for any tour operator, whether specializing in the straight or gay and lesbian market, not to have its own web site. Some mainstream travel web sites such as Orbitz (US) and Octopus (UK) have gay travel micro-sites. There are also a number of web sites established by gay businesses in a destination with a view to encouraging tourists, such as that of the 'Gay Toronto Tourism Guild'. The promotion of the town as 'a top gay tourism destination' was, in part, a reason for Bournemouth Pride revamping its web site (*Gay Times*, January 2005).

The Internet offers particular advantages to gays and lesbians for both information gathering and for booking, if some degree of confidentiality is required, though it may be used more for the former purpose than for the latter. It is considered important that suppliers of holidays and travel services maintain direct lines of communication through e-mail or phone for bookings and for queries, especially related to more complicated or expensive arrangements (Andrew Roberts, AMRO, Borehamwood, UK, 2004, personal communication). The need for the 'personal touch' has not disappeared and consumers may consider that quicker as well as more personal responses can be obtained by telephone. The UK tour operator Respect reports that the Internet still accounts for only 20% of direct sales (Rob Harkavy, Respect, London, 2004, personal communication).

In the USA, gays and lesbians spend over three-quarters of 'their travel dollars' online compared with 59% of other travellers (Trucco, 2004) and one-third booked more than half of leisure travel online compared with 23% of the rest of the population (Kolko, 2003). In a survey of Australian and North American gay travellers, the Internet was used by 54% to research their vacations and by 57% to book. The remainder were divided equally between the use of travel agents to book their holidays or direct booking (http://www.gaytravelguides.info, 2004).

Research in an Australian survey stated that gays made more use of the Internet for travel information and booking than did heterosexuals (15% as opposed to 10–11% of all), but were also more likely to have used a travel agent (used for booking the last trip by 20% of gays compared with 12% for all) (Roy Morgan Research, 2003). UK gays and lesbians also showed a greater use of the Internet for holiday booking than did the rest of the population: in the Mintel (2000a) survey, 11% had used the Internet at a time when less than 2% of total holiday market was booked through the Internet. The Internet was particularly used for booking 'flight only' (59% of Internet users) but much less so for package holidays (18%), for which travel agents remained the most popular means. Equally high percentages of respondents to the Community Marketing surveys had booked their holidays through travel agents (80%) and the Internet (79%) (Community Marketing, 2001, 2003). Gay men were more likely to book air travel and hotels through the Internet, and cruises and packages through a travel agent.

How do Destinations Market themselves to the Gay and Lesbian Market?

Some of the most popular gay and lesbian destinations appear to have become that with little direct marketing on the part of the destination-marketing organizations. Cities such as New York, San Francisco and Amsterdam and beach destinations such as Provincetown, Sitges, Mykonos or Lesvos have become popular by reputation and word-of-mouth. Even these, with the pressure of increased competition, may feel the necessity to promote. It is usual to promote to the travel trade rather than directly to the target segment. This is done through (wholesale) travel fairs and familiarization tours for the trade and for the media so as to persuade the travel trade to include the destinations in their programme of offers and to persuade the media to publicize them.

A number of 'non-traditional' places have, however, recognized the apparent benefits of attracting such an apparently lucrative market and have set about deliberately targeting gays and lesbians. It has often been cities that have done this. Many cities have sought regeneration through tourism (Law, 2002), but inevitably they have had to address a number of issues including the fact that the tourism product is beyond the influence of any one agency. A city seeking to attract tourism is reduced largely to encouraging (perhaps incentivizing) others to develop suitable attractions, and the main activities of a destination-marketing organization become the creation of a favourable image, positioning the city-product as one that meets the needs of particular market segments and promoting to target segments. A destination-marketing organization has little option but to work with a given.

Considering the significance of gay-friendliness, toleration and the absence of homophobia in the destination choice it might be expected that places where these are apparent would capitalize on them to attract gays and lesbians. In some instances it may be a case of persuading potential tourists that these do exist, even if the reality is not particularly strong. The existence of gay-friendliness and absence of homophobia do not in themselves guarantee positive responses, and failure of a tourist board to target or acknowledge gay and lesbian visitors in its campaigns may in itself inhibit tourism. Although destination popularity may arise from many sources – especially word-of-mouth, literature, films, television and news reports – the nature of gay life is such that gay space or gay-friendliness may not register with potential visitors until given exposure in efforts to attract gays. Tourist board campaigns can dispel ignorance and modify image, and the lack of such campaigns may mean a continuing ignorance of a destination's potential. Lack of knowledge of a destination's attributes may mean that it does not even enter a tourist's 'awareness set'. Even if aware of a destination, potential tourists may shun it in favour of destinations that, through targeted marketing, do recognize their existence and which are supportive of their needs.

Ignorance of a destination may not be the case for Hawaii, but the Hawaii VCB has, none the less, been criticized in the past for not marketing to gays, allegedly out of fear of anti-gay protests (Gomes, 1999). The Hawaiian islands do not offer the same holiday experience as other popular gay destinations such as San Francisco or Key West, but do have unique natural attractions, a reputation for gay-friendliness and a significant number of gay-owned or gay-oriented accommodation, bars, clubs and restaurants. They are undoubtedly a popular destination for gays and, despite the lack of destination marketing, a 1999 survey showed that Hawaii was the second most popular US vacation destination for gay Americans (Link, 2002). Although this neglect of the gay and lesbian market appeared to have caused no great harm, it did overlook intensifying competition for gay tourism and the positive responses from gays and lesbians to destinations that had made affirmative, reassuring approaches to them.

Communities and villages

Drives to attract gay and lesbian tourists often highlight the existing resident gay and lesbian population, usually described as 'a community'. The gay and lesbian part of Melbourne tourist board's web site states that 'the large gay, lesbian, bisexual and transgender community ensures that Melbourne has it all'. Along with this goes a focus on the 'gay scene', though in the case of Philadelphia it was acknowledged that it was small. 'You've got to have that strong gay infrastructure. That's why

Fort Lauderdale succeeds as a destination but Orlando wouldn't' (Fort Lauderdale hotelier quoted in Trucco, 2004). Vienna's web site also refers to the 'sizeable gay and lesbian scene' and a consequent variety of venues. The existence of a gay scene of bars, clubs, restaurants and the like may act as an indicator of gay-friendliness even if those facilities are not used by visitors.

More pointedly, a concentration of gay venues in an identifiable quarter is implicitly regarded as a selling point. Gay leisure space within a defined locality has the convenience factor associated with all forms of tourism cluster and, in addition, there are associated perceptions of safety and of empowerment. The significance of tourism was an element in a proposal to develop a gay quarter at South William Street in Dublin (Battles, 1998). The gay scene has become more visible in the Irish capital but the gay quarter concept, following the model of Manchester (UK), would have given a focus and generated a higher profile.

Friendliness

Friendliness is a common word in tourism marketing directed at both straight and gay segments. In addition, acceptance and celebration of diversity is a frequent theme in gay and lesbian marketing. A spokesperson for the Greater Philadelphia Tourism Marketing Corporation (GPTMC) identified Philadelphia's 'history of diversity' as being a significant issue in the decision to target the gay and lesbian market (Trucco, 2004). Cosmopolitanism is associated with acceptance of difference, whether that is of ethnicity or sexuality. Melbourne (Australia) is described by the tourist board in its gay and lesbian tourist publicity material as a destination 'where world cultures blend and diversity is an everyday thing ... Diversity is embraced' (http://www.visitmelbourne.com). The web site of the Gay Toronto Tourism Guild claims that the city 'boasts one of the most diverse, multi-cultural populations in the world, a city where closets are for clothes'. 'Gay and Lesbian Miami', published by the Greater Miami CVB, portrays the city as one that 'revels in its diversity and offers a mixture of cultures that can be found no place elsewhere'. The Australian Tourist Commission's guide to gay and lesbian travel refers to the country's diverse population leading to it being a place where 'understanding and acceptance of difference is necessary'.

'Gay-friendly' is also commonly encountered in descriptions and promotion of destinations. It has no precise meaning, though it may be assumed that customers and visitors will be allowed full access to all the services and amenities that are available to others and on the same terms (i.e. no discrimination). Many would also believe that it has a more attitudinal dimension which, at the least, amounts to toleration. At best, it refers to gays and lesbians being fully accepted by service providers and locals in positive relationships that are mutually respectful and without condescension – a difference between being tolerated and being embraced. 'That means no one bats an eye when two men or women request one king-size bed. The concierge should be knowledgeable about gay activities, events, neighbourhoods and night life' (Trucco, 2004, p. 2). Tourism Vancouver's web site has a 'gay-friendly' section which refers to gay-related events, facilities and things to do as well as accommodation.

No matter what the intent of the users of the term, the reality may well not match expectations. 'It takes more than a rainbow flag and a Kylie Minogue soundtrack to make a location and a tour operator gay-friendly' (Levitt, 2004). The New Zealand Gay and Lesbian Tourism Association (NZGLTA) is a trade association that seeks to develop gay and lesbian tourism in the country and, to that end, attempted to ensure from 1998 that use of the term 'gay/lesbian friendly' was restricted. It has, in 2004, been replaced by the term 'Rainbow Tourism Accreditation', which can be used only if owners are 'committed in supporting gay and lesbian lifestyle and are not seen to be exploiting gay and lesbian travellers' (http://www.nzglta.org.nz). Further, it is expected that gays and lesbians would be able to 'express their lifestyle openly'.

Some destination campaigns

Philadelphia (USA) has not usually been thought of as a gay and lesbian tourist destination but the city did, in 2003, launch a 3-year US$900,000 marketing campaign targeted at this segment as part of an on-going wider strategy to attract leisure tourists (Haber, 2003). The marketing plan of the GPTMC (Philadelphia) was based on strategies that included targeting several segments such as Afro-American and gay and lesbian travellers. (Afro-Americans increased to 25% of all the city's visitors in 2000 from 14% in 1997, when targeted marketing started (Sharp, 2003).)

The gay and lesbian campaign was claimed to be the largest and most comprehensive of its kind in the USA, with a primary focus on the north-eastern states, though it was also hoped to attract tourists from Canada and Europe. Tourism officials believed that, despite not having an image comparable to more established gay destinations, a combination of the city's historical, cultural and sporting attractions and the city's small but 'thriving' gay scene would capture this market. The marketing would be on television, on the revamped web site and in print and would include gay-friendly press kits and use slogans such as 'Get your history straight and your nightlife gay' and 'Philadelphia, the place that loves you back'. Advertisements included Benjamin Franklin flying a rainbow kite and the city's links with the early days of US independence were capitalized on in its promotion as the 'birthplace of life, liberty and the pursuit of happiness', suggesting an atmosphere that would be particularly tolerant (Philadelphia CVB, 2004).

The prominence of gays in Philadelphia politics and business was referred to as a sign of openness and integration. Apart from this apparent tolerance and the historical and cultural sites of the city, the 'gayborhood' – the centre of gay business and nightlife – was also identified as a reason for visiting. GPTMC claimed that the return on advertising was greater for targeted gay advertising than it was for that targeted at the general population: direct visitor spending of US$153 and US$92, respectively, for every dollar of advertising expenditure (Johnson, 2005a).

The success of Cape Town as a destination for international gays and lesbians has owed more to spontaneous growth than to promotion, though the promotional aspects have accelerated (Visser, 2002). It has identifiable gay space and significant gay and lesbian events have developed, but its promotion has relied also on the cultural and natural resources of South Africa. An additional promotional advantage is the country's 1996 constitution, which ensures equality for all and that no person should be discriminated against on grounds that include sexual orientation. This is the first instance of constitutional protection for gays and lesbians and reference to it is made in tourism material. The country is also referred to as the 'rainbow nation', largely because of its multi-cultural composition, but the term obviously has a particular significance for gays and lesbians. Legislation relating to same-sex sexual activity and to ages of consent for such activity are frequently referred to in destination guides. Despite this, tolerance or acceptance of gay lifestyles is not widespread in South Africa and cultural mores, strong religious beliefs and the legacy of a macho apartheid society inhibit openness.

Washington, DC adopted the slogan 'Where more than just the cherry blossoms come out' in its drive to attract gay and lesbian visitors (Reilley, 2004). A similar theme, 'Come out and play', was reportedly to be used by Bloomington (Indiana) as it endeavoured to enter this market for the first time. The town would also have a redesigned logo, in rainbow colours, for its campaign. The appeal of Bloomington, a relatively small town of 65,000 inhabitants, was considered to lie in its open, college-town atmosphere (a 'cool college town') alongside a number of conventional historic, cultural and scenic attractions. It is not, however, generally recognized as a place with a particularly active gay scene.

The success of targeted marketing campaigns is illustrated by Fort Lauderdale (Florida) which, from 1995, sought to turn around its identification as a spring break destination for college students. The town had long attracted gay and lesbian visitors but had been openly targeting the market, with considerable success, since the mid-1990s. In 2003 it was estimated that 660,000 gays and lesbians would visit the area, spending about US$600m (Sharp, 2003). It is now believed that the gay market accounts for 12% of the city's tourism revenue and Fort Lauderdale ranks as one of the most popular US gay destinations (Reilley, 2004). Product development has included commitment ceremonies for same-sex couples, such as a 4-day event for about 150 couples in September 2003 (Van Drake, 2003).

In the UK, the city of Manchester launched a campaign in 1999 to attract gay and lesbian tourists, especially from North America (Hughes, 2003). This, as in the case of Philadelphia, was one part of a wider set of markets that were to be targeted. Its underpinning was the well-established 'Gay Village', but also in conjunction with strong cultural assets such as theatres, museums and art galleries, as well as diverse and upscale retail and restaurant sectors. The city also has the advantage of an international airport with daily direct flights from and to major US cities such as New York, Chicago, Atlanta and Washington, DC.

Brighton (UK) is already a popular place for gays and lesbians to live and to holiday but it too launched a campaign in 2003 targeting US gays. Significantly, the town strengthened its campaign by initially linking with London, only later focusing on Brighton alone (http://www.uk.gay.com, 2003).

The coastal city of Hull (UK) is not particularly known for its gay life nor as a tourist destination, but has aimed to attract gay and lesbian tourists and, to that end, the city council arranged a familiarization visit for journalists from the gay media during 2004 (Branigan, 2004b). Hull, on the Yorkshire coast, was originally a major fishing port and not a seaside resort but it has, since the demise of the fishing industry, endeavoured to tap into tourism through attractions such as 'the Deep', an aquarium complex. Its image as a fishing port may initially have been a hindrance to the attraction of tourists but tourism earnings have, it is claimed, quadrupled from the mid-1990s to 2002. The attention to the gay and lesbian market was stimulated by a recent rapid growth of gay venues in the city (from one to eight within a year). As in many places seeking to attract gays and lesbians, the city's tourism manager is reported as stressing the city's tradition of 'tolerance, freedom and understanding towards others' (Branigan, 2004b).

Local gay space is not always welcomed as a tourist asset, however. It is claimed that gay venues in Belfast (Northern Ireland) draw people from outside Belfast but businesses have argued that the potential for tourism from wider afield has not developed. This is believed to be because of an apparent reluctance of the city council and local tourist boards to refer to gay venues and events in tourist guides and promotional literature (McDonald, 2004).

Conclusions

The discussion in the early part of the chapter relating to market segments is fundamental to much of the discussion in the rest of this book. By reference to the usual criteria for identifying a market segment, there does appear to be a gay and lesbian market segment. There is an identifiable group of people with distinctive characteristics and needs who have sufficient purchasing power to make it worthwhile to target. There are ways of reaching this market through, for instance, gay and lesbian media, and there is confidence that the size of the market is unlikely to diminish. The interest of marketers is confined, however, more to gay men than it is to lesbians, who are generally considered to have fewer of the desirable upscale characteristics that make the males an attractive marketing target. Even so, the basis for the more favourable view of gay men is itself subject to some reservations.

Market research data about gays and lesbians are derived from surveys, but the extent to which these can be taken to represent gays and lesbians is a contentious issue. They inevitably cover only those gays and lesbians who are willing to identify as such and, even then, surveys are often confined to readers of particular magazines, customers at particular bars or visitors to particular events – and may not even be representative of them. In some respects this market segment exists only because marketers have created it: they have identified features that they have combined into a model of what it means to be gay or lesbian. A gay or lesbian, according to this argument, is a marketing construction and is a consumerist one. Some of the implications of this are explored in the next chapter.

A market segment exists as long as marketers believe it does, and many producers of goods and services have turned their attention to the market as being a particularly profitable growth one. Approaches to targeting this market (assuming it can be categorized as a uniform one) will vary according to the type of product being marketed. In many cases, existing products may simply be advertised in gay or lesbian media and, in others, some modification of the advertising message, perhaps with gay and lesbian imagery or indications of gay-friendliness, may be deemed more appropriate.

There are, however, products especially associated with leisure and tourism that have features that are specific to gays and lesbians. These invariably require dedicated marketing strategies, some of which will include product development or modification as, for instance, 'gay holidays' or 'gay accommodation'. For products such as bars, clubs, holidays and destinations, a positioning as gay-friendly without appropriate modification in the form of considerate service, or perhaps restriction to gays and lesbians (in the case of bars) is unlikely to be successful. For tour operators, travel agents, airlines, accommodation and destinations which potentially serve the whole population, the same product may be positioned in a different way to the gay and lesbian market. Others (some tour operators' programmes, some accommodation) that are exclusive to gays and lesbians will not require this multi-positioning approach and can develop strategies that are targeted solely at this market.

Whatever approach is considered to be appropriate, the Internet is likely to become increasingly important, as it has a particular significance in the marketing of gay and lesbian holidays. Undoubtedly its role is expanding across the whole sphere of tourism, but for gays and lesbians it has an extra dimension of helping to avoid possible embarrassment and breach of confidentiality. Information about gay and lesbian destinations and accommodation can be researched without having to seek it from people who might not have that information or who are unsympathetic – or even hostile. Many destinations have dedicated gay and lesbian tourism web sites, whereas there are numerous gay and lesbian web sites of a general magazine nature that have travel sections. The opportunity to access relevant information is now considerable. Tourists may be a little less willing to book than to research through the Internet, but this opportunity is offered by most gay and lesbian tour operators if not yet by all accommodation providers.

In addition to the issues of a consumerist gay identity, some of the wider repercussions of the aspects of marketing discussed in this chapter will be considered further in the next chapter.

Holidays, Marketing and Implications for Homosexuality

8

Introduction

Gays and lesbians appear to be more likely to take holidays and to take more holidays than the rest of the population. In this respect, they share in the 'good life' associated with modern society and may be considered to be 'privileged' members of that society. The willingness of travel companies and of holiday destinations (coastal and urban) to target gays and lesbians as tourists may also be regarded as an indicator of acceptance by the heterosexual world. The readiness with which heterosexuals attend gay and lesbian festivals, at least as spectators, may be considered to be a similar indicator.

It has been seen too how holidays may have a particular significance for gays and lesbians in facilitating the adoption and affirmation of a gay identity and providing necessary opportunities to be oneself. Gays and lesbians on holidays may face fewer restrictions on their behaviour than when at home and can therefore be more open about their sexual orientation. For those who have yet to adjust to identifying as gay or lesbian, the distance from the home environment may grant anonymity and confidentiality to explore sexuality with other gays and lesbians. Others who are more comfortable with their homosexuality will look on holidays less as an opportunity for exploring sexuality but more for confirming it, or at least having the opportunity to be oneself. As with most tourists, there will be a concern to avoid a holiday experience which might mean behaving less freely than when at home. This is especially important when home environments, whether of family, friends or employment, are restrictive – as they can be for gays and lesbians, as was discussed in Chapter 2.

The holiday experience is likely to be of considerable significance to many gays and lesbians. Holidays provide opportunities to 'escape' from problems of social censure, prejudice and isolation at home and to construct, confirm and live a desired identity. The overall holiday experience can and does offer considerable satisfaction to gays and lesbians and the fulfilment of their tourist motivations. Despite the risks and limitation of choice a substantial number of desirable destinations are left for consideration.

There are then many positive aspects of the holiday profiles of gays and lesbians. Their holidays do have, however, significance for a number of issues that are wider than those of the beneficial effects to individuals, and wider than those of the holidays themselves. Some of these issues are examined in this chapter. Initially, the significance of the linking of gay identity with consumption or patterns of expenditure is discussed, as are the implications for 'citizenship'. The issue of contested space was raised in Chapter 2 and is pursued here in the context of tourism. This has several tourism dimensions, as do gay and lesbian parades and festivals. These have implications for the relationships between homosexuals and heterosexuals generally, as much as they have for the development of gay and lesbian 'communities'.

Some of these issues may be of little direct concern either to gays and lesbians themselves or to those who supply holidays or who market them. It is important to recognize these, however, and to acknowledge the wider societal effects of decisions taken and actions carried out by individuals and organizations who are pursuing their own best interests.

Consumerism and Gay Identity

Holidays have come to be one of the defining characteristics of what it means to be gay or lesbian. In itself this is not a problem, but it is part of the wider issue of gay identity being channelled in a particular direction which has been reductive of sexuality. A gay and lesbian identity has become associated with the pursuit of a particular lifestyle, rather than associated primarily with sexuality. As discussed in the previous chapter, the image constructed by marketers has been one associated with conspicuous consumption. Identifying as gay or lesbian has come to imply a particular way of life, including wearing distinguishing clothes and following certain leisure activities, including patronizing gay bars, clubs and similar facilities and frequent holiday-taking (Schofield and Schmidt, 2005). This is, in some ways, no more than a wider societal preoccupation with constructing identity through consumption, display of goods and services and leisure (Featherstone, 1987). A consumer constructs and demonstrates an identity according to the meanings attached to goods and services and gay identity has become a commoditized and commercialized form of identity (Kates, 1998). The significance of other possible aspects of a gay identity has been minimized so that 'what it means to be gay becomes increasingly articulated through what it means to be a gay consumer' (Sender, 2004, p. 144).

The emergence of a gay identity and community does owe a great deal to the attention of commercial institutions (including bars and clubs) to the supposed market potential of gays (Badgett, 2001). The gay community's meeting places and sites of identity formation have been bars, clubs (Haslop *et al.*, 1998) and holiday destinations, so it is not too surprising that being gay (or lesbian) has come to be defined as following a particular lifestyle, including drinking, clubbing and holiday-taking, rather than by other criteria (Bell and Binnie, 2000; Badgett, 2001). Undoubtedly, though, this has meant gays and lesbians have been able to identify as gay in positive ways.

Many gays and lesbians, though, cannot readily relate to the 'typical lifestyle' and, as a result, are unable to identify comfortably with being gay or lesbian. 'Not having the financial capability seriously compromises one's attempts to lead a "modern gay lifestyle"' (Binnie, 2000, p. 171) leading to exclusion from the 'community' for many. It is exclusionary as much as it is inclusionary. It has been noted earlier, for instance, that a particular holiday image can only be applied to a (unknown) proportion of gays and lesbians. Those who cannot afford such a holiday profile and who therefore do not fit into the picture of the 'typical' homosexual may feel alienated from what it means to be gay or lesbian. It is evident also that for those who do go on holiday, destination choice is limited – more so than for other holidaymakers, and the freedom associated with holidays is circumscribed by the need to modify behaviour and avoid situations that could be problematic.

Distraction

A further implication of this linking of gay identity with consumerism is that is has been perceived by some to have distracted from the pursuit of more fundamental freedoms and from the pursuit of political ends, whether of an assimilationist or of a more radical nature. It is commonly argued that 'consumerism diminishes political agency rather than strengthening it' (Ingebretsen, 1999, p. 134) and gays and lesbians have been distracted by the pursuit of material gain (such as holiday-taking) from remedying significant issues relating to their lives, such as removing societal disapproval and eliminating anti-gay, or at least inequitable, legislation (Whittle, 1994; Field, 1995; Gluckman and Reed, 1997b; Ingebretsen, 1999).

Consumerism may well be an opportunity to assert economic power, but this may be a freedom that is illusory (Binnie, 1995). This freedom – to consume, to go on holiday – has been fostered and is considered accept-able by the rest of society which, none the less, restricts freedom to that dimension and determines its limits so as to restrict any threat to hetero-sexual hegemony (Field, 1995; Richardson, 2001). The 'thriving gay and lesbian market' may be regarded as progress but also as encouraging indi-vidualism at the expense of a more collective and community ethos and deterring participation in political activity (Rimmerman, 2002). Intensive holiday-taking, the existence of a large number of gay and lesbian parades and festivals, sporting events and circuit parties can be regarded as progress, though they can equally be considered as distractions from the pursuit of equality. One observer commented that it would be 'naïve to conflate public visibility with social progress; . . . the high level of visibility that [Sydney] Mardi Gras now enjoys may conceal systematic oppression, homophobia and discrimination' (Markwell, 2002, p. 83); the underlying issues remain. The apparent conflict between consumerism and the drive for acceptance and equality can be summed up in the comments of the Director of the National Gay and Lesbian Task Force (USA) about the re-election of President G. W. Bush: 'we can either fight or we can go on dancing' (quoted in Beaumont, 2004).

Not only might gays and lesbian be distracted but, in addition, the portrayal of gays and lesbians as prosperous and living a leisure-oriented life carries the risk that others will fail to recognize or acknowledge legal and social discrimination and disapproval. They have been portrayed as a privileged group with the opportunity and desire to pursue pleasure and their own interests, who are therefore undeserving of civil rights protec-tion. Stereotypes are reinforced and the images can be counter-productive in that they further alienate gays and lesbians from the rest of society. Some will then denounce the call for legal equality (Gluckman and Reed, 1997b; Badgett, 2001).

Citizenship

The arguments about gay identity being a commodified, consumerist one and its effects on the pursuit of political ends, are related to the issue of 'citizenship' – a sense of membership of a community or nation. The sup-posed ability of gays and lesbians to consume, such as holiday-taking, portrays an impression of being full 'citizens' in the sense of being fully able to enjoy material rewards. Holidays have come to be regarded as a 'necessary' part of contemporary life and this has been the case for some considerable time. It was reported, for instance, in a 1985 study, that 63% of the UK population considered a 1-week holiday away from home per year (not staying with relatives) to be a 'necessity' (Mack and Lansley, 1985). Urry (1990) considered that 'not to go away is like not possessing a car or nice house. It is a matter of status in modernist societies' (p. 4).

One study of people who could not go on holiday, because of adverse economic and social conditions, concluded that 'opportunities to go on holiday should be treated as an important indicator of social well-being' (Haukeland, 1990, p. 179). Gays and lesbians can therefore be considered to have achieved citizenship, at least in the consumerism interpretation of the term. This refers to the rights of citizens as consumers (Evans, 1993), the right to live according to society's prevailing standards and to consume goods and services that are generally considered to be 'the norm'. The perception of high holiday propensity and intensive holiday-making of gay men (and possibly lesbians) would seem to suggest that they are not excluded from this consumerist aspect of citizenship. Gay men and women would appear to be full citizens in that they are able to consume services that are widely considered to be desirable or even necessary.

It has been noted previously, however, that the 'typical' holiday profile is unlikely to apply to all. In addition, limited destination choice and behaviour adaptation on holiday are limitations on full inclusion in society and the marketing moment has thus not delivered full citizenship (Hughes, 2005). 'We do not think of tourism as a citizenship right until our freedom to travel is threatened' (Rojek, 1998, p. 291). Awareness of the limited choices and of the desire of some places to exclude gay and lesbian visitors and the 'fantasy' of gay-friendliness not materializing on a holiday, for whatever reason, may also have an adverse effect on self-esteem.

Regardless of whether gays and lesbians are 'consumer citizens', citizenship has dimensions other than consumerism. In most of Western Europe there has been a predisposition towards a 'liberal' interpretation of the concept of citizenship as, for instance, formulated by Marshall (1950). The concept is a complex one, though in a basic sense it relates to 'nationality', rights of abode and of entitlement to services (especially state services such as health and education), rights to participate in the political system, equality before the law and freedom to be able to do certain things without hindrance. This Marshallian perspective and subsequent developments have been criticized for failing to recognize that 'some citizens are able . . . to assert more successfully their citizenship rights. This success is, in turn, shaped by a citizen's place in the class structure, his or her gender or ethnic origin and so on' (Faulks, 1998, p. 177).

As the concept of citizenship 'is closely associated with the institutionalisation of heterosexuality' (Richardson, 2001, p. 157), gays and lesbians in many countries may not experience equality of rights relating to sexual activity, nor equal access to general rights (such as marriage). These are sometimes referred to as 'sexual citizenship', in which respect gays and lesbians have not achieved full citizenship (Weeks, 1998). Homosexuality has frequently been regarded as a threat to the nation state, which is often based on such concepts as family (Richardson, 1998) and it is only in the sphere of 'citizenship as consumerism that non-heterosexuals seem to be most acceptable as citizens' (Richardson, 2001, p. 162). In the non-consumer sphere it is argued that gays and lesbians have not achieved full citizenship and, although holiday-taking is seen as inclusion, even there, there may be less than full citizenship. In addition, it, along with other aspects of consumerism, has served to distract from and further delay full citizenship.

Contested Space

A further general issue to which tourism contributes is that of 'contested space'. It is evident that tensions exist within many societies between local gays and lesbians and the rest of the population. It has also been discussed how 'space' was important in the construction of identity, but how most space was heteronormative. The desire of gays and lesbians to express their sexuality may therefore give rise to 'contested space'. This relates not solely to the use of buildings, facilities or open space (streets, parks, squares, etc.), but more generally to the ability of gays and lesbians to be open about their sexuality without contestation. This has a local, domestic dimension but there can also be a tourism dimension superimposed on it.

Local dimension

With respect to the local dimension of contested space, the success and acceptance of the Manchester gay space, for instance, has led to an influx of local non-gay customers and it has become space that is directly contested between gays and straights. Similar concerns have arisen in Belfast and Newcastle-upon-Tyne (Kitchin and Lysaght, 2003; Casey, 2004). Whilst gay space has particular advantages for gays and lesbians it can also be problematic by signalling 'presence', and thus providing a focus for homophobes and for physical and verbal abuse. Contestation does not solely take the form of abuse, however, but also the threat of it and, at a more subtle level, simply by the presence of non-gays. The attraction of the Manchester Village to non-gays has been its novelty and trendiness (and curiosity value) and, at one stage, because of a bar and club scene elsewhere in the city that was mature and limited. The presence of all-male heterosexual groups has been considered threatening by both lesbians and gay men, and there has been a fear of homophobic intrusion, abuse and violence (Pritchard *et al.*, 2002). Heterosexual women wishing to avoid the masculine culture of night-time cities have also used gay space for 'safety' (Skeggs, 1999). Lesbians, though, feel marginalized in their own space by this, as heterosexual women destabilize the nature of the gay space. Straight women who may have no difficulty relating to gay men may also regard lesbians as threatening (Casey, 2004).

Further contestation in respect of gay space has arisen within the gay and lesbian population itself because of the apparent focus on 'the young and the beautiful' (Whittle, 1994, p. 38). Manchester's Village has excluded as much as it included and 'among the marginalized groups are lesbians, ethnic minorities and older gay men' (Hindle, 2000, p. 26). It is not uncommon for lesbians to experience intolerance from some gay men, as they reinforce notions of patriarchal society (Pritchard *et al.*, 2002). The Le Marais district of Paris has been a similar commercial gay space and has, in effect, excluded the poor, the old, the unattractive and women (Sibalis, 2004). Alienation of some gays and lesbians can also be the effect of gay and lesbian parades and festivals also, because of an inability to identify with them or the images generated. The Sydney Mardi Gras, for instance, is relatively expensive and its organization, participation and representation are dominated by white, urban, middle-class gays (Markwell, 2002). The West Hollywood Pride (known as Christopher Street West Pride from 1978) was initially dominated by working-class men, but city council concern about mismanagement in 2000 made its grant conditional on it becoming more professional (Ward, 2003). It lost its transgressive nature and became 'predictable, contained, bureaucratic, welcoming to heterosexuals and produced in co-operation with police and other symbols of power and authority' (Ward, 2003, p. 89).

Non-gay tourists and contested space

Tourism will add a further dimension to these 'contested space' issues. In the same way as the local gay and lesbian population may resent the intrusion of local non-gays, there may also be a tension that arises from heterosexual tourists visiting local gay and lesbian venues. A strong local gay and lesbian community and gay space may have a positive effect on non-gay tourism flows. In the case of San Francisco, for instance, gay and lesbian sites are featured in non-gay travel guides (Howe, 2001). These are considered one of the attractions of the city and suitable objects for the tourist gaze: 'the sexual other takes the place of the primitive other on which to gaze' (Howe, 2001, p. 47). Manchester's Gay Village is also featured in mainstream tourist guides as a place to go.

In both instances, however, the presence of non-gay tourists in local gay space (or in 'gay holiday destinations') may not be welcomed by local gay and lesbian populations (or by gay and lesbian tourists). Some gays may believe that the use of gay space by straight tourists represents acceptance – and therefore 'success' – in overcoming heterosexual hegemony, but there are some unfavourable aspects to it. Gays and their way of life become objects for the 'tourist gaze'. The presence of heterosexuals – local and tourist – promotes concerns of being exposed or of feeling a need to be inhibited in behaviour and a dislike of being the object of the gaze.

'The [Manchester] Village has turned itself into a . . . zoo where the wider population can come and gawp at the gay inhabitants' (Wilson, 2001, p. 20). The promotion of gay space as a tourism commodity also entails a 'watering-down of queerness' (Rushbrook, 2002, p. 198) and the creation of an image that will be acceptable to a heteronormative society (Binnie and Skeggs, 2004). This further minimization of the diversity of homosexual experience, though, will not be acceptable to some gays and lesbians who use the gay space.

Whatever the tensions that might arise from the interaction of gays and lesbians and non-gays, gay space and gay events are, in effect, 'de-gayed' – they lose their character and meaning and it contributes to a feeling of 'disempowerment, disenfranchisement and the loss of control over crucial places and spaces' (Pritchard *et al.*, 1998, p. 280). Given the importance of gay space and gay events for identity formation, and the perception of gay space as a place of security and safety and where privacy and confidentiality can be assured, this de-gaying may be of considerable significance.

Gay and lesbian tourists and contested space

In addition to straight tourists being an issue, so might gay and lesbian tourists be, as local gays and lesbians can feel displaced by the tourists. The supposed existence of an international community of gays and lesbians, and a greater empathy for fellow homosexuals in other countries than for heterosexual society at home, may lead to the assumption that gay tourists will be welcomed. They may, nevertheless, physically 'crowd out' locals from their space, promote a feeling of loss of ownership of the space, damage the bindings of local communities and be a source of irritation in much the same way as any tourist can be to local residents. The Castro district of San Francisco is an extremely popular destination for gay and lesbian visitors, though it evolved as a residential and commercial community neighbourhood. Local gays and lesbians may resent the treatment of their space as a tourist sight but, in addition, such a place risks a transformation into serving the tourist trade rather than the local population, and thus losing its community spirit. In Cape Town, apart from a homophobic backlash from some elements of the local population, there has been concern about the gentrification of the Waterkant area and a loss of community. The development has, in addition, served to alienate elements of the local gay and lesbian community, especially lesbians, blacks and coloureds. It 'welcomes the empowered gay play-boy whilst, at the same stroke, marginalizing the already dis-empowered of Cape Town' (Visser, 2003, p. 186). It is possible too that local gays and lesbians may find some difficulty identifying with the image of their town or country that is projected to encourage homosexual tourists.

A more positive aspect of the inflow of gay and lesbian tourists, though, may be the development of gay and lesbian space such as bars, clubs and restaurants in some parts of the world where they were poorly developed previously. Such an infrastructure may owe more to servicing the needs of tourists than to a local population, which may be small or 'undeveloped'. Cape Town has become a popular destination for gay and lesbian visitors from Europe and North America. The number and range of bars, clubs, saunas and guest houses are associated with this tourism and not with a local population (Visser, 2003). There is a similar lack of a gay residential concentration in Amsterdam, and the extensive gay space would not exist if not for tourists to the city (Hughes, 1998).

Local non-gay residents

A further dimension of contested space, apart from the tourism impact on local gay and lesbian populations, is that of the impact on the local non-gay population. It has been noted previously how the presence of gay and lesbian tourists may give rise to tensions between them and locals, or between them and heterosexual tourists. Also, the promotion of a place as a gay and lesbian tourist destination can cause local residents disquiet because of the 'inappropriate' image portrayed. The reaction to the 1999 gay tourism campaign for Manchester (UK) was noted earlier. Some destinations may become both spatially and symbolically transformed by their popularity with gay and lesbian tourists. The physical appearance of a town or city, or at least parts of it, may be altered by the use of indicators such as rainbow flags and other symbols of gay space, by signs and shop displays and by the changed use of buildings, for instance, into gay bars or shops or saunas.

The concentration of usage into particular areas gives rise to identifiable gay space, such as the three or four separate clusters of Amsterdam (Hughes, 1998). The whole atmosphere of a place may be altered by the presence of gay and lesbian tourists; symbolic transformation may also occur when a town or city becomes known as 'a place for gays and lesbians' or a 'gay capital'. Manchester's Gay Village (UK) has been held to foster an image of the city which is not acceptable to all. A national Sunday newspaper report on the 1999 Mardi Gras (Pride) festival concluded: 'This city built its reputation with its export of high-quality machines and textiles, now it is reduced to peddling homosexual bars and clubs – and sex' (Hillmore, 1999, p. 38). Any or all of this can give rise to hostility from local non-gay residents, though in some cases spatial transformation – especially in some large cities – may owe more to local development than to tourism. Subsequent symbolic transformation may be down to efforts of destination-marketing organizations.

One of the more unfortunate impacts of gay and lesbian tourism may be the reinforcement of any anti-gay feelings within the local community.

High-profile gay and lesbian tourism introduced into communities that are already unsympathetic to homosexuality, such as in parts of the Caribbean, may stimulate a backlash for 'native' gays and lesbians (Puar, 2001).

Some of the opposition to gay and lesbian tourism is couched in terms of its possible adverse effect on other forms of tourism. Potential tourists may be deterred from visiting a destination which promotes itself as a gay destination or which is known to be popular with gays and lesbians. None the less, it is possible that these points may, in practice, have a positive effect on non-gay tourism. The tourism dimension of gay pride parades and festivals has been mentioned earlier. In addition, the presence and acceptance of gay and lesbian tourists may be interpreted as indicating tolerance and diversity, and can have a positive effect on tourist flows even if those tourists do not interact with gay and lesbian tourists. Any place that openly welcomes gay and lesbian visitors may be viewed by more liberal-minded tourists as a potentially attractive destination.

Gay space in a holiday destination may also attract tourists through 'novelty' value and its reassurance as 'safe' space. Some non-gay tourists may perceive gays and lesbians to be, in some way, better behaved on holiday. One UK newspaper columnist took his family (wife and children) on holiday to Sitges, in part because it was a gay resort 'and therefore seems likely to discourage the loutish, public-vomiting element' (Hogan, 2003, p. 6). In a similar vein, a director of the tour company Respect believed that gays were popular with hoteliers 'because they tend not to get their hotel rooms or apartments smashed up and they tend not to get complaints from other residents about terrible drunken revelry at four o'clock in the morning' (Walker, 2000).

Parades and Festivals

A further source of contestation between gays and straights may be gay and lesbian parades and festivals which, in large measure, are intended to intrude into heteronormative space. They have no necessary connection with tourism but it is evident that many have such a dimension and that spectators may be heterosexuals. Part of the basis for parades may have been the desire to challenge heteronormativity of society through increased visibility, the claim of gays and lesbians on public space and the requirement to be accepted during parades and festivals. This is achieved by a demonstration of 'difference', but that very display 'can reinforce the notion that gays and lesbians comprise a minority qualitatively different from the putative heterosexual majority' (Graham, 2002, p. 36) and reinforces and emphasizes the difference and increases heterosexual anxiety. The exaggerated portrayals of gays and lesbians (especially as drag queens, disco bunnies or butch leather boys) serve to confirm and perpetuate stereotypes in heterosexuals' minds.

Heterosexuals may be willing spectators at parades and festivals, but only if sexuality and difference are contained and not allowed to become permanently visible. It is only a temporary challenge to heteronormative society and it is 'authorised transgression' (Markwell, 2002, p. 90). It is similar to gays and lesbians being 'allowed' to be citizens in the consumer sense. Straights may watch only out of curiosity and a desire for entertainment, whilst maintaining a view of 'deviant other' about gays and lesbians. The invisibility of homosexuality is lifted and it becomes less of a threat, making heterosexuals more comfortable about themselves (Johnston, 2001), though the intrusion of sexuality into the public sphere may also create unease. Gay and lesbian festivals in New Zealand have, in the past, been criticized in the 'straight' press for exhibitionism and the flaunting and glamorizing of homosexuality; by implication, this should have been confined to the private sphere (Brickell, 2000).

Heterosexual spectators at gay and lesbian festivals and parades may, though, in a reverse sequence, be considered to be intruding into what are considered by some to be essentially gay and lesbian events. They may, in addition, intrude into physical gay space. The Manchester (UK) lgbt festival is considered to have added to tensions for, as the *Guardian* newspaper commented, 'straights pour into the [Gay] Village for the event' (Anon., 1999, p. 13). Space is contested between homosexuals and heterosexuals, whether they are locals or tourists, in the way that the gay space of bars, clubs and residences can be.

'De-gaying' and depoliticization

Tourism is also associated with further significant issues to do with such festivals and parades. Many are believed to have become 'de-gayed', as well as depoliticized and over-commercialized (Hughes, 2006). Pride political parades have become festivals and have been promoted, and rationalized, as tourist attractions. The Sydney Mardi Gras, for instance, 'is now inextricably framed within a global gay and lesbian tourist industry that demands spectacle [and] consumption of experience' (Markwell, 2002, p. 85). The construction of parades and festivals for a straight audience (locals and tourists) and for gay and lesbian tourists who equally want entertainment and spectacle rather than transgression, combined with the desire to project an 'acceptable' image of gays and lesbians, has meant that they have become sanitized and depoliticized. For many, their ownership and meaning have been modified, and political protest and struggle has arguably been sidelined in pursuit of other, more material, objectives. The sense of ownership of many events may have been diminished because of the use by tourism. Parades may no longer be the outcome of a desire to make a political gesture or to express gay identity, but are the outcome of a need to attract tourists. The meaning of many parades has been diluted and their form changed; they have become devalued and distorted. Opportunities for self-expression and the ability to establish and consolidate gay identity have been undermined through this erosion by tourism, whether gay or non-gay.

The significance of tourism in this apparent shift of lgbt festivals from politics to party is, however, arguable. The promotion of gay festivals as tourist attractions has been a key factor in the development of some, and as such may be considered to have been beneficial. It has also, however, strengthened the perception of festivals as being concerned with 'party' and contributed to the depoliticization of many. Tourism has, from this perspective, been the 'cause'.

An alternative view is that the shift towards 'party' and depoliticization has been occurring anyway (related to a more general consumerism and reduced interest in politics throughout the population as a whole). This shift, through more emphasis on carnival and festival, has created tourism. Tourism, from this perspective, has been the 'effect'. The situation is evidently not clear-cut and the two are intertwined: non-locals cause 'more party' and 'more party' attracts non-locals. In the specific case of gays and lesbians, of course, it can be argued that there has been an 'inevitable' shift as political gains have been made and the need for protest has diminished. Nevertheless, it is clear that the shift was occurring before such achievements and in countries where political gains have not been as great as in others.

Exploitation

Gay parades and festivals have been used by tourist boards for the purpose of promoting a destination to visitors, both homosexual and heterosexual, and also for place-marketing. Part of this strategy is to suggest diversity and tolerance, as exemplified by gayness (Rushbrook, 2002), but it can lead to a sense of exploitation and manipulation for the advantage of others. This argument has been applied equally to similar usage of gay space and communities, so that 'gay sexuality is being exploited as an urban spectacle' (Quilley, 1997, p. 291). This may add to tensions existing already: between gays and straights and between locals and visitors (Hughes, 2003, 2006). Gay space is diluted as a centre of empowerment and cultural strength and gay people no longer feel 'ownership'. Gay space is 'touristified' and, whilst it is a sign of heterosexual acceptance, it also establishes heterosexual control (Pritchard *et al.*, 1998).

This is not confined to tourism, as cities market themselves in order to attract inward investment and migration as well as visitors. This, though, necessitates a dilution of the spirit of the gay space. The growth of

Manchester's gay space was spontaneous rather than planned and was a case of redevelopment of a run-down commercial area by entrepreneurs (Hindle, 2000). This was only later enlisted by local government for place-marketing in encouraging a more positive image of the city and consequent inward investment as well as tourism. It 'was due more to the area's economic importance in marketing the city' (Quilley, 1997, p. 284) than out of concern for social equity (Kitchin, 2002; Rushbrook, 2002). The city was anxious to generate a vision of progressiveness, liberalism and cosmopolitanism as competitive tools in place-marketing, but it has furthered the shift from 'ownership' of the Village by locals to appropriation by others for their own ends.

Community and Force for Change

A further issue relates to the idea of the universal homosexual community. Gays and lesbians may be characterized as a 'quasi-ethnic community' (see Chapter 2), and this concept has been extended further to envisage a worldwide homosexual community. The concept of gay ethnicity or a gay nation is attributed by Cox (2001) to the interaction of the tourists themselves. It is also likely, though, that tourism provides 'models' for gays and lesbians in societies where gay life is less open, encourages local homosexuals to be more open and brings with it the previously unfamiliar concept of a gay or homosexual identity. Changes in Mexican homosexual subculture were believed to be the outcome of an indigenous gay and lesbian movement but were also 'intimately linked to queer tourism' (Cantu, 2002, p. 139). Local gay communities and networks may be encouraged by the visibility of gay and lesbian tourists. Similarly, 'local' tourists to places such as the USA may return with a desire to replicate developments there. Mexican gay men who had been to the USA have had an influence on the emergence of gay networks and communities in Mexico (Sanchez-Crispin and Lopez-Lopez, 1997).

Alternative lifestyles are explored and valued and a sense of community with a trans-national dimension is established. It may seem reasonable to assume that, with globalization (the standardization and homogenization of cultures), a worldwide homosexual community exists (Manalansan, 1995, 2000) and that 'tourism . . . is one of the most important aspects of the globalization of sexuality and sexual identities' (Puar, 2002a, p. 1). Altman (2001) considers that globalization has helped create an international gay and lesbian identity of people who have more in common across boundaries than with others in their own societies. He recognizes, though, that globalization does not necessarily mean homogenization, but more a modification of global factors by local cultural pressures and that race and nationality remain important aspects of identity.

Binnie (2000) dismisses a universal homosexual identity as being a 'romantic myth' (p. 174), largely on the grounds that the identity is grounded in Western consumerist and urban lifestyles. The concept of a 'gay identity' is a Western import that can, unthinkingly, be assumed to be the desirable norm for other societies. Such an assumption may be considered to be a form of neo-colonialism in the same way as is gay tourism which is based on the inequality of commercial sex tourism and the concept of the 'exotic foreign other' to be exploited. As such, it could not realistically be conceived of as a contribution to the construction of a universal homosexual community (Altman, 1997; Cantu, 2002).

Finally, gays and lesbians travelling may be a force with the potential to change attitudes of heterosexuals. They are making homosexuality visible and challenging society's heteronormativity and, as such, they are part of an 'agenda of liberationist human rights' (Puar, 2001, p. 1046). This 'visibility politics' promotes a vision of a gay and lesbian world associated with relative affluence and leisure time which may fuel the aspirations of others. It provides, though, a distorted vision of what it means to be gay or lesbian, as the behaviour, demeanour and dress of tourists is unlike that at home. It is also often a vision that is unattainable for many in destinations and can therefore be more disruptive than bonding (Puar, 2002b).

Conclusions

Organizations and destinations that seek to meet or stimulate the tourism demand from gays and lesbians may not only be pursuing profit but, from an altruistic perspective, are also contributing to the significant role that holidays play in the creation of gay identity, both individual and collective.

In this chapter, the view has been discussed that identifying and targeting a gay and lesbian market has contributed to a particular gay and lesbian identity that is grounded in consumerism. This identity, it has been argued, has eliminated the diversity of sexual orientation and reduced it to a particular model. It has, too, encouraged gays and lesbians to aspire to that identity and consider themselves fulfilled once achieved, but at the expense of failing to pursue full citizenship. The apparently enhanced ability to go on holiday may have been but one of many pleasurable distractions from the pursuit of equality in the political sphere. Gays and lesbians may have been too busy enjoying themselves to bother too much about remedying disapproval and discrimination.

Gay and lesbian tourism has also exacerbated a number of existing tensions related to the contestation of what is ostensibly heteronormative space. It has become another dimension of the struggle between the ascendancy of heteronormativity and the requirement that sexuality be confined to the private sphere. It is another aspect of the struggle for acceptance of gays and lesbians by the rest of society.

Not only does sexual orientation influence the holiday abilities and decisions of gays and lesbians, but there is also an inverse effect: tourism and the marketing of it engage with the nature of homosexuality and have an influence upon it. Perhaps, most evidently, the development of homosexual identity is facilitated and modified through being away from home and also through a wider exposure to gays and lesbians than is possible at home. An enhanced opportunity to holiday may also raise self-esteem of gays and lesbians. Tourism can also encourage the development of homosexual (and gay) identities and communities in places where they have not existed before. A further outcome is that homosexual life and heterosexual acceptance of homosexuality are influenced by gay and lesbian tourism. To the dynamics of interaction between local gays and local non-gays are added interactions between tourists and locals (gays and non-gays). Tourism may result in the appropriation of hetero space by gays, and vice versa. The former case may be considered by homosexuals as 'progress', whereas the latter may not.

Whether or not such issues should feature in the promotion of gay and lesbian holidays is contentious. Bodies or individuals are generally commercial and profit-oriented, and wider issues such as this cannot necessarily be expected to feature in decision-making (Schlegelmilch, 1998; Ferrell et al., 2002; Hosmer, 2003; Desmond and Crane, 2004). There is considerable discussion about to whom participants in the free-market system should owe some degree of responsibility and what that social responsibility should be. This, in turn, will be influenced by legal restraints, cultural norms and by ethical philosophies ascribed to. There is common ground that marketers should adhere to codes of ethics about matters such as collecting market data, representing the product, health and environmental issues and pricing. Issues relating to representations of the consumer and to the social effects of promoting the product are less frequently addressed, but these are significant issues with respect to gay and lesbian tourism.

Tourism has particular implications for various aspects of gay and lesbian life, some of which are positive and others arguably less so. These issues are discussed here without an imperative (implicit or explicit) that 'something should be done'. In the case of advertising, some commentators have felt strongly that it 'can . . . change how we think about each other' (Ricker and Witeck, 2003, p. 1) and, as a consequence, there should be an obligation, according to GLAAD (2002), to show more representative and inclusive and less stereotypical images of gays and lesbians. The view that 'the overuse of idealised images of young, muscular, blond, hairless young men should be eschewed' (Kates, 1998, p. 191) may have particular resonance in the case of holiday promotional strategies. This, and especially the other issues addressed in this chapter, may be recognized by the tourism industry but, given the commercial nature of most of it, individual and isolated action to respond to them is unlikely. Opportunities for profit stimulate activity and the provision of goods and services. Amendment of strategies in response to some of these wider matters is unlikely if it is seen to interfere with commercial success. Awareness and consideration of these issues will, though, contribute something to the development of Tribe's (2002) 'philosophic practitioner', who is more than an unfettered and unconcerned capitalist.

Conclusions and Implications 9

This book has examined the holidays of gays and lesbians from a perspective that owes much to marketing. This has not been a marketing book but rather a book that has indicated the relationship between homosexuality and holidays, and this within a broadly marketing context. In this short chapter, conclusions from earlier chapters will be revisited and some ideas for future research briefly outlined.

The intent was to examine gay and lesbian holidays, in part because this is something that is currently under-researched. This mattered not only from a practical marketing perspective but also because of the insight it could give into homosexuality itself. Tourism studies have also tended to focus on the mainstream, but are beginning to recognize the diversity of tourism needs and experiences. A study of homosexuality and tourism would serve the purpose of filling gaps in tourism studies and contribute to an awareness of diversity, in a similar way as has the increasing attention to studies of women's leisure and tourism. A significant practical issue, however, in reviewing this field was the limited number of existing sources – research is in its early stages and, as yet, there is relatively little on which to base conclusions. As a consequence, a diversity of sources was consulted, some of which were less reliable than were others.

The desire to consider the two-way relationship between marketing and holiday-taking was based on the consideration of work in the wider gay and lesbian studies sphere, where it was evident that marketing to gays and lesbians was believed to have had significant repercussions beyond those simply of successful (or not) sales figures.

In examining the nature and characteristics of homosexuality, it was clear that the concept itself was nebulous and that any attempt to describe or analyse the holidays of homosexuals, therefore, faced some considerable difficulty. It was evident, however, that homosexuals, especially males, were marginalized in many societies. This had its origin in the 19th century construction of the homosexual concept and the bipolar classification of 'normal' heterosexuals and 'deviant' homosexuals. This marginalization meant that adjusting to and living with one's sexual orientation was a difficult process. Some societies had progressed further in accepting and tolerating homosexual lifestyles than had others, but currently gays and lesbians continue to be disapproved of and discriminated against in many parts of the world.

The importance of the leisure sphere and gay space (or the gay scene) as a forum for 'safe' socialization and for the ability of gays and lesbians to formulate an identity was noticeable. Many in Western Europe and North America now lead relatively open gay lifestyles and there had been, in some countries, significantly increased acceptance and progress in achievement of 'rights'. Other issues of possible significance to tourism included the fact that gay identity and community tended to be associated with 'the West' and with urban areas. There was also a conventional wisdom that, despite marginalization, gays (and lesbians less so) were desirable alpha consumers with considerable discretionary spending power and leisure time, and with particularly carefree and style-conscious consumption patterns.

These features were utilized to explain the apparently favourable holiday profiles of gays and lesbians. Most sources revealed a fairly upbeat view of gay and lesbian holidays and about prospects for this market. As with surveys about market characteristics of gays and lesbians, the influence of US material on general perceptions of the market has probably been considerable. In broad terms, however, there is an evident lack of information relating to the holidays of lesbians of either their needs, profiles or destinations. The information about gay men is restricted to a limited, well-defined group of individuals, and knowledge of the holidays of others in the gay population is restricted. Even in the surveys that have been completed, there are issues that remain unclear, especially relating to the role, for instance, of gay space, gay-friendliness or sexual activity in holiday decision-making, or about behaviour (sexual and other) and activities when on holiday. Past holiday destinations are often ascertained in an unhelpful way, as is the part played by gay-friendliness in influencing purchase decisions as opposed to favourably disposing gays and lesbians. It is arguably more important in the case of holidays (and other leisure pursuits) where it is part of the 'product', the holiday experience, than it is for purchases of cars or food.

With respect to 'market knowledge' there is the insuperable problem of carrying out surveys that will capture respondents who are representative of the gay and lesbian population. Given the difficulties in defining the nature of homosexuality, it would appear that limited surveys that cover only a self-selecting, 'out' section of that population will continue to dominate. Attempts to increase the representative nature of even these restricted respondents may be advisable. It has to be recognized too that, given the nature of the gay and lesbian surveys, making comparisons with the rest of the population may be difficult to justify. Further, data referred to in this book relate mostly to gays and lesbians in the USA and the UK, largely because of convenience. Such data may well exist for other tourist-generating countries in the rest of Europe, North America and Asia and could contribute to a more complete and global picture of gay and lesbian tourism. Much could be revealed also through small-scale investigations exploring attitudes and opinions in depth. These may not be representative of the population but they have the potential to reveal a wealth of material about feelings expressed in words that have meaning for the 'informants'. Such studies can often demonstrate people's views and innermost positions more clearly than can surveys.

It is argued, none the less, that holidays do have a special significance for gays and lesbians. A theme throughout this book has been how the 'push' of disapproval and discrimination has stimulated the desire to get away in order to be oneself. This may involve spending a short period of leisure time in a proximate city centre or travelling further and staying for a longer period of time somewhere on holiday. Apart from this specific impetus for holidaying, the reasons gay and lesbians go on holiday are similar to those of the rest of the population, but there may well be additional factors taken into account in assessing a potential destination. In many cases it is likely that varying degrees of gay-friendliness and absence of homophobia will be key desired attributes; it is important that the social environment is no less favourable than it is at home. Sexual activity as a reason for travel might be expected to be significant, given the problems faced by some in finding sexual partners at home. There is little to suggest, however, that this is the case.

Destination choice of gays and lesbians is a little more risky than for many others, given the hostility towards homosexuals in many parts of the world. Such general hostility may be discerned through word-of-mouth or sources such as news media, or more particularly through reports of anti-gay feeling directed towards tourists. There are many such instances reported which would be expected to affect choice decisions. The reaction of local residents and organizations appears to have an important influence on gay and lesbian holiday choices, but has not been researched in any systematic way. The extent and manner of the host–guest interaction and the effects of gay and lesbian tourism upon local cultural values are significant issues for further exploration. What gays and lesbians do on holiday and how their activities and behaviour compare with those of other tourists is also unknown.

Where gays and lesbians do choose to go on holiday is not altogether clear either, though there are certain places that feature regularly in tour operators' programmes and in gay and lesbian travel guidebooks. There would appear to be a number for places that are especially popular with US and British gays and lesbians, and these include coastal, sea and sun destinations and cities which have a reputation for gay-friendliness. Some of this would appear to be due to a strong local gay or lesbian community or, at least, a local community that has welcomed unconventional migrants and visitors.

The special holiday needs identified by many gays and lesbians have led to the emergence of tour operators and travel agents who specialize in that market. Some accommodation providers have also sought to target that market. The matter of gay-friendliness of destinations and accommodation seems to be of importance to gays and lesbians, and to some extent this can be determined by their own personal research, especially through the Internet. As a consequence, most gays and lesbians seem content to book holidays through mainstream suppliers. Apartments rather than hotels may have a particular attraction in order to maintain privacy. The supply side of gay and lesbian tourism has, though, been considerably under-researched. The structure of the tour operator sector and the nature of the competition within it raise particular issues with respect to choice options, price and brand loyalty. Specialist tour operators may also have played a significant role in facilitating gay and lesbian travel, and they may have a greater concern for the sustainability of particular destinations than do other tour operators.

Apart from the usual sights and events that attract tourists, there are a number of specific events that have a particular appeal to gay and lesbian tourists. These include the Gay Games (and the newer OutGames), gay pride parades and festivals and, particularly in the USA, circuit parties. Their influence on tourist flows is generally considered to be considerable, though is not known with much certainty.

There is an implicit assumption in much of the work that is available about gay and lesbian tourism that such a market does exist. This view was explored further and it was concluded that, in a sense, it was a circular argument – a gay and lesbian market existed because marketers had created it. Particularly favourable characteristics of gays, in particular, that surfaced in several surveys were the inevitable outcome of the survey methods and the desires of the promoters. Marketers choose to categorize people in certain ways. Sexual orientation could have been omitted from categorization and gays and lesbians targeted under other classifications, in so far as it is believed that sexual orientation has little or no impact on preferences and spending. The underlying assumption of perceiving a gay and lesbian market to exist is that sexual orientation will have an effect on expenditure patterns. Certainly, for those who have revealed their preferences and patterns with respect to holidays, this seems to be the case – the 'gayness' factor does influence purchase decisions.

The nature of the surveys on which these and other characteristics are based is such, however, that some reservations need to be held about their reliability. Despite this, marketers target the supposed market in the belief that it does exist (at least for men), is relatively upscale and, in the case of tourism, many target it successfully. Access to this market is becoming easier as the number of gay and lesbian magazines and magazine web sites increases. Dedicated marketing takes the form of 'modified' products – gay (or lesbian) holidays in gay accommodation organized by gay tour operators – or promotion that emphasizes gay-friendliness and understanding.

Although sexual orientation does play a role in holiday consumer behaviour, there is also a reverse sequence of holiday-taking influencing homosexuality. It has already been commented how holidays can facilitate the adoption of a gay identity and a sense of community. The identity created – and to which others might aspire – is one, however, that is associated with a particular consumerist lifestyle. This may have reduced the sexual aspect of that identity but, perhaps more importantly, this lifestyle – which includes holiday-taking – may be argued as having distracted gays and lesbians from endeavouring to improve their 'rights'. Gays and lesbians may be consumerist citizens, but they continue to experience less than full citizenship in other respects.

Gay and lesbian tourists can, in some parts of the world, stimulate the development and emergence of local gay space or gay and lesbian communities. It may be, however, that their presence causes resentment either among a local gay community that feels crowded out or among non-gays who have a hostility to gays and lesbians anyway. Existing issues of contested space are exacerbated. In a similar way, pride festivals or gay sporting events can generate strong feelings of empowerment for gays and lesbians, but can be a catalyst for contesting space between gays and non-gays. Although these events are not necessarily tourist-oriented, they often do have a considerable tourism dimension which adds to the issue. Heterosexual spectators at these, and heterosexual tourists who perceive gay villages and communities as tourist sights, may reduce the sense of ownership of these and contribute to 'de-gaying'. It may also contribute to a feeling among local gays of being 'used', especially where local councils, development agencies or tourist boards deliberately employ the community as an indicator of liberalism for reasons, including tourism, that are little to do with supporting gay and lesbian communities for their own sake. Issues such as de-gaying, contested space and exploitation are frequently asserted, but the reality of the interaction between gays and non-gays remains largely unexplored.

In conclusion, it has been shown that the holiday patterns of gays and lesbians are apparently different from those of most of the rest of the population. This is true at least of those who are represented in surveys which appear to capture similar people. The differences are explained by sexual orientation and the disapproval and discrimination experienced by homosexuals. The differences vary within the gay and lesbian population but are sufficient to cause accommodation providers, tour operators and others to deal with the market in a different way. One of the purposes of this book was to consider how holiday-taking and the marketing of holidays might affect gay and lesbian life. Significantly, holidays contribute to the development of gay identity but they also have consequences that go beyond that to affect relationships between gays and non-gays. It is apparent, too, that by studying homosexuality within the context of tourism, it has served to illuminate a number of issues relating to this sexual orientation. In particular, these include continuing difficulties faced by gays and lesbians and the extra dimensions of the difficulties. Frequently, gays and lesbians are only able to be fully open about their sexual orientation when in the leisure sphere including, in some instances, when being on holiday. The prospect of disapproval or discrimination when on holiday, a period of time when this is least desired, may be particularly daunting.

It may seem obvious that this study has raised more questions than have been answered. Some of these questions have been touched on in this chapter but a reading of any of the previous chapters reveals how much remains to be discovered. Much of what is written about gay and lesbian tourism is speculative or based on sources whose reliability may be questionable. Some of the arguments in this book are based on drawing out the implications of particular arguments and perspectives rather than on the firmer foundations of rigorous research. The scope for further work is therefore considerable. Given the significance of holidays to gays and lesbians, their influence on relationships between homosexuals and heterosexuals – and thus the significance for the evolution of gay and lesbian lives, some degree of importance can be attached to pursuing this field of research.

Holidays are a domain which contributes to the meaning of homosexual life and to the awareness and acceptance (or intolerance) of homosexuality. As a consequence, gay and lesbian tourism should be of interest and concern to more than merely commercial suppliers or market researchers. Holidays are opportunities for many gays and lesbians to 'make sense' of their lives. Hopefully, this book will stimulate others to undertake further investigations of this important field. Hopefully, too, it has made some small contribution to meeting the aspirations Schuyf and Sandfort (2000) and Weeks (2000) expressed for the study of gays and lesbians (as quoted in Chapter 1).

References

Adetunji, L. (2002) Gay staff treated unequally despite progress. *The Financial Times* (14 August), p. 8.

Aitchison, C. (1999) New cultural geographies; the spatiality of leisure, gender and sexuality. *Leisure Studies* 18, 19–39.

Aldrich, R. (1993) *The Seduction of the Mediterranean: Writing, Art and Homosexual Fantasy*. Routledge, London.

Aldrich, R. (1996) Colonialism and homosexuality. *Thamyris* 3 (1), 175–191.

Aldrich, R. (2004) Homosexuality and the city: an historical overview. *Urban Studies* 41 (9), 1719–1737.

Allcock, J. and Young, A. (eds) (2000) *Black Lambs and Grey Falcons: Women Travelling in the Balkans*, 2nd edn. Berghahn Books, New York.

Altman, D. (1997) Global gaze/global gays. *GLQ* 3, 417–436.

Altman, D. (2001) *Global Sex*. University of Chicago Press, Chicago, Illinois.

Amnesty International (2001) *Crimes of Hate, Conspiracy of Silence: Torture and Ill-treatment Based on Sexual Identity*. Amnesty International Publications, London.

Amnesty International UK (1997) *Breaking the Silence: Human Rights Violations Based on Sexual Orientation*. Amnesty International UK, London.

Anderson, A. (2000) Lesbos falls out of love with lesbian tourists. *The Independent on Sunday* (17 September), p. 23.

Anderson, B. (1991) *Imagined Communities: Reflections on the Origin and Spread of Nationalism*, Revised edn. Verso, London.

Anderton, B. (2004) *Is Rehoboth Turning into Ocean City?* (www.washingtonblade.com, 28 May, accessed 27 January 2005).

Andriotis, K. and Vaughan, R. (2003) Urban residents' attitudes towards tourism development: the case of Crete. *Journal of Travel Research* 42, 172–185.

Anon. (1999) Majorities unwelcome. *The Guardian* (30 August), p. 13.

Anon. (2002) Did you hear the one about the hotel that welcomed dogs but kicked out gays? *Gay Times* (September), p. 19.

Anon. (2004) World in brief: Solomon Islands. *Gay Times* (February), p. 67.

Anon. (2005a) Co-op asks Christian Voice to quit. *The Guardian* (24 June), p. 21.

Anon. (2005b) Russia. *Gay Times* (July), p. 78.

Apostolopoulos, Y. and Sonmez, S. (2001) Working producers, leisured consumers: women's experiences in developing regions. In: Apostolopoulos, Y., Sonmez, S. and Timothy, D. (eds) *Women as Producers and Consumers in Developing Regions*. Praeger, Westport, Connecticut, pp. 3–17.

Arabsheibani, R., Marin, A. and Wadsworth, J. (2004) In the pink: homosexual–heterosexual wage differentials in the UK. *International Journal of Manpower* 25 (3–4), 343–354.

Arguelles, L. and Rich, B. (1984) Homosexuality, homophobia and revolution: notes toward an understanding of the Cuban lesbian and gay male experience, part I. *Signs: Journal of Women in Culture and Society* 9 (4), 683–699.

Badgett, L. (1997a) Beyond biased samples: challenging the myths on the economic status of lesbians and gay men. In: Gluckman, A. and Reed, B. (eds) *Homo Economics: Capitalism, Community and Lesbian and Gay Life*. Routledge, London, pp. 65–71.

Badgett, L. (1997b) Vulnerability in the workplace. *Angles* 2 (1), 1–4.

Badgett, L. (2001) *Money, Myths and Change: the Economic Lives of Lesbians and Gay Men*. University of Chicago Press, Chicago, Illinois.

Badgett, L. and King, M. (1997) Lesbian and gay occupational strategies. In: Gluckman, A. and Reed, B. (eds) *Homo Economics: Capitalism, Community and Lesbian and Gay Life*. Routledge, London, pp 73–86.

Baer, B. (2002) Russian gays/Russian gaze: mapping (homo)sexual desire in post-Soviet Russia. *GLQ* 8 (4), 499–521.

Baird, V. (2004) *Sex, Love and Homophobia*. Amnesty International UK, London.

Banks, C. (2003) *The Cost of Homophobia: Literature Review on the Human Impact of Homophobia in Canada*. Gay and Lesbian Health Services of Saskatoon, Saskatoon, Canada.

Banks, C. (2005) Climate change. *Gay Times* (June), pp. 61–62.

Barrington, J. (1998) Beds. In: Bledsoe, L. (ed.) *Lesbian Travels: a Literary Companion*. Whereabouts Press, San Francisco, California, pp. 59–64.

Batalla-Duran, E., Oakeshott, P. and Hay, P. (2003) Sun, sea and sex? Sexual behaviour of people on holiday in Tenerife. *Family Practice: an International Journal* 20 (1), 493–494.

Bates, S. (2005a) Vengeance in the air as churches face expulsion. *The Guardian* (22 June), p. 8.

Bates, S. (2005b) Baptists end Disney boycott. *The Guardian* (24 June), p. 19.

Battles, J. (1998) Pink power seeks Dublin gay quarter. *Sunday Times* (11 January), p. 7.

Bauer, T. and McKercher, B. (2003) (eds) *Sex and Tourism: Journeys of Romance, Love and Lust*. Haworth Hospitality Press, New York.

Beaumont, P. (2004) Gay community fears new era of intolerance. *The Observer* (7 November), p. 17.

Bell, D. (1991) Insignificant others: lesbian and gay geographies. *Area* 23 (4), 323–329.

Bell, D. and Binnie, J. (2000) *The Sexual Citizen: Queer Politics and Beyond*. Polity Press, Cambridge, UK.

Bell, D. and Valentine, G. (1995) Introduction: orientations. In: Bell, D. and Valentine, G. (eds) *Mapping Desire: Geographies of Sexualities*. Routledge, London, pp. 1–27.

Bellis, M., Hughes, K., Thomson, R. and Bennett, A. (2004) Sexual behaviour of young people in international tourist resorts. *Sexually Transmitted Infections* 80 (1), 43–47.

Bennett, A. (2004) A common assault. *London Review of Books* 26 (21), 25–29.

Berno, T. and Ward, C. (2005) Innocence abroad: a pocket guide to psychological research on tourism. *American Psychologist* 60 (6), 593–600.

Besculides, A., Lee, M. and McCormick, P. (2002) Residents' perceptions of the cultural benefits of tourism. *Annals of Tourism Research* 29 (2), 303–319.

Bess, A. (2004) Marketers come out of the closet to target gays. *The Tribune* (www.hrc.org, 26 August, accessed 3 November 2004).

Beyond Barriers (2002) *First Out: Survey of Lesbian, Gay, Bisexual and Transgender People in Scotland*. Beyond Barriers, Glasgow, UK.

Beyond Barriers (2003) *System Three Poll Reveals Shocking Levels of Racism and Homophobia in Glasgow*. Beyond Barriers, Glasgow, UK (www. beyondbarriers.org.uk, accessed 4 April 2003).

Bhatia, S. (1997) Millions from Britain for Luxor killers. *The Observer* (23 November), p. 2.

Binnie, J. (1995) Trading places, consumption, sexuality and the production of queer space. In: Bell, D. and Valentine, G. (eds) *Mapping Desire: Geographies of Sexualities*. Routledge, London, pp. 182–199.

Binnie, J. (1997) Invisible Europeans: sexual citizenship in the New Europe. *Environment and Planning A* 29, 237–248.

Binnie, J. (2000) Cosmopolitanism and the sexed city. In: Bell, D. and Haddour, A. (eds) *City Visions*. Pearson, Harlow, UK, pp. 166–178.

Binnie, J. and Skeggs, B. (2004) Cosmopolitan knowledge and the production and consumption of sexualised space: Manchester's gay village. *The Sociological Review* 52 (1), 39–61.

Binnie, J. and Valentine, G. (1999) Geographies of sexuality – a review of progress. *Progress in Human Geography* 23 (2), 175–187.

Birkett, D. (2000) Bucks, brides and useless baggage: women's quest for a role in their Balkan travels. In: Allcock, J. and Young, A. (eds) *Black Lambs and Grey Falcons: Women Travelling in the Balkans*, 2nd edn. Berghahn Books, New York, pp. 208–216.

Black, D., Gates, G., Sanders, S. and Taylor, L. (2000) Demographics of the gay and lesbian populations in the United States: evidence from available systematic data sources. *Demography* 37 (2), 139–154.

Black, P. (2000) Sex and travel: making the links. In: Clift, S. and Carter, S. (eds) *Tourism and Sex: Culture, Commerce and Coercion*. Pinter, London, pp. 250–264.

Blackstock, C. (2004) B&B owner refused double bed for gays. *The Guardian* (30 June), p. 6.

Bledsoe, L. (ed.) (1998a) *Gay Travels: a Literary Companion*. Whereabouts Press, San Francisco, California.

Bledsoe, L. (ed.) (1998b) *Lesbian Travels: a Literary Companion*. Whereabouts Press, San Francisco, California.

Bledsoe, L. (1998c) Preface. In: Bledsoe, L. (ed.) *Gay Travels: a Literary Companion*. Whereabouts Press, San Francisco, California, pp. xi–xiv.

Bouthillette, A. (1997) Queer and gendered housing: a tale of two neighbourhoods in Vancouver. In: Ingram, G., Bouthillette, A. and Retter, Y. (eds) *Queers in Space: Communities, Public Places, Sites of Resistance*. Bay Press, Seattle, Washington, pp. 213–232.

Boyd, N. (1997) Homos invade SF! San Francisco's history as a wide-open town. In: Beemyn, B. (ed.) *Creating a Place for Ourselves: Lesbian, Gay and Bisexual Community Histories*. Routledge, London, pp. 73–96.

Boyd, N. (2003) *Wide Open Town: a History of Queer San Francisco to 1965*. University of California Press, Berkeley, California.

Branigan, T. (2004a) Beenie Man concert axed over homophobia fears. *The Guardian* (25 June), p. 8.

Branigan, T. (2004b) Sydney, Brighton and now . . . Hull? *The Guardian* (7 August), p. 4.

Bravmann, S. (1994) The lesbian and gay past: it's all Greek to whom? *Gender, Place and Culture* 1 (2), 149–167.

Brickell, C. (2000) Heroes and invaders: gay and lesbian pride parades and the public/private distinction in New Zealand media accounts. *Gender, Place and Culture* 7 (2), 163–178.

Brophy, K. (2004) Gay tourist victimisation: an investigation involving perceptions, reactions and recommendations for the tourist industry. MSc thesis, Business School, University of Plymouth, Plymouth, UK.

Brown, B. (1998) Foreword. In: Bledsoe, L. (ed.) *Lesbian Travels: a Literary Companion*. Whereabouts Press, San Francisco, California, pp. vii–ix.

Brown, J. (2004) On gay circuit, the party never ends. *New York Times* (www.travel2.nytimes.com/mem/travel, 30 April, accessed 3 November 2004).

Browne, K., Church, A. and Smallbone, K. (2005) *Do it with Pride in Brighton and Hove: Lesbian, Gay, Bisexual and Trans Lives and Opinions*. Survey report, School of the Environment, University of Brighton, Brighton, UK.

Brunt, P. and Courtney, P. (1999) Host perceptions of sociocultural impacts. *Annals of Tourism Research* 26 (3), 493–515.

Buhalis, D. (1998) Strategic use of information technologies in the tourism industry. *Tourism Management* 19 (5), 409–423.

Bunzl, M. (2000) The Prague experience: gay male sex tourism and the neo-colonial invention of an embodied border. In: Derdahl, B., Bunzl, M. and Lampland, M. (eds) *Altering States: Ethnographies of Transition in Eastern Europe and the Former Soviet Union*. University of Michigan Press, Ann Arbor, Michigan, pp. 70–95.

Burrows, G. (2004) *Gay and Ethical Shopping can Work* (www.ethicalmatters.co.uk/articles, accessed 3 November 2004).

Butler, J. (1990) *Gender Trouble: Feminism and the Subversion of Identity*. Routledge, London.

Butler, K. (1995) Independence for western women through tourism. *Annals of Tourism Research* 22 (2), 487–489.

Butler, R. (1980) The concept of the tourist area cycle of evolution: implications for management of resources. *Canadian Geographer* 24 (1), 5–12.

Campbell, D. (1999) US airline recognises gay workers' partners. *The Guardian* (2 August).

Cant, B. (1997) (ed.) *Invented Identities? Lesbians and Gays Talk about Migration*. Cassell, London.

Cantu, L. (2002) De ambiente: queer tourism and the shifting boundaries of Mexican male sexualities. *GLQ* 8 (1–2), 139–166.

Carey, S., Gountas, Y. and Gilbert, D. (1997) Tour operators and destination sustainability. *Tourism Management* 18 (7), 425–431.

Carter, S. and Clift, S. (2000) Tourism, international travel and sex: themes and research. In: Clift, S. and Carter, S. (eds) *Tourism and Sex: Culture, Commerce and Coercion*. Pinter, London, pp. 1–19.

Casey, M. (2004) De-dyking queer space(s): heterosexual female visibility in gay and lesbian spaces. *Sexualities* 7 (4), 446–461.

Chou, W. (2000) Individual strategies for tongzhi empowerment in China. In: Drucker, P. (ed.) *Different Rainbows*. Gay Men's Press, London, pp. 193–206.

Chrisafis, A. (2005) Gays and lesbians under siege as violence and harassment soar in Northern Ireland. *The Guardian* (6 June), p. 13.

Clark, D. (1993) Commodity lesbianism. In: Abelove, H., Barale, M. and Halperin, D. (eds) *The Lesbian and Gay Reader*. Routledge, New York, pp. 186–201.

Clift, S. and Carter, S. (2000) (eds) *Tourism and Sex: Culture, Commerce and Coercion*. Pinter, London.

Clift, S. and Forrest, S. (1999a) Gay men and tourism: destinations and holiday motivations. *Tourism Management* 20 (5), 615–625.

Clift, S. and Forrest, S. (1999b) Factors associated with gay men's sexual behaviours and risk on holiday. *AIDS Care* 11 (3), 281–295.

Clift, S. and Forrest, S. (2000) Tourism and the sexual ecology of gay men. In: Clift, S. and Carter, S. (eds) *Tourism and Sex: Culture, Commerce and Coercion*. Pinter, London, pp. 179–199.

Clift, S. and Page, S. (eds) (1996) *Health and the International Tourist*. Routledge, London.

Clift, S., Callister, C. and Luongo, M. (2002a) Gay men, holidays and sex: surveys of gay men visiting the London Freedom Fairs. In: Clift, S., Luongo, M. and Callister, C. (eds) *Gay Tourism: Culture, Identity and Sex*. Continuum, London, pp. 231–249.

Clift, S., Luongo, M. and Callister, C. (eds) (2002) *Gay Tourism: Culture, Identity and Sex*. Continuum, London.

Cock, J. (2003) Engendering gay and lesbian rights: the equality clause in the South African constitution. *Women's Studies International Forum* 26 (1), 35–45.

Community Closet Association (2003) *Mainstream Advertising Best Practices* (July). Community Closet Association, New York.

Community Marketing Inc. (2001) *Gay and Lesbian Travel Demographics 2001: 7th Annual Gay and Lesbian Travel Survey*. Community Marketing Inc., San Francisco, California (www.mark8ing.com, accessed 3 March 2003).

Community Marketing Inc. (2003) *Press Release and Executive Summary: 8th Annual Gay and Lesbian Travel Survey*. Community Marketing Inc., San Francisco, California (www.mark8ing.com, accessed 12 May 2003).

Connell, R. (1995) *Masculinities*. Polity Press, Cambridge, UK.

Cope, R. (2002) European leisure groups. *Travel and Tourism Analyst* 4, 2–20.

Copestake, A. (2004a) Winter warmers. *Gay Times* (February), pp. 115–132.

Copestake, A. (2004b) Scotland wants to win back gay tourists. *Gay Times* (August), p. 75.

Copestake, A. (undated) www.gaytimestravel.co.uk, accessed 24 September 2005.

Corteen, K. (2002) Lesbian safety talk: problematising definitions and experiences of violence, sexuality and space. *Sexualities* 5 (3), 259–280.

Cox, M. (2001) Gay holidaymaking: a study of tourism and sexual culture. PhD thesis, University College, University of London, London.

Crawford, B. (ed.) (1994) *Best Guide to Amsterdam and the Benelux,* 5th edn. Bookscene, Amsterdam.

Cunningham, M. (2004) *Land's End: a Walk Through Provincetown.* Vintage, London.

Czyzselska, J. (2003) Shipwrecked! *The Pink Paper* (11 July), pp. 20–22.

Davidson, P. (1996) The holiday and work experiences of women with young children. *Leisure Studies* 15 (2), 89–103.

Davis, G. (2004) Going cheap. *Gay Times* (April), pp. 137–139.

Davis, T. (1995) The diversity of queer politics and the redefinition of sexual identity and community in urban spaces. In: Bell, D. and Valentine, G. (eds) *Mapping Desire: Geographies of Sexualities.* Routledge, London, pp. 284–303.

Deem, R. (1996) No time for a rest? *Time and Society* 5 (1), 5–25.

Deem, R. (1999) How do we get out of the ghetto? Strategies for research on gender and leisure for the twenty-first century. *Leisure Studies* 18, 161–177.

De Kadt, E. (ed.) (1979) *Tourism: Passport to Development?* Oxford University Press, Oxford, UK.

De Lind van Wijngaarden, J. (1999) Between money, morality and masculinity: bar-based male sex work in Chiang Mai. In: Jackson, P. and Sullivan, G. (eds) *Lady Boys, Tom Boys, Rent Boys: Male and Female Homosexualities in Contemporary Thailand.* Harrington Park Press, Binghampton, New York, pp. 193–218.

Department of Trade and Industry (Women and Equality Unit) (2003) *Civil Partnership: a Framework for the Legal Recognition of Same-sex Couples.* Department of Trade and Industry, London.

Desmond, J. and Crane, A. (2004) Morality and the consequences of marketing action. *Journal of Business Research* 57 (11), 1222–1230.

Diaz, R. and Ayala, G. (2001) *Social Discrimination and Health: the Case of Latino Gay Men and HIV Risk.* National Gay and Lesbian Task Force Policy Institute, New York.

Doxey, G. (1975) A causation theory of visitor-resident irritants: methodology and research inferences. In: *Conference Proceedings: Sixth Annual Conference of the Travel Research Association,* San Diego, California, pp. 195–198.

Drucker, P. (ed.) (2000a) *Different Rainbows.* Gay Men's Press, London.

Drucker, P. (2000b) Introduction: remapping sexual identities. In: Drucker, P. (ed.) *Different Rainbows.* Gay Men's Press, London, pp. 9–41.

Duggan, L. (2002) The new homonormativity: the sexual politics of neoliberalism. In: Castronovo, R. and Nelson, D. (eds) *Materialising Democracy: towards a Revitalised Cultural Politics.* Duke University Press, Durham, North Carolina, pp. 175–194.

Duncan, N. (1996) Renegotiating gender and sexuality in public and private spaces. In: Duncan, N. (ed.) *BodySpace: Destabilising Geographies of Gender and Sexuality.* Routledge, London, pp. 127–145.

Dunne, G. (1997) *Lesbian Lifestyles: Women's Work and the Politics of Sexuality.* Macmillan, Basingstoke, UK.

Duval Smith, A. (1997) Angry southern Baptists declare boycott of 'pro-gay' Disney. *The Guardian* (19 June), p. 14.

Duyves, M. (1995) Framing preferences, framing differences: inventing Amsterdam as gay capital. In: Parker, R. and Gagnon, J. (eds) *Conceiving Sexuality: Approaches to Sex Research in a Post-modern World*. Routledge, London, pp. 51–66.

Egginton, J. (2004) Boys from Brazil. *Gay Times* (June), pp. 142–144.

Elliott, L., Morrison, A., Ditton, J., Farrall, S., Short, E., Cowan, L. and Gruer, L. (1998) Alcohol, drug use and sexual behaviour of young adults on a Mediterranean dance holiday. *Addiction Research* 6 (4), 319–340.

Elwood, S. (2000) Lesbian living spaces: multiple meanings of home. In: Valentine, G. (ed.) *From Nowhere to Everywhere: Lesbian Geographies*. Harrington Park Press, Binghampton, New York, pp. 11–27.

English Tourism Council, Wales Tourist Board, VisitScotland and Northern Ireland Tourist Board (2002) *The UK Tourist: Statistics 2000*. English Tourism Council, London.

Enloe, C. (1990) *Bananas, Beaches and Bases: Making Feminist Sense of International Politics*. University of California Press, Berkeley, California.

Erens, B., McManus, S., Prescott, A. and Field, J. (2003) *National Survey of Sexual Attitudes and Lifestyles II: Reference Tables and Summary Report*. National Centre for Social Research, London.

Esterberg, K. (1997) *Lesbian and Bisexual Identities*. Temple University Press, Philadelphia, Pennsylvania.

Evans, D. (1993) *Sexual Citizenship: the Material Construction of Sexualities*. Routledge, London.

Evans, G. (2002) In search of tolerance. In: Park, A., Curtice, J., Thomson, K., Jarvis, L. and Bromley, C. (eds) *British Social Attitudes: the 19th Report*. Sage, London, pp. 213–230.

Evans, N. (2001) The UK air inclusive tour industry: a reassessment of the competitive positioning of the independent sector. *International Journal of Tourism Research* 3 (6), 477–492.

Faulks, K. (1998) *Citizenship in Modern Britain*. Edinburgh University Press, Edinburgh, UK.

Featherstone, M. (1987) Lifestyle and consumer culture. *Theory, Culture and Society* 4 (1), 55–70.

Federation of Gay Games (2003) *Image of the Gay Games*. Strategic Planning Committee, Federation of Gay Games, Chicago, Illinois.

Fejes, F. and Lennon, R. (2000) Defining the lesbian/gay community? Market research and the lesbian/gay press. *Journal of Homosexuality* 39 (1), 25–42.

Fenton, K., Mercer, C., McManus, S., Erens, B., Wellings, K., Macdowall, W., Byron, C., Copas, A., Nanchahal, K., Field, J. and Johnson, A. (2005) Ethnic variations in sexual behaviour in Great Britain and risk of sexually transmitted infections: a probability survey. *Lancet* 365, 1246–1255.

Ferber, L. (2001) *Out (and About) in Cancún, Mexico* (www.uk.gay.com, 21 May, accessed 25 January 2005).

Ferrell, O., Fraedrich, J. and Ferrell, L. (2002) *Business Ethics: Ethical Decision Making and Cases*, 5th edn. Houghton Mifflin, Boston, Massachusetts.

Fickling, D. (2003) Lycra and lucre at Mardi Gras. *The Observer* (2 March), p. 23.

Fickling, D. (2004) Switch for gay resort in doldrums. *The Guardian* (8 January).

Field, N. (1995) *Over the Rainbow: Money, Class and Homophobia*. Pluto Press, London.

Florida, R. (2002) *The Rise of the Creative Class*. Basic Books, New York.

Forest, B. (1995) West Hollywood as symbol: the significance of place in the construction of a gay identity. *Environment and Planning D: Society and Space* 13, 133–157.

Forsyth, A. (2001) Sexuality and space: nonconformist populations and planning practice. *Journal of Planning Literature* 15 (3), 339–358.

Fugate, D. (1993) Evaluating the US male homosexual and lesbian population as a viable target market segment. *Journal of Consumer Marketing* 10 (4), 46–57.

Galliano, J. (2004) Eastern promise. *Gay Times* (October), pp. 73–75.

Gartner, W. (1993) Image formation process. *Journal of Travel and Tourism Marketing* 2 (2/3), 191–215.

Gartner, W. and Bachri, T. (1994) Tour operators' role in the tourism distribution system: an Indonesian case study. *Journal of International Consumer Marketing* 6 (3/4), 161–179.

Gevisser, M. (2000) Mandela's stepchildren: homosexual identity in post-apartheid South Africa. In: Drucker, P. (ed.) *Different Rainbows*. Gay Men's Press, London, pp. 111–136.

Ghaziani, A. (2005) The circuit party's Faustian bargain. *The Gay and Lesbian Review Worldwide* 12 (4) (www.glreview.com, accessed 13 September 2005).

Gibson, H. (2001) Gender in tourism: theoretical perspectives. In: Apostolopoulos, Y., Sonmez, S. and Timothy, D. (eds) *Women as Producers and Consumers in Developing Regions*. Praeger, Westport, Connecticut, pp. 19–43.

Gibson, O. (2004) Cash boost for gay station. *The Guardian* (www.media.guardian. co.uk, 13 December, accessed 13 December 2004).

GLAAD (Gay and Lesbian Alliance against Defamation) (2002) New study asks are advertisers missing out on the diverse gay and lesbian market? (www. glaad.org/publications, 4 September, accessed 11 July 2004).

GL Census Partners (2001) *The 2001 Gay and Lesbian Consumer Online Census*. GL Census Partners (Syracuse University, OpusComm Group, GSociety Inc.), New York.

GL Census Partners (2002) *The 2002 Gay and Lesbian Consumer Online Census*. GL Census Partners (Syracuse University, OpusComm Group, GSociety Inc.), New York.

GL Census Partners (2004–2005) *The 2005 Gay and Lesbian Consumer Online Census*. GL Census Partners (Syracuse University, OpusComm Group), New York.

Gluckman, A. and Reed, B. (eds) (1997a) *Homo Economics: Capitalism, Community and Lesbian and Gay Life*. Routledge, London.

Gluckman, A. and Reed, B. (1997b) The gay marketing moment. In: Gluckman, A. and Reed, B. (eds) *Homo Economics: Capitalism, Community and Lesbian and Gay Life*. Routledge, London, pp. 3–9.

Golden, C. (1994) Our politics and choices: the feminist movement and sexual orientation. In: Greene, B. and Herek, G. (eds) *Lesbian and Gay Psychology: Theory, Research and Clinical Applications*. Sage, Thousand Oaks, California, pp. 54–70.

Goldenberg, S. (2003) Gay in the USA. *The Guardian* G2 (15 July), pp. 6–7.

Golding, C. (2003) The pink pound. *Caterer and Hotelkeeper* (1 May), pp. 26–28.

Goldstein, R. (2002) *The Attack Queers*. Verso, London.

Gomes, A. (1999) Hawaii gives gay a cold shoulder. *Pacific Business News* (26 April).

Goni, U. (2004) Last tango for machismo as gay tourists flock to Argentina. *The Observer* (27 June), p. 21.

Goodson, L. and Phillimore, J. (2004) The inquiry paradigm in qualitative tourism research. In: Phillimore, J. and Goodson, L. (eds) *Qualitative Research in Tourism: Ontologies, Epistemologies and Methodologies.* Routledge, London, pp. 30–45.

Gough, J. (1989) Theories of sexual identity and the masculinisation of the gay man. In: Shepherd, S. and Wallis, W. (eds) *Coming on Strong.* Unwin Hyman, London, pp. 119–136.

Graham, M. (2002) Challenges from the margins: gay tourism as cultural critique. In: Clift, S., Luongo, M. and Callister, C. (eds) *Gay Tourism: Culture, Identity and Sex.* Continuum, London, pp. 17–41.

Gregory, N. (2004) Trouble in paradise. *Gay Times* (August), pp. 55–58.

Gronchfelder, S. (2003) Cry freedom. *Gay Times* (August), pp. 54–55.

Grossman, C. (2003) Is homosexual backlash a permanent trend or mere blip? *USA Today* (30 July).

Gunn, C. (1988) *Vacationscapes: Designing Tourist Regions.* Van Nostrand Reinhold, New York.

Haber, P. (2003) Brotherly love comes out in Philly campaign (www.gfn.com/ news, 17 November, accessed 16 March 2004).

Haggard, L. and Williams, D. (1992) Identity affirmation through leisure activities: leisure symbols of the self. *Journal of Leisure Research* 24 (1), 1–18.

Halifax, N. (1988) *Out, Proud and Fighting: Gay Liberation and the Struggle for Socialism.* Socialist Workers Party, London.

Hall, C. (2004) Reflexivity and tourism research: situating myself and/with others. In: Phillimore, J. and Goodson, L. (eds) *Qualitative Research in Tourism: Ontologies, Epistemologies and Methodologies.* Routledge, London, pp. 137–155.

Hall, D. and Kinnaird, V. (1994) A note on women travellers. In: Kinnaird, V. and Hall, D. (eds) *Tourism: a Gender Analysis.* Wiley, Chichester, UK, pp. 188–209.

Halwani, R. (1998) Essentialism, social constructionism and the history of homosexuality. *Journal of Homosexuality* 35 (1), 25–51.

Hamer, D., Hu, S., Magnuson, V., Hu, N. and Pattatucci, A. (1993) A linkage between DNA markers on the X chromosome and male sexual orientation. *Science* 261, 321–327.

Hanna, J. (2005a) How advertising depicts gays and lesbians. *HarvardBusiness School Working Knowledge* (www.workingknowledge.hbs.edu, accessed 18 September 2005).

Hanna, J. (2005b) Marketing to gay and lesbian consumers. *Harvard Business School Working Knowledge* (www.workingknowledge.hbs.edu, accessed 18 September 2005).

Haslop, C., Hill, H. and Schmidt, R. (1998) The gay lifestyle: spaces for a subculture of consumption. *Marketing Intelligence and Planning* 16 (5), 318–326.

Haukeland, J. (1990) Non-travellers: the flip side of motivation. *Annals of Tourism Research* 17, 172–184.

Healey, D. (1999) Moscow. In: Higgs, D. (ed.) *Queer Sites: Gay Urban Histories since 1600.* Routledge, London, pp. 38–60.

Heckert, J. (2000) Beyond identity? Questioning the politics of pride. MSc dissertation. School of Social and Political Studies, University of Edinburgh, UK.

Hekma, G. (1999) Amsterdam. In: Higgs, D. (ed.) *Queer Sites: Gay Urban Histories since 1600*. Routledge, London, pp. 61–88.

Hencke, D. (2004) Holiday firm ends ban on gay couples. *The Guardian* (12 October) p. 13.

Herbert, I. (2005) Liverpool courts pink pound as the capital for gay weddings. *The Independent* (3 February).

Herold, E., Garcia, R. and DeMoya, T. (2001) Female tourists and beach boys: romance or sex tourism? *Annals of Tourism Research* 28 (4), 978–997.

Herrera, S. and Scott, D. (2005) We gotta get out of this place: leisure travel among gay men living in a small city. *Tourism Review International* 8, 249–262.

Heyer, H. (2005) The debate over gay tourism. *eTurboNews* (www.travelwirenews. com, 15 April, accessed 10 May 2005).

Higgs, D. (ed.) (1999a) *Queer Sites: Gay Urban Histories since 1600*. Routledge, London.

Higgs, D. (1999b) Introduction. In: Higgs, D. (ed.) *Queer Sites: Gay Urban Histories since 1600*. Routledge, London, pp. 1–9.

Hill, A. (2002) Pink bank slips into the red. *The Observer* (17 February), p. 10.

Hillmore, P. (1999) Madness of the gay ghetto where being normal is a crime. *Mail on Sunday* (29 August), p. 38.

Hindle, P. (1994) Gay communities and gay space in the city. In: Whittle, S. (ed.) *The Margins of the City: Gay Men's Urban Lives*. Arena, Aldershot, UK, pp. 7–25.

Hindle, P. (2000) The influence of the Gay Village on migration to central Manchester. *The North West Geographer* 3, 21–28.

Hogan, P. (2003) You say pedalo, I say Picasso. *The Observer: Escape* (12 January), pp. 6–7.

Holcomb, B. and Luongo, M. (1996) Gay tourism in the United States. *Annals of Tourism Research* 23 (3), 711–713.

Holt, M. and Griffin, C. (2003) Being gay, being straight and being yourself: local and global reflections on identity, authenticity and the lesbian and gay scene. *European Journal of Cultural Studies* 6 (3), 404–425.

Horowitz, J. and Newcomb, M. (2001) A multidimensional approach to homosexual identity. *Journal of Homosexuality* 42 (2), 1–19.

Horsfall, A. (2004) Back to our roots. *Gay Times* (November), 70–72.

Hosmer, L. (2003) *The ethics of management*, 4th edn. McGraw-Hill, New York.

Howe, A. (2001) Queer pilgrimage: the San Francisco homeland and identity tourism. *Cultural Anthropology* 16 (1), 35–61.

Hughes, H. (1997) Holidays and homosexual identity. *Tourism Management* 18 (1), 3–7.

Hughes, H. (1998) Sexuality, tourism and space: the case of gay visitors to Amsterdam. In: Tyler, D., Guerrier, Y. and Robertson, M. (eds) *Managing Tourism in Cities: Policy, Process and Practice*. Wiley, Chichester, UK, pp. 163–178.

Hughes, H. (2002a) Gay men's holidays: identity and inhibitors. In: Clift, S., Luongo, M. and Callister, C. (eds) *Gay Tourism: Culture, Identity and Risk*. Continuum Press, London, pp. 174–190.

Hughes, H. (2002b) Gay men's holiday destination choice: a case of risk and avoidance. *International Journal of Tourism Research* 4 (4), 299–312.

Hughes, H. (2003) Marketing gay tourism in Manchester: new market for urban tourism or destruction of gay space? *Journal of Vacation Marketing* 9 (2), 152–163.

Hughes, H. (2004) A gay tourism market: reality or illusion, benefit or burden? *Journal of Quality Assurance in Hospitality and Tourism* 5 (3–4), 57–74.

Hughes, H. (2005) The paradox of gay men as tourists: privileged or penalised? *Tourism, Culture and Communication* 6, 19–35.

Hughes, H. (2006) Gay and lesbian festivals: tourism in the change from politics to party. In: Picard, D. and Robinson, M. (eds) *Festivals, Tourism and Social Change: Remaking Worlds*. Channel View Publications, Clevedon, UK (in press).

Human Rights Watch (2002) *World Report 2002. Special Issues and Campaigns: Lesbian, Gay, Bisexual and Transgender rights*. Human Rights Watch, New York.

Human Rights Watch (2004a) Hated to death: homophobia, violence and Jamaica's HIV/AIDS epidemic. *Human Rights Watch* 16, 6 (B).

Human Rights Watch (2004b) Fiji sodomy law convictions violate constitution (www.hrw.org, 2 April, accessed 9 June 2005).

Human Rights Watch (2005) Saudi Arabia: 'men behaving like women' face flogging (www.hrw.org, 7 April, accessed 9 June 2005).

Humberstone, B. (2004) Standpoint research: multiple versions of reality in tourism theorising and research. In: Phillimore, J. and Goodson, L. (eds) *Qualitative Research in Tourism: Ontologies, Epistemologies and Methodologies*. Routledge, London, pp. 119–136.

Humphreys, L. (1970) *Tearoom Trade: a Study of Homosexual Encounters in Public Places*. Duckworth, London.

Humphries, M. (1985) Gay machismo. In: Metcalf, A. and Humphries, M. (eds) *The Sexuality of Men*. Pluto, London, pp. 70–85.

Hyman, P. (2001) Lesbians and economic/social change: impacts of globalisation on our community(ies) and politics. *Journal of Lesbian Studies* 5 (1/2), 115–132.

Ingebretsen, E. (1999) Gone shopping: the commercialisation of same-sex desire. *Journal of Gay, Lesbian and Bisexual Identity* 4 (2), 125–148.

Ingram, G. (1997) Marginality and the landscapes of erotic alienations. In: Ingram, G., Bouthillette, A. and Retter, Y. (eds) *Queers in Space: Communities, Public Places, Sites of Resistance*. Bay Press, Seattle, Washington, pp. 27–52.

Ingram, G., Bouthillette, A. and Retter, Y. (eds) (1997) *Queers in Space: Communities, Public Places, Sites of Resistance*. Bay Press, Seattle, Washington.

Ioannides, D. (1998) Tour operators: the gatekeepers of tourism. In: Ioannides, D. and Debbage, K. (eds) *The Economic Geography of the Tourist Industry*. Routledge, London, pp. 139–158.

Ivy, R. (2001) Geographical variation in alternative tourism and recreation establishments. *Tourism Geographies* 3 (3), 338–355.

Jackson, P. and Sullivan, G. (eds) (1999a) *Lady Boys, Tom Boys, Rent Roys: Male and Female Homosexualities in Contemporary Thailand*. Harrington Park Press, Binghampton, New York.

Jackson, P. and Sullivan, G. (1999b) A panoply of roles: sexual and gender diversity in contemporary Thailand. In: Jackson, P. and Sullivan, G. (eds) *Lady Boys, Tom Boys, Rent Boys: Male and Female Homosexualities in Contemporary Thailand*. Harrington Park Press, Binghampton, New York, pp. 1–27.

Jacobson, S. and Samdahl, D. (1998) Leisure in the lives of old lesbians: experiences with and responses to discrimination. *Journal of Leisure Research* 30 (2), 233–255.

Jafari, J. and Brent Ritchie, J. (1981) Toward a framework for tourism education: problems and prospects. *Annals of Tourism Research* 8 (1), 13–34.

Jeffreys, S. (2003) Sex tourism: do women do it too? *Leisure Studies* 22, 223–238.

Jeffries, S. (2004) Nice place, unless you're gay. *The Guardian G2* (1 July), p. 4.

Johnson, C. (1999) Living the game of hide and seek: leisure in the lives of gay and lesbian young adults. *Leisure/Loisir* 24 (3–4), 255–278.

Johnson, I. (2005a) Gay travel marketing (www.gaymarketing101.blogspot.com, 5 August, accessed 25 August 2005).

Johnson, I. (2005b) Boston rolls out rainbow carpet (www.gaymarketing101. blogspot.com, 21 July, accessed 25 August 2005).

Johnson, I. (2005c) Lesbian and gay media expanding your view (www. gaymarketing101.blogspot.com, 17 August, accessed 25 August 2005).

Johnson, I. (undated) Post-Priscilla, now what? *Outlook* 4, 10–12.

Johnston, E. (2004) Canada law to fuel gay travel boom? (www.uk.gay.com, 15 December, accessed 25 January 2005).

Johnston, L. (2001) (Other) bodies and tourism studies. *Annals of Tourism Research* 28 (1), 180–201.

Jones, D. (1996) Discrimination against same-sex couples in hotel reservation policies. In: Wardlow, D. (ed.) *Gays, Lesbians and Consumer Behavior: Theory, Practice and Research Issues in Marketing*. Harrington Park Press, Binghampton, New York, pp. 153–159.

Joseph, S. and Dhall, P. (2000) No silence please, we're Indians – les-bi-gay voices from India. In: Drucker, P. (ed.) *Different Rainbows*. Gay Men's Press, London, pp. 157–178.

Josiam, B., Hobson, P., Dietrich, U. and Seaton, G. (1998) An analysis of the sexual, alcohol and drug related behavioural patterns of students on spring break. *Tourism Management* 19 (6), 501–513.

Kantsa, V. (2002) Certain places have different energy. Spatial transformations in Eresos, Lesvos. *GLQ* 8 (1–2), 35–55.

Kates, S. (1998) *Twenty Million New Customers! Understanding Gay Men's Consumer Behavior*. Haworth Press, New York.

Kinnaird, V. and Hall, D. (eds) (1994a) *Tourism: a Gender Analysis*. Wiley, Chichester, UK.

Kinnaird, V. and Hall, D. (1994b) Conclusions: the way forward. In: Kinnaird, V. and Hall, D. (eds) *Tourism: a Gender Analysis*. Wiley, Chichester, UK, pp. 210–216.

Kinnaird, V., Kothari, V. and Hall, D. (1994) Tourism: gender perspectives. In: Kinnaird, V. and Hall, D. (eds) *Tourism: a Gender Analysis*. Wiley, Chichester, UK, pp. 1–34.

Kirby, S. and Hay, I. (1997) (Hetero)sexing space: gay men and straight space in Adelaide, South Australia. *Professional Geographer* 49 (3), 295–305.

Kitchin, R. (2002) Sexing the city: the sexual production of non-heterosexual space in Belfast, Manchester and San Francisco. *City* 6 (2), 205–218.

Kitchin, R. and Lysaght, K. (2003) Heterosexism and the geographies of everyday life in Belfast, Northern Ireland. *Environment and Planning A* 35, 489–510.

Kivel, B. (1994) Lesbian and gay youth and leisure: implications for practitioners and researchers. *Journal of Park and Recreation Administration* 12 (4), 15–28.

Kivel, B. and Kleiber, D. (2000) Leisure in the identity formation of lesbian/gay youth: personal but not social. *Leisure Sciences* 22 (4), 215–232.

Klemm, M. and Parkinson, L. (2001) UK tour operator strategies: causes and consequences. *International Journal of Tourism Research* 3 (5), 367–375.

Knopp, L. (1995) Sexuality and urban space: a framework for analysis. In: Bell, D. and Valentine, G. (eds) *Mapping Desire: Geographies of Sexualities*. Routledge, London, pp. 149–161.

Kolko, J. (2003) *Gays are the Technology Early Adopters you Want*. Forrester Research, San Francisco, California.

Kramer, J. (1995) Bachelor farmers and spinsters: gay and lesbian identities and communities in rural North Dakota. In: Bell, D. and Valentine, G. (eds) *Mapping Desire: Geographies of Sexualities*. Routledge, London, pp. 200–213.

Laign, J. (2004) Family matters (www.porthole.com, accessed 1 February 2005).

Lang, T. (2000) The effect of the internet on travel consumer purchasing behaviour and implications for travel agencies. *Journal of Vacation Marketing* 6 (4), 368–385.

Lavers, M. (2004) Warning for tourists after gay man killed (www.uk.gay.com, 6 August, accessed 30 November 2004).

Law, C. (2002) *Urban Tourism: the Visitor Economy and the Growth of Large Cities*, 2nd edn. Continuum, London.

Lawson, R. and Thyne, M. (2001) Destination avoidance and inept destination sets. *Journal of Vacation Marketing* 7 (3), 199–208.

Lee, V. (2000) Wimbledon 2000. Women out in force: having a gay old time. *The Guardian* (25 June), p. 16.

Lee, V. (2002) Book quick for Easter: the Palm Springs gay and lesbian parties will clash. *The Observer* (24 February).

Leiper, N. (1981) Towards a cohesive curriculum in tourism: the case for a distinct discipline. *Annals of Tourism Research* 8 (1), 69–84.

Leiper, N. (1990) Tourist attraction systems. *Annals of Tourism Research* 17, 367–384.

LeVay, S. (1991) A difference in hypothalamic structure between heterosexual and homosexual men. *Science* 253, 1034–1037.

Levitt, R. (2004) Glad to get away – the same-sex guide to romantic holidays. *The Independent* (8 February).

Lillington, K. (2003) Dream ticket. *The Guardian* (16 October), p. 25.

Link, M. (2002) A case-study in contradictions: Hawaii and gay tourism. In: Clift, S., Luongo, M. and Callister, C. (eds) *Gay Tourism: Culture, Identity and Sex*. Continuum, London, pp. 63–87.

Long, S. (2003) *State-sponsored homophobia in Southern Africa*. Human Rights Watch and International Gay and Lesbian Human Rights Commission, New York.

Lukenbill, G. (1999) *Untold Millions: Secret Truths about Marketing to Gay and Lesbian Consumers*. Harrington Park Press, Binghampton, New York.

Lumsden, I. (1996) *Machos, Maricones and Gays: Cuba and Homosexuality*. Temple University Press, Philadelphia, Pennsylvania.

Lumsdon, L. and Swift, J. (1999) The role of the tour operator in South America: Argentina, Chile, Paraguay and Uruguay. *International Journal of Tourism Research* 1 (6), 429–439.

Lundberg, D. (1994) *The Hotel and Restaurant Business*, 6th edn. Van Nostrand Reinhold, New York.

Luongo, M. (2002) Rome's World Pride: making the eternal city an international gay tourism destination. *GLQ* 8 (1–2), 167–181.

Luongo, M. (ed.) (2004) *Between the Palms: a Collection of Gay Travel Erotica.* Harrington Park Press, Binghampton, New York.

Lutyens, D. (2003) The gay team. *The Observer Magazine* (26 October), pp. 29–38.

Macgregor, K. (2001) Faiths unite to fight gay invasion of Cape Town. *The Independent on Sunday* (18 March), p. 20.

Mack, J. and Lansley, S. (1985) *Poor Britain.* George Allen and Unwin, London.

Macleod, T. (2003) Out in Lesbos – and proud of it. *The Independent* (23 August).

Manalansan IV, M. (1995) In the shadows of Stonewall: examining gay transnational politics and the diasporic dilemma. *GLQ* 2, 425–438.

Manalansan IV, M. (2000) Diasporic deviants/divas: how Filipino gay transmigrants play with the world. In: Patton, C. and Sanchez-Eppler, B. (eds) *Queer Diasporas.* Duke University Press, Durham, North Carolina, pp. 183–203.

Mansergh, G., Colfax, G., Marks, G., Rader, M., Guzman, R. and Buchbinder, S. (2001) The circuit party men's health survey: findings and implications for gay and bisexual men. *American Journal of Public Health* 91 (6), 953–958.

MAPS (1998) *The Pink Pound 1998: Strategic Market Report.* Market Assessment Publications Ltd, London.

Marks, K. (2002) Anger as Sydney's Mardi Gras goes bust. *The Independent on Sunday* (11 August), p. 17.

Markwell, K. (1998) Space and place in gay men's leisure. *Annals of Leisure Research* 1, 19–36.

Markwell, K. (2002) Mardi Gras tourism and the construction of Sydney as an international gay and lesbian city. *GLQ* 8 (1–2), 81–99.

Marsh, I. and Galbraith, L. (1995) The political impact of the Sydney Gay and Lesbian Mardi Gras. *Australian Journal of Political Science* 30, 300–320.

Marshall, T. (1950) *Citizenship and Social Class.* Cambridge University Press, Cambridge, UK.

Mason, A. and Palmer, A. (1996) *Queer Bashing: a National Survey of Hate Crimes against Lesbians and Gay Men.* Stonewall, London.

Mburu, J. (2000) Awakenings; dreams and delusions of an incipient lesbian and gay movement in Kenya. In: Drucker, P. (ed.) *Different Rainbows.* Gay Men's Press, London, pp. 179–191.

McCamish, M. (1999) The friends thou hast: support systems for male commercial sex workers in Pattaya, Thailand. In: Jackson, P. and Sullivan, G. (eds) *Lady Boys, Tom Boys, Rent Boys: Male and Female Homosexualities in Contemporary Thailand.* Harrington Park Press, Binghampton, New York, pp. 161–191.

McDonald, H. (2004) Gay Belfast is new magnet. *The Observer* (9 May), p. 6.

McKenna, N. (2004) *The Secret Life of Oscar Wilde.* Arrow, London.

McKercher, B. and Bauer, T. (2003) Conceptual framework of the nexus between tourism, romance and sex. In: Bauer, T. and McKercher, B. (eds) *Sex and Tourism: Journeys of Romance, Love and Lust.* Haworth Hospitality Press, New York, pp. 3–17.

McLean, G. (2003) Boys' night out. *The Guardian* (28 October).

McMahon, B. (2005) Italy snaps over gay poster excess. *The Observer* (18 September), p. 21.

Mellor, R. (2002a) Red hot and pink. *The Observer Escape* (24 February), pp. 13–16.

Mellor, R. (2002b) Fun-fur flies as gay train rolls into town. *The Observer Escape* (24 February), pp. 2–3.

Miles, P. (2000) Where to spend the pink pound. *The Times* (14 October) p. 12.

Miles, P. (2003) Sweet and sour. *The Pink Paper* (11 July), pp. 20–21.

Miller, C. (2002) Better living through circuitry: lesbians and circuit parties. In: Clift, S., Luongo, M. and Callister, C. (eds) *Gay Tourism: Culture, Identity and Sex*. Continuum, London, pp. 214–227.

Mims, C. and Kleiner, B. (1998) Homosexual harassment in the workplace. *Equal Opportunities Journal* 17 (7), 16–20.

Mind (2002) Lesbians, gay men, bisexuals and mental health: fact sheet (www. mind.org.uk).

Mintel (2000a) *The Gay Holiday Market*. Mintel International Group, London.

Mintel (2000b) *The Gay Entertainment Market*. Mintel International Group, London.

Minto, D. (2005) End of an era. *Gay Times* (October), pp. 28–32.

Mizielinska, J. (2001) The rest is silence . . . Polish nationalism and the question of lesbian existence. *The European Journal of Women's Studies* 8 (3), 281–297.

Mogrovejo, N. (2000) Lesbian visibility in Latin America: reclaiming our history. In: Drucker, P. (ed.) *Different Rainbows*. Gay Men's Press, London, pp. 71–89.

Mowbray, T. (2003) Putting the gay back into Paris. *The Guardian* (18 January).

Murray, S. (1992) The 'underdevelopment' of modern/gay homosexuality in Mesoamerica. In: Plummer, K. (ed.) *Modern Homosexualities: Fragments of Lesbian and Gay Experience*. Routledge, London, pp. 29–38.

Myslik, W. (1996) Renegotiating the social/sexual identities of places: gay communities as safe havens or sites of resistance? In: Duncan, N. (ed.) *BodySpace: Destabilising Geographies of Gender and Sexuality*. Routledge, London, pp. 156–169.

Naphy, W. (2004) *Born to be Gay: a History of Homosexuality*. Tempus, Stroud, UK.

Nardi, P. (1992) That's what friends are for: friends as family in the gay and lesbian community. In: Plummer, K. (ed.) *Modern Homosexualities: Fragments of Lesbian and Gay Experience*. Routledge, London, pp. 108–120.

National Tour Association (2002) *Preliminary Market Appraisal: Gay and Lesbian Market*. National Tour Association, Lexington, Kentucky.

Nestle, J. (1997) Restriction and reclamation: lesbian bars and beaches of the 1950s. In: Ingram, G., Bouthillette, A. and Retter, Y. (eds) *Queers in Space: Communities, Public Places, Sites of Resistance*. Bay Press, Seattle, Washington, pp. 61–67.

Newman, B. (2005) Turks and Caicos chief minister responds to opposition leader over gay cruise. *eTurboNews* (www.eturbonews.com, 13 April).

New Mardi Gras Ltd (NMGL) (2002) *Mardi Gras: Dodo or Phoenix?: Background Paper* (November). New Mardi Gras Ltd, Sydney, Australia.

New Mardi Gras Ltd (NMGL) (2003) *New Mardi Gras Constitutional Committee: Objects Discussion Paper* (February). New Mardi Gras Ltd, Sydney, Australia.

New South Wales Attorney General's Department (Crime Prevention Division) (2003) *You Shouldn't Have to Hide to be Safe: a Report on Homophobic Hostilities and Violence against Gay Men and Lesbians in New South Wales*. New South Wales Attorney General's Department, Sydney, Australia.

Newton, E. (1993) *Cherry Grove, Fire Island: Sixty Years in America's First Gay and Lesbian Town*. Beacon Press, Boston, Massachusetts.

Oakenfull, G. and Greenlee, T. (2004) The three rules of crossing over from gay media to mainstream media advertising: lesbians, lesbians, lesbians. *Journal of Business Research* 57 (11), 1276–1285.

Office of the Attorney General, State of Florida (2004) *Hate Crimes in Florida 2003*. Office of the Attorney General, Tallahassee, Florida.

Offices of the Congregation of the Doctrine of the Faith (2003) *Considerations Regarding Proposals to Give Legal Recognition to Unions between Homosexual Persons*. Offices of the Congregation of the Doctrine of the Faith, Rome.

Offices of the Congregation of the Doctrine of the Faith (2004) *Letter to the Bishops of the Catholic Church on the Collaboration of Men and Women in the Church and the World*. Offices of the Congregation of the Doctrine of the Faith, Rome.

O'Hara, M. (2005) Fear and loathing. *The Guardian: Society* (29 June), p. 2.

Oppermann, M. (1999) Sex tourism. *Annals of Tourism Research* 26 (2), 251–266.

Patton, C. (2000) Migratory vices. In: Patton, C. and Sanchez-Eppler, B. (eds) *Queer Diasporas*. Duke University Press, Durham, North Carolina, pp. 15–37.

Peake, L. (1993) Race and sexuality: challenging the patriarchal structuring of urban social space. *Environment and Planning D: Society and Space* 11, 415–432.

Pearce, D. (2002) New Zealand holiday travel to Samoa: a distribution channels approach. *Journal of Travel Research* 41 (2), 197–205.

Penaloza, L. (1996) We're here, we're queer and we're going shopping! A critical perspective on the accommodation of gays and lesbians in the US marketplace. In: Wardlow, D. (ed.) *Gays, Lesbians and Consumer Behavior: Theory, Practice and Research Issues in Marketing*. Harrington Park Press, Binghampton, New York, pp. 9–41.

Pennington-Gray, L. and Kerstetter, D. (2001) What do university-educated women want from their pleasure travel experiences? *Journal of Travel Research* 40, 49–56.

Philadelphia Convention and Visitor Bureau (2004) *Philadelphia: Gay and Lesbian Travel Guide*. PCVB, Philadelphia, Pennsylvania.

Philipp, S. (1999) Gay and lesbian tourists at a southern USA beach event. *Journal of Homosexuality* 37 (3), 69–86.

Phillips, P. (2003) Ad nausea. *Gay Times* (September), pp. 67–70.

Picano, F. (1998) Foreword. In: Bledsoe, L. (ed.) *Gay Travels: a Literary Companion*. Whereabouts Press, San Francisco, California, pp. vii–x.

Pilcher, J. and Whelehan, I. (2004) *50 Key Concepts in Gender Studies*. Sage, London.

Pitts, B. (1999) Sports tourism and niche markets: identification and analysis of the growing lesbian and gay tourism industry. *Journal of Vacation Marketing* 5 (1), 31–50.

Plummer, K. (1992) Speaking its name: inventing a gay and lesbian studies. In: Plummer, K. (ed.) *Modern Homosexualities: Fragments of Lesbian and Gay Experience*. Routledge, London, pp. 3–25.

Poria, Y. and Taylor, A. (2001) I am not afraid to be gay when I'm on the net: minimising social risk for lesbian and gay consumers when using the internet. *Journal of Travel and Tourism Marketing* 11 (2/3), 127–142.

Potgieter, C. (1997) From apartheid to Mandela's constitution: black South African lesbians in the nineties. In: Greene, B. (ed.) *Ethnic and Cultural Diversity among Lesbians and Gay Men*. Sage, Thousand Oaks, California, pp. 88–116.

Predrag, S., Gajsek, A. and Rodgerson, G. (2002) First Pride march in Croatia ends in tears. *Gay Times* (August), p. 59.

Pritchard, A. and Morgan, N. (1997) The gay consumer: a meaningful market segment? *Journal of Targeting, Measurement and Analysis for Marketing* 6 (1), 9–20.

Pritchard, A., Morgan, N. and Sedgley, D. (2002) In search of lesbian space? The experience of Manchester's gay village. *Leisure Studies* 21 (2), 105–123.

Pritchard, A., Morgan, N., Sedgley, D. and Jenkins, A. (1998) Reaching out to the gay market: opportunities and threats in an emerging market segment. *Tourism Management* 19 (3), 273–282.

Pritchard, A., Morgan, N., Sedgley, D., Khan, E. and Jenkins, A. (2000) Sexuality and holiday choices: conversations with gay and lesbian tourists. *Leisure Studies* 19 (4), 267–282.

Pruitt, M. (2002) Size matters: a comparison of anti- and pro-gay organisations' estimates of the size of the gay population. *Journal of Homosexuality* 42 (3), 21–29.

Puar, J. (2001) Global circuits: transnational sexualities and Trinidad. *Signs* 26 (4), 1039–1065.

Puar, J. (2002a) Introduction. *GLQ* 8 (1–2), 1–6.

Puar, J. (2002b) Circuits of queer mobility: tourism, travel and globalisation. *GLQ* 8 (1–2), 101–137.

Puar, J. (2002c) A transnational feminist critique of queer tourism. *Antipode* 34 (5), 935–946.

Puar, J., Rushbrook, D. and Schein, L. (2003) Sexuality and space: queering geographies of globalisation. *Environment and Planning D: Society and Space* 21, 383–387.

Quest, R. (1998) *Business: the Economy. Gay Travel Boom*. BBC News online network (www.bbc.co.uk, accessed 3 November 2004).

Quilley, S. (1997) Constructing Manchester's new urban village: gay space in the entrepreneurial city. In: Ingram, G., Bouthillette, A. and Retter, Y. (eds) *Queers in Space: Communities, Public Places, Sites of Resistance*. Bay Press, Seattle, Washington, pp. 275–292.

Quittner, J. (2004) Gavin's gay gamble. *The Advocate* (30 March), pp. 28–31.

Rahim, S. (2000) Out in Africa. *New Internationalist* 328 (www.newint.org/issue 328, accessed 28 January 2004).

Rankin, S. (2003) *Campus Climate for Gay, Lesbian, Bisexual and Transgender People: a National Perspective*. National Gay and Lesbian Task Force Policy Institute, New York.

Reid, D., Weatherburn, P., Hickson, F., Stephens, M. and Hammond, G. (2004) *On the Move: Findings from the UK Gay Men's Sex Survey 2003*. Sigma Research, London.

Reid-Smith, T. (2003) Pride will be back despite not paying park this year. *The Pink Paper* (26 September), p. 4.

Reilley, M. (2004) Let's all visit . . . Indiana! (www.washingtonblade.com, 9 January 2004, accessed 27 January 2005).

Richards, G. (2001) The market for cultural attractions. In: Richards, G. (ed.) *Cultural Attractions and European Tourism*. CAB International, Wallingford, UK, pp. 31–53.

Richardson, D. (1998) Sexuality and citizenship. *Sociology* 32 (1), 83–100.

Richardson, D. (2001) Extending citizenship: cultural citizenship and sexuality. In: Stevenson, N. (ed.) *Culture and Citizenship*. Sage, London, pp. 153–166.

Richardson, D. and Seidman, S. (2002) Introduction. In: Richardson, D. and Seidman, S. (eds) *Handbook of Lesbian and Gay Studies*. Sage, London, pp. 1–12.

Ricker, J. and Witeck, B. (2003) *Understanding the Gay, Lesbian, Bisexual and Transgender Market and how it Influences Marketing Communications*. Harris Interactive Inc. (www.witeckcombs.com, accessed 15 February 2005).

Ridgeway, J. (2005) First gay pride parade in Romania. *Gay Times* (July), p. 79.

Rimmerman, C. (2002) *From Identity to Politics: the Lesbian and Gay Movements in the United States*. Temple University Press, Philadelphia, Pennsylvania.

Robinson, A. and Williams, M. (2003) *The Stonewall Cymru Survey*. Stonewall Cymru, Cardiff, UK.

Robinson, J. (1990) *Wayward Women: a Guide to Women Travellers*. Oxford University Press, Oxford, UK.

Robinson, M. and Novelli, M. (2005) Niche tourism: an introduction. In: Novelli, M. (ed.) *Niche Tourism: Contemporary Issues, Trends and Cases*. Elsevier Butterworth-Heinemann, Oxford, UK, pp. 1–11.

Robinson, P. (2002) *Opera, Sex and Other Vital Matters*. University of Chicago Press, Chicago, Illinois.

Robinson, P. (2005) *Queer Wars: the New Gay Right and its Critics*. University of Chicago Press, Chicago, Illinois.

Rodgerson, G. (2004a) The States and our unions. *Gay Times* (April), pp. 60–62.

Rodgerson, G. (2004b) World watch: Egypt. *Gay Times* (July), p. 78.

Rogstad, K. (2004) Sex, sun, sea and STIs: sexually transmitted infections acquired on holiday. *British Medical Journal* 329, 214–217.

Rojek, C. (1998) Tourism and citizenship. *Cultural Policy* 4 (2), 291–310.

Roper, A. (1996) Resort hotels. In: Innes, P. (ed.) *Introduction to Hospitality Operators*. Cassell, London, pp. 50–60.

Roth, T and Luongo, M. (2002) A place for us 2001: tourism industry opportunities in the gay and lesbian market. In: Clift, S., Luongo, M. and Callister, C. (eds) *Gay Tourism: Culture, Identity and Sex*. Continuum, London, pp. 125–147.

Roth, T. and Paisley, D. (with Chesnut, M.) (2004) *Gay and Lesbian Travel: a Lifestyle Specialist Course*. The Travel Institute, Wellesley, Massachusetts.

Rothenburg, T. (1995) And she told two friends: lesbians creating urban social space. In: Bell, D. and Valentine, G. (eds) *Mapping Desire: Geographies of Sexualities*. Routledge, London, pp. 165–181.

Roy Morgan Research (2003) *Key Trends in Gay Leisure Travel*. Roy Morgan Research Pty Ltd, Melbourne, Australia.

Rubenstein, W., Sears, R. and Sockloskie, R. (2003) *Some Demographic Characteristics of the Gay Community in the United States*. The Williams Project, UCLA School of Law, University of California, Los Angeles, California.

Rushbrook, D. (2002) Cities, queer space and the cosmopolitan tourist. *GLQ* 8 (1–2), 183–206.

Russell, P. (2001) The world gay travel market. *Travel and Tourism Analyst* 2, 37–58.

Rutherford, N. (2005) No room at the inn for B&B double-room couple. *The Pink Paper* (15 September), p. 6.

Ryan, C. and Hall, M. (2001) *Sex Tourism: Marginal People and Liminalities*. Routledge, London.

Said, E. (1978) *Orientalism: Western Conceptions of the Orient*. Routledge and Kegan Paul, London.

Sanchez-Crispin, A. and Lopez-Lopez, A. (1997) Gay male places in Mexico City. In: Ingram, G., Bouthillette, A. and Retter, Y. (eds) *Queers in Space: Communities, Public Places, Sites of Resistance*. Bay Press, Seattle, Washington, pp. 197–212.

Sanchez Taylor, J. (2001) Dollars are a girl's best friend? Female tourists' sexual behaviour in the Caribbean. *Sociology* 35 (3), 749–764.

Sanders, D. (2002) Some say Thailand is a gay paradise. In: Clift, S., Luongo, M. and Callister, C. (eds) *Gay Tourism: Culture, Identity and Sex.* Continuum, London, pp. 42–62.

Sandfort, T. (2000) Homosexuality, psychology and gay and lesbian studies. In: Sandfort, T., Schuyf, J., Duyvendak, J. and Weeks, J. (eds) *Lesbian and Gay Studies: an Introductory, Interdisciplinary Approach.* Sage, London, pp. 14–45.

Schlegelmilch, B. (1998) *Marketing Ethics: an International Perspective.* International Thomson Business Press, London.

Schofield, K. and Schmidt, R. (2005) Fashion and clothing: the construction and communication of gay identities. *International Journal of Retail and Distribution Management* 33 (4), 310–323.

Schuyf, J. (1992) The company of friends and lovers: lesbian communities in the Netherlands. In: Plummer, K. (ed.) *Modern Homosexualities: Fragments of Lesbian and Gay Experience.* Routledge, London, pp. 53–64.

Schuyf, J. (2000) Hidden from history? Homosexuality and the historical sciences. In: Sandfort, T., Schuyf, J., Duyvendak, J. and Weeks, J. (eds) *Lesbian and Gay Studies: an Introductory, Interdisciplinary Approach.* Sage, London, pp. 61–79.

Schuyf, J. and Sandfort, T. (2000) Conclusion: gay and lesbian studies at the crossroads. In: Sandfort, T., Schuyf, J., Duyvendak, J. and Weeks, J. (eds) *Lesbian and Gay Studies: an Introductory, Interdisciplinary Approach.* Sage, London, pp. 215–227.

Scott-Clark, C. and Levy, A. (2005) Where it's really hurting. *The Guardian: Weekend* (10 September), pp. 26–33.

Scraton, S. and Watson, B. (1998) Gendered cities: women and public leisure space in the postmodern city. *Leisure Studies* 17 (2), 123–137.

Sears, R. and Badgett, M. (2004) *The Impact on California's Budget of Allowing Same-sex Couples to Marry.* The Williams Project, UCLA School of Law, University of California, Los Angeles, California.

Seidman, S., Meeks, C. and Traschen, F. (1999) Beyond the closet? The changing social meaning of homosexuality in the United States. *Sexualities* 2 (1), 9–34.

Selby, M. (2004) *Understanding Urban Tourism: Image, Culture and Experience.* I B Tauris, London.

Sender, K. (2004) *Business, not Politics: the Making of the Gay Market.* Columbia University Press, New York.

Sharp, D. (2003) Cities come out about wooing gays – and their dollars. *USA Today* (7 December).

Shenker, S. (2005) US gay couples head to Canada to wed (www.newsvote. bbc.co.uk, accessed 29 September 2005).

Shilts, R. (1988) *And the Band Played on: Politics, People and the AIDS Epidemic.* Penguin, London.

Sibalis, M. (1999) Paris. In: Higgs, D. (ed.) *Queer Sites: Gay Urban Histories since 1600.* Routledge, London, pp. 10–37.

Sibalis, M. (2004) Urban space and homosexuality: the example of the Marais, Paris, gay ghetto. *Urban Studies* 41 (9), 1739–1758.

Simpson, M. (2004) Forget new man. Now you're hetero, retro or metro. *The Observer: 'Man Uncovered' supplement* (27 June), pp. 51, 53.

Skeggs, B. (1999) Matter out of place: visibility and sexualities in leisure spaces. *Leisure Studies* 18, 213–232.

Skinner, T. (1995) Gay couple denied room in top hotel. *The Pink Paper* (24 November), p. 6.

Smith, H. (1996) Welcome home for Sappho's daughters. *The Observer* (4 August), p. 21.

Smith, M. (2003) *Issues in Cultural Tourism Studies*. Routledge, London.

Smith, R. (2002) Is this the end for Mardi Gras? *Gay Times* (September), p. 41.

Smith, R. (2004a) Our man in Tashkent. *Gay Times* (February), pp. 42–44.

Smith, R. (2004b) The rise and rise of a gay phenomenon. *Gay Times* (March), pp. 37–38.

Sonmez, S. and Graefe, A. (1998) Determining future travel behaviour from past travel experience and perceptions of risk and safety. *Journal of Travel Research* 37 (2), 171–177.

Sonmez, S. and Sirakaya, E. (2002) A distorted destination image? The case of Turkey. *Journal of Travel Research* 41 (2), 185–196.

Spencer, C. (1995) *Homosexuality: a History*. Fourth Estate, London.

Stagg Elliott, V. (1998) Pink sails in the sunset. *The Guardian* (4 June), p. 12.

Steele, N. (2004) Suite smarts. *Metrosource* (April/May), p. 51.

Stephenson, M. (2002) Travelling to the ancestral homelands: the aspirations and experiences of a UK Caribbean community. *Current Issues in Tourism* 5 (5), 378–425.

Stonewall (2001) *Profiles of Prejudice: a Survey by MORI for Citizenship 21 Project*. Stonewall, London.

Stonewall (2005) *Stonewall Corporate Equality Index 2005: the Top 100 Employers for Gay People in Britain*. Stonewall, London.

Stormbreak (2000) *Gay Life and Style New Millennium Survey* (www.stormbreak. co.uk).

Stuber, M. (2002) Tourism marketing aimed at gay men and lesbians: a business perspective. In: Clift, S., Luongo, M. and Callister, C. (eds) *Gay Tourism: Culture, Identity and Sex*. Continuum, London, pp. 88–124.

Sullivan, A. (1995) *Virtually Normal*. Picador, London.

Sullivan, G. and Jackson, P. (1999) Introduction: ethnic minorities and the lesbian and gay community. *Journal of Homosexuality* 36 (3–4), 1–28.

Summerskill, B. (2001) Package holiday giant dares to think pink. *The Observer* (25 March), p. 7.

Summerskill, B. (2002) Pop to the shops with the Queen who's a pin-up. *The Observer: Escape* (24 Feb), pp. 6–7.

Swain, M. (1995) Gender in tourism. *Annals of Tourism Research* 22 (2), 247–266.

Swain, M. (2004) (Dis)embodied experience and power dynamics in tourism research. In: Phillimore, J. and Goodwin, L. (eds) *Qualitative Research in Tourism: Ontologies, Epistemologies and Methodologies*. Routledge, London, pp. 102–118.

Swift, S. (2005a) Tennis hero cruises into travel team. *The Pink Paper* (26 May), p. 48.

Swift, S. (2005b) Revellers defy nature and God to parade through New Orleans. *The Pink Paper* (15 September), p. 10.

Tapper, R. (2001) Tourism and socio-economic development: UK tour operators' business approaches in the context of the new international agenda. *International Journal of Tourism Research* 3 (5), pp. 351–366.

Tatchell, P. (2002) Even the whales are gay down Mexico way. *The Observer: Escape* (24 February), pp. 8–9.

Tatchell, P. (2003) Man overboard. *The Pink Paper* (11 July), p. 25.

Tatchell, P. (2004a) Paradise found. *Gay Times* (February), pp. 117–119.

Tatchell, P. (2004b) Shortbreaks Sardinia. *Gay Times* (July), p. 149.

Tatchell, P. (2004c) We've come a long way baby but . . . *Gay Times* (July) pp. 81–82.

Theobald, S. (2002) Cautionary tales for omelette makers. *The Observer: Escape* (24 February), pp. 10–11.

Theobald, S. and Howard, M. (2000) Lesbians go mad in Lesbos. *The Guardian* (14 September), p. 8.

Thiede, H., Valleroy, L., MacKellar, D., Celentano, D., Ford, W., Hagan, H., Koblin, B., LaLota, M., McFarland, W., Shehan, D. and Torlan, L. (2003) Regional patterns and correlates of substance use among gay young men who have sex with men in seven US urban areas. *American Journal of Public Health* 93 (11), 1915–1921.

Thomas, M. (2000) Exploring the contexts and meanings of women's experiences of sexual intercourse on holiday. In: Clift, S. and Carter, S. (eds) *Tourism and Sex: Culture, Commerce and Coercion*. Pinter, London, pp. 200–220.

Tourism Queensland (2002) *Gay and Lesbian Tourism*. Research Department, Tourism Queensland, Brisbane, Australia.

Townley, B. (2004) British Airways may face gay discrimination claim (www.uk.gay.com/headlines, 18 October, accessed 30 October 2004).

Townsend, C. (2004) Heading north to Vancouver (www.uk.gay.com, 8 July, accessed 25 January 2005).

Tremlett, G. (2005) Bishops to lead gay law protest. *The Guardian* (17 June), p. 18.

Tribe, J. (1997) The indiscipline of tourism. *Annals of Tourism Research* 24 (3), 638–657.

Tribe, J. (2002) The philosophic practitioner. *Annals of Tourism Research* 29 (2), 338–357.

Trucco, T. (2004) Courting gay travellers. *The New York Times* (www.nytimes.com, 16 May, accessed 3 November 2004).

Tuck, A. (1998) Book a double room? Not if you're gay, sir. *The Independent on Sunday* (8 February), p. 5.

Tuller, D. (1996) *Cracks in the Iron Closet: Travels in Gay and Lesbian Russia*. Faber and Faber, Boston, Massachusetts.

Um, S. and Crompton, J. (1992) The role of perceived inhibitors and facilitators in pleasure travel destination decisions. *Journal of Travel Research* 30 (3), 18–25.

Urry, J. (1990) *The Tourist Gaze: Leisure and Travel in Contemporary Society*. Sage, London.

Valentine, G. (1995) Out and about: geographies of lesbian landscapes. *International Journal of Urban and Regional Research* 19, 96–112.

Valentine, G. (1996) Re-negotiating the heterosexual street: lesbian production of space. In: Duncan, N. (ed.) *BodySpace: Destabilising Geographies of Gender and Sexuality*. Routledge, London, pp. 146–155.

Valentine, G. (2000) Introduction. In: Valentine, G. (ed.) *From Nowhere to Everywhere: Lesbian Geographies*. Harrington Park Press, Binghampton, New York, pp. 1–9.

Valentine, G. and McDonald, I. (2004) *Understanding Prejudice: Attitudes toward Minorities*. Stonewall, London.

Valentine, G. and Skelton, T. (2003) Finding oneself, losing oneself: the lesbian and gay scene as a paradoxical space. *International Journal of Urban and Regional Research* 27 (4), 849–866.

Van Drake, S. (2003) Commitment pageant to bring tourism business. *South Florida Business Review* (18 August).

Van Gelder, L. and Brandt, P. (1991) *Are You Two . . . Together? A Gay and Lesbian Travel Guide to Europe.* Random House, New York.

Vasagar, J. (2004) Zanzibar's gay community fears tough new law will force it into twilight zone. *The Guardian* (2 June), p. 15.

Verkaik, R. (2001) Airline told transsexual to remove dress and wig if he wanted to fly. *The Independent* (7 September), p. 5.

Visser, G. (2002) Gay tourism in South Africa: issues from the Cape Town experience. *Urban Forum* 13 (1), 85–94.

Visser, G. (2003) Gay men, tourism and urban space: reflections on Africa's gay capital. *Tourism Geographies* 5 (2), 168–189.

Von Metzke, R. (2005) Massachusetts gay weddings mean big bucks for Provincetown (www.lesbianation.com, accessed 11 October 2005).

Walker, M. (2000) Boy zone. *The Guardian* (18 March).

Want, P. (2002) Trouble in paradise: homophobia and resistance to gay tourism. In: Clift, S., Luongo, M. and Callister, C. (eds) *Gay Tourism: Culture, Identity and Risk.* Continuum Press, London pp. 191–213.

Ward, J. (2003) Producing pride in west Hollywood: a queer cultural capital for queers with cultural capital. *Sexualities* 6 (1), 65–94.

Wardlow, D. (1996) (ed.) *Gays, Lesbians and Consumer Behavior: Theory, Practice and Research Issues in Marketing.* Harrington Park Press, Binghampton, New York.

Warner, J., McKeown, E., Griffin, M., Johnson, K., Ramsay, A., Cort, C. and King, M. (2004) Rates and predictors of mental illness in gay men, lesbians and bisexual men and women. *British Journal of Psychiatry* 185 (6), 479–485.

Wearing, B. and Wearing, S. (1992) Identity and the commodification of leisure. *Leisure Studies* 11 (1), 3–18.

Weeks, J. (1992) The body and sexuality. In: Bocock, R. and Thompson, K. (eds) *Social and Cultural Forms of Modernity.* Polity Press, Cambridge, UK, pp. 219–266.

Weeks, J. (1998) The sexual citizen. *Theory, Culture and Society* 15 (3–4), 35–52.

Weeks, J. (2000) The challenge of lesbian and gay studies. In: Sandfort, T., Schuyf, J., Duyvendak, J. and Weeks, J. (eds) *Lesbian and Gay Studies: an Introductory, Interdisciplinary Approach.* Sage, London, pp. 1–13.

Wells, D. (2001) Around the world with David Tours. *QTMagazine* (May) (via: www.davidtours.com, accessed 1 December 2004).

Wells, M. (2002) Club gayteen-30. *The Guardian* (30 November).

Wells, M. (2004) Mag that made it cool to be gay. *The Guardian: Media* (26 April), p. 9.

Whittle, S. (1994) Consuming differences: the collaboration of the gay body with the cultural state. In: Whittle, S. (ed.) *The Margins of the City: Gay Men's Urban Lives.* Arena, Aldershot, UK, pp. 27–41.

Wilke, M. (2004) Wyndham, Westin and W Hotels bed gays. *San Francisco Spectrum* 7 (4), 7.

Wilke, M. (2005) From the executive director (www.commercialcloset.org, accessed 18 September 2005).

Williams, M. (2001) Religious outrage over pink tourism (www.iol.co.za, 17 February, accessed 2 February 2005).

Wilson, J. (2005) Texas abortion law sparks protests. *The Guardian* (7 June), p. 13.

Wilson, N. (2001) Gaychester RIP. *Attitude* 84, 65–67.

Wiltshier, P. and Cardow, A. (2001) The impact of the pink dollar: Wellington as a destination for the gay market. *Pacific Tourism Review* 5 (3), 121–130.

Witeck-Combs Communications and Harris Interactive (2003a) *National Survey Reveals Gays and Lesbians are Frequent and Discerning Business Travellers.* Witeck-Combs Communications and Harris Interactive, Rochester, New York.

Witeck-Combs Communications and Harris Interactive (2003b) *Why Market to the Gay Community? Answers to the Top Ten Questions Asked by Smart Marketers.* Witeck-Combs Communications and Harris Interactive, Rochester, New York.

Witeck-Combs Communications and Harris Interactive (2004) *National Survey Reveals Gay Consumers Prefer Equality-minded Companies.* Witeck-Combs Communications and Harris Interactive, Rochester, New York.

Witeck-Combs Communications and Harris Interactive (2005) *National Survey Shows Gay-specific Marketing Practices may Influence Brand Loyalty and Purchase Decisions of Gays, Lesbians and Bisexuals.* Witeck-Combs Communications and Harris Interactive, Rochester, New York.

Witeck-Combs Communications Inc. (2004) *Gay Issues and the 2004 Election.* Witeck-Combs Communications Inc., Washington, DC.

Wood, L. (1999) Think pink! Attracting the pink pound. *Insights*, A107–A110.

World Tourism Organization (1981) *Guidelines for the Collection and Presentation of Domestic and International Tourism Statistics.* World Tourism Organization, Madrid.

Wright, L. (1999) San Francisco. In: Higgs, D. (ed.) *Queer Sites: Gay Urban Histories since 1600.* Routledge, London, pp. 164–189.

Yang, A. (1999) *From Wrongs to Rights 1973–1999. Public Opinion on Gay and Lesbian Americans' Moves toward Equality.* National Gay and Lesbian Task Force Policy Institute, New York.

Yates, R. (ed.) (2002) Sex uncovered. *The Observer Supplement* (27 October).

Young, C. (2000) Sin city: Dublin branded sex disease capital of Europe by medics. *The Mirror* (23 November), p. 1.

Younge, G. (2004) Chilling call to murder as music attacks gays. *The Guardian* (26 June), p. 14.

YouthNet (2003) *Shout: Research into the Needs of Young People in Northern Ireland who Identify as Lesbian, Gay, Bisexual and/or Transgender.* YouthNet, Belfast, UK.

Zarra, E. and Ward, D. (2003) Europe's biggest gay festival to be held in UK. *The Guardian* (11 February), p. 12.

Web site references

www.365gay.com (2003): Sandals upholds its anti-gay policy (accessed 29 October 2004).

www.abc.org.uk (accessed 19 August 2005).

www.afrol.com/articles (2004): Zanzibar threatened with tourism boycott (27 April, accessed 30 October 2004).

www.atc.australia.com/markets (2004): Gay and lesbian tourism (accessed 17 June 2004).

www.axm-mag.com (accessed 19 August 2005).

www.capetown.tv (2004): Gay Pride festival 2004 (19 January, accessed 28 June 2004).

www.city.ac.uk: City News (6 December 2004, accessed 15 December 2004).

www.cnsnews.com (2003): Financially ailing airline blasted for link to bisexuality event (2 September, accessed 3 November 2004).

www.commercialcloset.org/portrayals: Mess (accessed 18 September 2005).

www.damron.com (accessed 30 November 2004).

www.ethicalmatters.co.uk/articles (2004): Gideon Burrows says gay and ethical shopping can work (undated, accessed 3 November 2004).

www.fco.gov.uk/knowbeforeyougo: Travellers' checklists: gay, lesbian, bisexual and transgender travellers (accessed 4 November 2004).

www.freedomclub.co.uk (accessed 1 December 2004).

www.friendsofdot.com (accessed 23 October 2004).

www.gay.com.uk (accessed 6 September 2004).

www.gayaustraliaguide.com (accessed 13 February 2005).

www.gayday.com/history (accessed 15 June 2004).

www.gaydealsbrighton.co.uk (accessed 10 October 2005).

www.gaygames.com (accessed 6 February 2003).

www.gayplaces4u.com (accessed 23 October 2004).

www.gaytimes.co.uk/diva (accessed 19 August 2005).

www.gaytimes.co.uk/gt (accessed 19 August 2005).

www.gaytimestravel.co.uk (accessed 24 Sept 2005).

www.gaytravelguides.info (2004): Gay travel guides: gay Canada guide: online market research study (prepared by Grant Thornton LLP, Victoria BC, on behalf of Gay Travel Guides, Sydney).

www.gmax.co.za/look04 (2004): Zanzibar legislators pass bill to outlaw homosexual sex (15 April, accessed 30 October 2004).

www.iglta.org (accessed 11 March 2003).

www.interpride.org (accessed 11 March 2003).

www.lesbianation.com (accessed 4 November 2004).

www.lesbianlife.about.com (accessed 4 November 2004).

www.lezziecamp.co.uk (accessed 1 December 2004).

www.magazine.org (accessed 19 August 2005).

www.mantrav.co.uk/about us (accessed 7 November 2004).

www.mardigras.com.au (accessed 16 November 1999).

www.navigaytion.com (accessed 4 November 2004).

www.nzglta.org.nz (accessed 21 January 2005).

www.octopustravel-gay.com (accessed 10 October 2005).

www.odyusa.com (accessed 30 November 2004).

www.outandabout.com (accessed 4 November 2004).

www.outnowconsulting.com (accessed 25 August 2005).

www.outrage.nabumedia.com (accessed 15 February 2003).

www.outwestadventures.com (accessed 1 December 2004).

www.pinkotel.com (accessed 20 September 2005).

www.pinkpaper.com (accessed 19 August 2005).

www.pinkpassport.com (accessed 20 August 2005).

www.pinkroute.co.za (accessed 5 February 2005).

www.planetout.com/news, 1997: Bauer buddies target American (12 March, accessed 1 November 2004).

www.planetout.com/news, 1998: Bahamians protest gay cruise (5 February, accessed 1 November 2004).

www.planetout.com/news, 1999: American Airlines goes DP (5 August, accessed 3 November 2004).

www.qtmagazine.com (accessed 5 November 2004).

www.qtmagazine.com, 2004: World's first health resort and spa for gay and lesbian travellers opens (20 October, accessed 1 December 2004).

www.rainbowholidays.com (accessed 10 May 2005).

www.sbu.ac.uk/stafflag: Mattachine Society (accessed 6 February 2003).

www.tourismvancouver.com (accessed 1 December 2004).

www.uk.gay.com/headlines, 2002: Gay tourists attacked in South Africa (17 December, accessed 1 November 2004).

www.uk.gay.com/headlines, 2003: Brighton targets US pink pound (28 October, accessed 5 February 2005).

www.usnewswire.com, 2004: American Airlines again earns 100% score on HRC Corporate Equity Index (6 October, accessed 3 November 2004).

www.visitmelbourne.com (accessed 1 December 2004).

www.wien.info (accessed 1 December 2004).

www.womenstaynewzealand.com (accessed 29 June 2004).

Index

Over 300 places are mentioned in the text; only those with the more significant input are indexed here.